Th. Emil Homerin

THE GREEK HISTORIANS

Herma of Herodotus and Thucydides

THE GREEK HISTORIANS

Introduction and Selected Readings

Edited by NORMAN AUSTIN
Assistant Professor of Classics and Humanities
University of California (Los Angeles)

HERODOTUS · THUCYDIDES · POLYBIUS · PLUTARCH

VAN NOSTRAND–REINHOLD COMPANY
New York   Toronto   London   Melbourne

VAN NOSTRAND REGIONAL OFFICES: *New York, Chicago, San Francisco*

D. VAN NOSTRAND COMPANY, LTD., *London*

D. VAN NOSTRAND COMPANY (Canada), LTD., *Toronto*

D. VAN NOSTRAND AUSTRALIA PTY. LTD., *Melbourne*

Copyright © 1969, by AMERICAN BOOK COMPANY

All rights reserved. No part of this work covered by the copyrights hereon may be reproduced or used in any form or by any means—graphic, electronic, or mechanical, including photocopying, recording, taping, or information storage and retrieval systems—without written permission of the publisher. Manufactured in the United States of America.

Published simultaneously in Canada by
D. VAN NOSTRAND COMPANY (Canada), LTD.

Library of Congress Catalog Card No. 68–54717

The map on the cover and page 134 is reproduced by kind permission of New York Graphic Society Ltd. from REALMS OF GOLD by Leonard Cottrell.

PRINTED IN THE UNITED STATES OF AMERICA

FOR MY PARENTS

PREFACE

IN ANY course in Classical Literature or in Western Civilization the Greek poets are treated with the respect that is their due, but the Greek historians are generally passed over with short shrift. The complete works of the major Greek historians are too large for a survey course which must deal also with ancient epic and tragedy. It is a natural inclination, therefore, to relegate the historians to specialists in ancient history. This is regrettable, because history shares with philosophy the distinction of being the outstanding achievement of the Greeks in prose writing. No consideration of Greek thought can be adequate which does not recognize the intellectual struggle which gave birth to historiography. We might even say that historiography is a more significant manifestation of the Greek mind than the poetic forms which the Greeks produced, for poetry was virtually their norm, while historiography was something alien to the Greek genius. *Oedipus Rex* is viewed as a monument in the development of Western thought and art, and rightly so, but perhaps Thucydides' *History of the Peloponnesian War* is a greater monument. It is no disparagement of the Greek dramatists to suggest that it was perhaps easier for a fifth-century Athenian to write an *Oedipus* than a contemporary history.

It is my hope that this selection from the Greek historians will be useful in correcting the imbalance that favors Homer and the dramatists. In my introductory essay on Greek historiography, I have been concerned to show the obstacles which Greek historiography had to face in its difficult progress in becoming a serious and intellectual rigorous discipline. I have laid particular emphasis on the difference between a predominantly oral culture and a predominantly literate culture and on the effect of the orientation on the culture's concept of history. This difference is rarely discussed at any length, but without an awareness of it we can scarcely appreciate the difficulties under which an ancient historian labored. An accurate chronology, for example, we now assume as an elementary foundation of historical studies, but the assumption was not available for the Greeks. Time was important in certain religious observances, in agriculture, and in business transactions, but otherwise the Greeks were blithely indifferent to it. Chronology had to be invented, and that invention was one of the Greek historians' most serious concerns. Thucydides' attempt to establish an accurate and systematic chronology out of the haphazard systems of his day must have seemed as pedantic to most of his contemporaries as it seems essential to us today. His insistence on chronology was a truly Quixotic stand. Here I acknowledge a special debt, among many which will be readily obvious to scholars, to Professors E. A. Havelock's *Preface to Plato* (Cambridge, Mass., 1963) for its analysis of some conspicuous differences between a nonliterate and a literate culture. His analysis centers on the conflict between philosophy and poetry in fifth-century Athens rather than on the problems of historiography. The conclusions which I draw are, therefore, my own, but for many insights into the nature of Greek culture I am grateful to Professor Havelock.

An editor is only too well aware of the inadequacies inherent in any volume of selections. This sense of inadequacy is particularly acute when the editor faces writers such as Herodotus and Thucydides, whose works are so comprehensive and varied. Recognizing the obvious limitations of abridgments, I have not tried to restrict the selections to narratives of the notable historical events. It will be obvious enough that this volume is less a documentary history of Greece than a documentary history of historiography. For the historian the complete works of the ancients are essential. I have attempted to make selections which will give a fair representation of the range of the authors' interests, their critical principles, their methods, and their narrative style. This edition cannot stand as a substitute for the complete works of the historians. It will have served its purpose even if it does no more than illustrate the salient problems of ancient historiography and the solutions attempted by the outstanding historians.

NORMAN AUSTIN

CONTENTS

Preface	vii
Greek Historiography	1
The Genesis of Historiography	1
Homer and Poetic Vision	7
Rise of the Critical Spirit	13
The Logographers	21
Hecataeus	22
Herodotus	26
Thucydides	44
Greek Historiography After Thucydides	65
Selections	
HERODOTUS: *The Histories*	77
THUCYDIDES: *The History*	135
POLYBIUS: *History*	193
PLUTARCH: *Pericles*	239

SUMMARY CHRONOLOGY

B.C. 1184   Traditional date for the fall of Troy

ARCHAIC PERIOD

B.C. 776	Olympic Games instituted
?	Homer
594	Archonship of Solon at Athens
545–510	Peisistratid tyranny at Athens
499–494	Ionian Revolt
490–479	Persian Wars
490	Battle of Marathon
480	Battle of Salamis
478	Foundation of Delian League; beginning of growth of Athenian Empire

CLASSICAL PERIOD

431–404	Peloponnesian War
399	Death of Socrates
359–336	Philip II King of Macedon
336–323	Reign of Alexander the Great
322	Death of Aristotle

HELLENISTIC PERIOD

146   Destruction of Corinth by Rome

GREEK HISTORIOGRAPHY

THE GENESIS OF HISTORIOGRAPHY

It is a paradox that the Greeks, who are rightly credited with the invention of historiography, conspicuously lacked any true historical sense. In the remarkable series of inventions of the Greeks in the archaic and classical periods, history was a latecomer, but late as it was, it was a premature discovery. History as a separate intellectual discipline was wrested from the province of mythology with considerable effort, and its success was sadly short-lived; some may say the effort was abortive, for history quickly lapsed into mythology again. We who consider history an essential part of the educational curriculum find it hard to realize that the Greeks did not hold that history was either natural or essential.

The systematic investigation and analysis of the past remained rather alien to Greek thought. This is not to say that the Greeks were insensitive to their past. On the contrary, their sense of the past and of the enduring reality of that past in their present was probably more acute than ours. It has been asserted, in fact, that the political failure of the Greeks was partly due to their rigid fixation upon the past, which impaired their judgment in the political crises which faced them in the fifth and fourth centuries B.C. The Greeks were much preoccupied with their past, and yet, in contrast to their contemporaries the Egyptians and Persians, they kept minimal records and showed scant interest in such records. In an earlier age the Greeks had been more record-conscious. The Linear B tablets found at Pylos have shown us that the Mycenean Greeks had a veritable addiction to records. Scarcely any artifact was too insignificant to be catalogued. The contrast between the highly organized bureaucratic Myceneans and the later Greeks of the historical period is striking. Though the later Greeks kept records of such things as treaties between cities, they seem to have shown a vast indifference to the value of such records.

The Greeks' faulty historical perspective is primarily the effect of a culture which is oral rather than literate. Between the time of the Linear B tablets (after which writing apparently disappeared from Greece) and the rediscovery of writing in the seventh and eighth centuries B.C., Greek culture was for several centuries completely oral. Even after the Greeks borrowed the art of writing from their eastern neighbors, their culture remained predominantly oral. Writing was, of course, in use in the classical period, as contemporary inscriptions testify, and was taught in the schools, but the Greeks did not become readers, at least not before the end of the fifth century.* They did not go to books for their information, but relied mainly on what was orally presented: legends and anecdotes which could be passed from one person or community to another, and, of course, poetry.

A widespread diffusion of writing and literacy frequently gives rise to a heightened interest in records and documents. The evidence leads us to conclude that such an interest did not prevail in Greece until after the classical period. Sheer accident has preserved much epigraphic and numismatic evidence from the classical period, but what survived by deliberate design rather than by the caprices of events is not historical documents but literature. The Greeks, we may say, saw the value of writing chiefly in its potential for preserving their poetry. In this way they betray the bias which they were to retain throughout the classical period in favor of artistic discourse against documentary records.

The reason for their bias is not far to seek. An oral culture encourages a certain kind of preservation of the past, but at the same time inhibits historical perspective because its particular means of transmitting information discourages the development of

---

* Eric A. Havelock, *Preface to Plato* (Cambridge, Mass., 1963) has given us an excellent study of the effect of the oral culture on the mode of thought of the Greeks. Mircea Eliade, *The Myth of the Eternal Return*, tr. W. R. Trask, Bollingen Series XLVI (New York: Pantheon Books, 1954) offers many perceptive comments on the relationship between history and myth in such early societies.

exact chronological consciousness. All information passed on in such cultures must be memorized and transmitted orally from generation to generation. In the absence of writing and written records there is no objective evidence against which to test a man's telling of the past. One man's memory can be compared with another man's; this is the only kind of verification possible. We are all too familiar with how variable memory can be. When oral transmission is the only means to preserve the past, the past inevitably undergoes transformation. Oral poetry can be remarkable for its accuracy. Some facts are tenaciously preserved for centuries, once they have become a part of oral tradition. Nevertheless, imperceptibly, sometimes deliberately for aesthetic or chauvinistic reasons, sometimes quite unconsciously, the details of a story will change from one telling to the next. One may find several variants of a story in circulation at the same time, and no variant with any more claim to legitimacy than the others.

A consequence of oral transmission which is continued over a period of centuries is that time telescopes. Stories which may have originally been concerned with events occurring over a great temporal and spatial expanse slowly cluster around an important event or an outstanding figure.* Characters who originally may have belonged to quite separate periods find themselves caught up in a single cycle of legend and the events of their lives brought into harmony with some event momentous enough to embrace all heroes. We can surmise that such a metamorphosis of history took place in the Homeric poems. The two poems, the *Iliad* and the *Odyssey*, have as their background the Trojan War in which heroic Greece confronted the concentrated might of Asia. The origins and the transmission of the poems are lost in obscurity, but with the help of archaeology and the results of modern studies of oral poetry

---

* Compare the way in which the Incas enhanced the authority of any newly promulgated law by attributing its authorship to the first Inca. See *The Incas: The Royal Commentaries of Garcilaso the Inca,* ed. 2nd intro. Alain Gheerbrant (New York: Orion, 1961), p. 17. In a literate culture such tampering with facts necessitates wholesale destruction of certain documents, forging new documents, and rewriting old documents. It is interesting that the officials of modern totalitarian states have, in their revisions of history, occasionally resorted to methods which are appropriate to an oral culture but highly anachronistic in an age of literacy.

we can assume that the poems as we have them incorporate varying customs and perhaps even historical events from several centuries. Whether there ever was a Trojan War of ten years' duration we have no way of knowing, though classical archaeologists, still under Homer's influence, often assume it as a fact. That there was a conflict between the Trojans and the Greeks we may accept as a reasonable conjecture. But it is probable that what Homer preserves is the memory not of a single war, whether of one or of ten years' duration, but of a protracted struggle between Asia and Greece. It is possible that Homer has exaggerated a shorter war into a ten-year siege of superhuman proportions. It is just as possible that he has telescoped the frequent conflicts of a long period into a single heroic and dramatic struggle.

The peculiar timelessness which continued to characterize the Greeks, at least until the Alexandrian period, may be observed in their attitude toward the Homeric poems. The poems, though they are the culmination of centuries of traditions and legends, were never perceived as such by the Greeks but were accepted as the representation of a single brief period in their past. It was obvious to the more sceptical and observant Greeks of a later period that the conditions presented in Homer did not correspond to those of their own time, but of the full extent of the differences between the two periods they never became aware. They were quick to note what we should call the mythical elements—the easy association of gods with men—but about the enormous sociological differences between the two periods they showed little curiosity. The poems, though they maintained a coherent internal chronology, stood outside of time altogether. They embodied the past of the Greeks and were therefore their history; yet it was really a past outside of history.

To account for the difference between Homeric and later times the Greeks resorted to a myth of the Ages of the World, proceeding from a paradisaical beginning through gradual stages of degeneration of the Age of Man. Just before the contemporary Age of Man they interpolated a transition stage, the Age of Heroes. With this kind of mythical perspective, the Greeks posited, in effect, only two periods of human history: the heroic age, when gods conversed with men, and the modern nonheroic age. Between the two there was an abrupt break, but to the events which caused that break the Greeks gave no consideration. Thus, though the myth of successive Ages suggests an evolutionary process, in fact the Greeks never developed an evolutionary consciousness. One period had simply disappeared and another had taken its place. Later, as their historical interest grew, the Greeks tried to bring Homer into history, to put Homer, as it were, into time, by tracing ancestries back to the Homeric heroes. These efforts were of the most elementary sort. There was no attempt to trace an evolutionary development in political conditions, but merely the need to fix Homer at some point in time by counting the generations between him and the present day. Even in this effort the Greeks betrayed their lack of historical perspective. An anecdote which Herodotus tells is highly illustrative. Herodotus relates that his predecessor Hecataeus, in his conversation with the priests of Thebes in Egypt, had traced his ancestry back to a god in the sixteenth generation. Hecataeus was giving, therefore, sixteen generations, or about 500 years, as the length of time from the heroic age to his own day. We might consider that 500 years indicated a certain degree of time consciousness, but Hecataeus was talking to Egyptians. The priests, by way of answer, showed him the wooden statues of their high priests, whose office had descended from father to son. They could count 345 generations of high priests and still they did not trace their ancestries back to the gods. What the Egyptians were telling Hecataeus, as they were later to tell Herodotus, and as Herodotus was to tell the Greeks in his *Histories,* is that any nation which put an upper limit of 500 years on human history had a ridiculous sense of time. An approximately analogous situation might be one in which an American boasted to the present-day descendants of Julius Caesar that he could trace his ancestry back to the *Mayflower* and there it became lost in the Dark Ages.

The Incan civilization offers another instructive parallel. The Incans differed from the Greeks in the high level of bureaucracy which they maintained, but in their lack of writing they possessed an oral culture which presents similarities. The Incans preserved their records, which by all accounts were prodigious, by two methods: a purely mechanical system of knots on a cord (*quipu*), and the oral method of stories and poems. By means of the quipus they could preserve anything which could be put into numerical form—not only accounts and catalogues, but historical dates. Specially trained experts, the *quipucamayus,* gave substance to the mere facts which they itemized on their quipus by memorizing stories to accompany each knot on their cords. The quipus were their mechanical aids to memory. The quipucamayus could, by passing the cord through their fingers, recite a wealth of memorized information about historical events, laws, ceremonies, and institutions. There were also "philosophers" who turned royal speeches and diplomatic events into simple fables which could be easily remembered by the people and transmitted orally with little substantial change; and to poets fell the task of incorporating important events and speeches into poems which could be memorized and recited at festivals.*

In the Incan civilization, in which all history was oral, we see something of the same foreshortening of time as in Greek civilization. When Garcilaso the Inca asked his uncle how long the Inca civilization had endured, his uncle replied that the time when the Sun had sent his first children to Earth "demands calculation beyond my memory; let us say that it was at least four hundred years ago."** Garcilaso's uncle's conjectural 400 years are the period of the twelve Incas. His uncle recognized that there had existed some primitive species of humans before the creation of the Inca civilization, but that primitive period was of no consequence. It is clear that for him the creation of the Incas marked the beginning of time. He could scarcely conceive that time could stretch back much farther than four centuries. Before that was creation, an act of divine fiat. This is the historical way of thinking of an oral culture.

A literate culture develops its chronological consciousness by inscribing its historical moments on some fairly permanent material, on stone or wood, clay or paper. It thereby fixes its historical events to a particular time and place. Printing further encourages this kind of historicity by making copies of the permanently in-

---
* *The Royal Commentaries* 159–160.
** *The Royal Commentaries,* p. 8.

scribed records widely available. Original documents can be destroyed by a single dictator, but only a general holocaust can destroy all the world's libraries. Our modern method of dating by consecutively numbered years rather than by generations or by some regularly recurring ceremony such as a presidential election, testifies to the way in which literacy has affected our historical consciousness. Such chronological exactitude has been in existence for a long time, but in its intensive application to the minute details of daily life it is a thoroughly modern European habit, directly attributable to inexpensive mechanical means of printing and duplicating records.

HOMER AND POETIC VISION

IN AN oral culture, since the only history the society possesses is that which is preserved by the poets, the poet is exalted to a high status. He knows the past and is the only link between present and past. In Homer the poet is called a *demiourgos,* a man who lives not as a private person, but as a public servant. The poet, like the physician, devotes himself to the common good. In a society in which the poet is the custodian of the past, the attitude toward history is very different from our modern attitude. To introduce the long Catalogue of Ships in the *Iliad,* Homer invokes the aid of the Muses. "For you are goddesses," he says, "and know everything. But we mortals hear only by report and know nothing." Elsewhere Homer talks of the poet's personal skill which sets him above his competitors; yet this invocation of the Muses is indicative of the essential fact that knowledge of the past is a possession of the gods and not of men. The past is not something which can be searched out or corroborated. Knowledge of the past is given as it were by revelation. The poet is the recipient of the past from the Muses; he delivers that past to the people.

Scholars at times talk as if the later Greeks brought a religious reverence to the account which Homer had given of their early legends, as if Homer were an infallible authority. This is not quite the case, although Homer may occasionally have been cited as a weighty authority in territorial disputes. Homer's invocation of the

Muses pointedly acknowledges his own fallibility, as indeed the fallibility of all humans. In an oral culture truth belongs to the gods alone. It is they who know, for they are the only eyewitnesses who survive through time. Humans can only report from hearsay. The criterion of truthfulness is applicable to legal disputes but not to distant historical facts. The poet's account is accepted only because there is no other history. The poets were necessarily judged not by standards of historical accuracy but by aesthetic standards. The poet is a *mythopoios,* literally a mythmaker. And the myth—a word which originally signified only a story with no implication as to veracity or probability—was outside the spheres of life in which canons of truth and falsehood could legitimately be applied.

Homer was not accepted as the infallible truth, but his tales were, quite simply, beyond the reach of critical investigation. The Athenian dramatists felt free to draw on a great number of variants of the same myths, and perhaps even to invent their own variants. Occasionally, too, a poet would allude to a version of a myth which contradicted the version given by Homer. Such conflicting versions could coexist quite peaceably. An oral culture cannot be dogmatic in its mythology, nor can it sustain any very efficacious censorship. Yet Homer did come to occupy an unrivaled position in Greek poetry. Though there must have been hundreds of oral poets through the centuries, and hundreds of legends told of the Greek heroes, the sustained force and beauty of Homer's narrative drove out all competition. He became the poet *par excellence* of the Greek people, and his poems their national history. But it was not history as we would think of history. It was not a chronological account with a beginning and an end. The Homeric poems did not offer a consecutive narrative of the past, but a brief moment in the past. What Homer did was to provide the Greeks with an idealized concept of their past. The very perfection of his idealization is what gave him his unquestioned authority. Moreover, it set a severe limit to historical perspective, for it crystallized the past into a form beyond competition or criticism. Other poets came along to complement Homer by filling in the gaps in his narrative or by elaborating on characters or incidents which had been only summarily treated in his poetry. But what Homer had treated, the wrath of

Achilles in the *Iliad* and the return of Odysseus from Troy in the *Odyssey*, no poet or historian ever treated again.

The powerful effect of an idealization is another manifestation of a predominantly oral culture and is therefore significant for Greek historiography. When history which we can accept as such came into existence in Greece, the same attitude arose towards the historians as had prevailed towards Homer. Herodotus gave the history of the Persian Wars, and thereafter that subject was beyond competition. Other historians might allude to events of the Persian Wars or to events mentioned by Herodotus, but no historian ever attempted to write a version either to correct or to supplement Herodotus' account. Similarly, after Thucydides had written the history of the Peloponnesian War, no historian ever attempted to write another history of that war. Thucydides' successors began their histories precisely at the point where his history left off. Following in his steps, they wrote sequels; but that it might have been desirable to cover from a different perspective what Thucydides had already covered was not something which occurred to them. What Homer had done for the Trojan War, Herodotus had done for the Persian and Thucydides for the Peloponnesian War. Each had taken the confused strands of events at a particular moment in Greek history and had woven them into a poetic whole. In their hands a formless mass of disparate events had crystallized into an ideal form. Later historians might venture doubts about a particular fact or a particular interpretation, but criticism of a minor detail never implied criticism of the whole. Just as Homer the poet became the historian, so the later historians became the poets of their ages, bequeathing the memorials of their own times to future generations. It is as if we thought it sufficient to have but one historian for the Revolution, one for the Civil War, one for the New Deal, one for World War II, and so on. Such a comparison underlines the great disparity between the ancient and our modern view of history and historiography.

The Greeks, then, largely because of their traditional preference of the spoken over the written word, held their poets in high esteem, and among the poets, on the highest pedestal of all, they placed Homer. They accepted poets as historians, educators, and philosophers, for it was the poets who "knew." The poets in their turn made what might seem today to be preposterous claims for the high importance of their educative function. Poetry, however, is a nonscientific way of looking at things. It calls for a sharply observant eye, but it transmutes keen visual perceptions into myths. It is by nature mythopoeic. A society which values poetry highly will be predictably poetic in its interpretation of life. It will respond to its poets because their mythopoeic imagination reflects the society's own mythopoeic vision.

The effect of this kind of poetic vision is perceptible in all aspects of Greek thought. Even in science, in which the Greeks made extraordinary advances, they consistently preferred the theoretic, the philosophic, to the strictly empirical. But the poetic vision of the Greeks had its most conspicuous effect in the sphere of human psychology, in what we may today loosely classify as social studies. The vagaries of changing social conditions were never as significant to the Greeks as the poetic essense of human nature.

It would be hard to imagine two societies more widely disparate than that of the Homeric poems and that of sixth- and fifth-century Athens. The old values were no longer tenable. There was little room for Homeric heroism in that later mercantile and democratic Athens. It is true that some of the lyric poets had written or were writing poetry of a very personal tone which was nonheroic and sometimes frankly antiheroic. Nevertheless, other poets, in particular the choral poets such as Pindar, were most incongruously addressing their bourgeois patrons as if they were the direct inheritors, and indeed the saviors, of the old Homeric codes of heroic valor. Such comparisons to values which had been outmoded for centuries were a pleasing flattery to the new bourgeoisie who were pulling down victories at the athletic contests, but they were more than mere time-serving flattery on the part of ambitious poets. They reveal the extent to which the historical Greeks, for all the obvious differences between themselves and their Mycenean forebears, recognized their essential identity in Homer's portraits. It was because the Greeks still could identify themselves so strongly with Homer's world that Homer remained the principal educational textbook so long after his ethic has lost its reason for existence.

Even Plato's attacks, which were perhaps the most stringent made on Homer in antiquity, are directed chiefly to the Homeric heroes' lapses from the high standards of their own ethic. Plato could have made a more telling attack on Homer by examining him on historical grounds. He could have demonstrated the absurdity of revering an authority whom historical evolution had already made antiquated. But Plato too accepted the heroic ethic of Homer. The philosopher seems, indeed, to have wanted to retain that kind of ethic as an ideal (suitable only for the guardians in his state), praiseworthy but in need of a few basic corrections. There is a suggestion in Plato that, for all his attacks on Homer, he would have favored a return to the Homeric way of life. It offered several features which were more in tune with Plato's temperament than the clamorous democracy in the fifth and fourth centuries. Plato, too, is as much a beneficiary of the Homeric *weltanschauung* as anyone else in Greece.

The art of fifth-century Athens, and presumably of other Greek cities if the evidence of numismatics and poetry is a reliable guide, evinces the continuing predominance of the mythical, the poetic, over the practicalities of daily life. Even Athenian comedy, which was firmly attached to the contemporary political scene, always rose into mythical realms of burlesque and fantasy, so that today it is difficult to know how closely the caricature figures in Aristophanes correspond to their namesakes in real life. If we compare Aristophanic comedy with some of the more directly political writings of Jonathan Swift, we can see at once how far Aristophanes is from engaging actively and concretely in the problems of his day.

Tragedy obviously dealt not with ephemeral manifestations but with themes of eternal importance: man in his relationship to the fates and the gods. Sometimes tragedies, using the old myths as vehicles, seem to raise issues of contemporary politics, but these issues are always presented in an ambiguous way. There is undoubtedly a certain topical relevance to political developments in such a play as Sophocles' *Antigone,* but the contemporary reality is viewed through the opaque screeen of ancient myth rather than in its immediate historical context. Whatever there is of the present in such a play loses its historical uniqueness by being merged into the timeless world of myth.

In Euripides the consciousness of the contemporary political turmoil is more noticeable. There is on his part a more determined effort to bring the action of tragedy out of the world of myth and closer to the present. Many of Euripides' plays were written while the Peloponnesian War was in progress and several of them reflect his antiwar sympathies. Yet, despite the forcefulness of his presentation and his psychological understanding, Euripides could not entirely break away from the mythical to consider the problems of specific individuals in a specific historical moment. Euripides was criticized in his own time for reducing tragedy to the level of contemporary realism but as we read Euripides now we find him far closer to Aeschylus and Sophocles than to the realism of modern playwrights.

In their plastic and decorative arts, too, the Greeks were far from modern realism. The themes of statuary and vase painting were almost all drawn from myth and legend, and when the themes were contemporary the representations were highly idealized studies of the human physique. Greek art was little interested in depicting scenes from daily life from their own sake. The history of Greek art is a history of steady progression towards realism, and yet even in the culmination of realism in the Hellenistic period Greek art remains, by modern standards, highly stylized.

The choice of themes which the Athenians made for the metopes of the Parthenon is a significant illustration of the Greeks' perspective on contemporary events. The Athenians erected the Parthenon after their defect of the Persians, and the metopes of the temple are their graphic representation of that victory. But rather than depict the victory explicitly they chose four mythical battles representing the triumph of order over disorder, of civilization over barbarism: the battles of the Centaurs and Lapiths, gods and giants, Greeks and Amazons, and Greeks and Trojans.* The Athenians celebrated

---

* Nowhere in Homer are the Trojans distinguished from the Greeks for their barbarism. From the time of the Persian Wars the word *barbaroi* becomes the standard epithet for all non-Greeks and particularly the Asians. Even so, the term "barbarians" had a far different connotation for the classical Greeks than it has for us today.

the Greek victory in the present in a symbolic way by reaching into the timeless realm of myth, thus transmuting the temporal into the eternal.

The historical temperament is the polar opposite of the mythopoeic temperament. Whether history is or can be a science need not concern us here. What is important is that the methods of history are those of science. History is rooted in the concrete, the here and now. It is wary of deceptive similarities and of the false logic so often inherent in analogy. What poetry joins together in metaphor and simile, science tears asunder. Poetry is akin to magic. Behind the real world it sees another and more real world alive with *mana;* behind external phenomena it sees a labyrinthine network of numinous powers. It finds in symbolic relationships a reality as cogent as that of scientific causality. It is within such a poetic context that Greek historiography had its beginnings and its zenith. Only by recognizing the antithetical nature of the two modes of vision, the historical and the poetic, can we understand the full achievement of the Greek historians. The extent of both the success and the failure of Greek historiography can be appreciated only when it is seen in the context of its own cultural milieu. In certain respects it overcame the formidable obstacles against which it had to contend in its cultural environment; in other respects, it fell victim to those hostile forces.

THE RISE OF THE CRITICAL SPIRIT

To THE eighth century the poems are probably to be dated which in antiquity, along with the *Iliad* and the *Odyssey,* constituted the Homeric corpus. Their authorship was disputed from very early times, but their themes are Homer's—i.e., the Trojan cycle of legends—and they were therefore classified with Homer. Except for the *Iliad* and *Odyssey,* these poems have survived only in summaries, but the summaries are sufficient to show us that they were not unified dramas around a central theme like the *Iliad* and the *Odyssey,* but were closer to chronicles, designed to narrate the events before and after the events in the *Iliad* and the *Odyssey.* They described the events at the beginning of the Trojan War, which are scarcely touched upon in the *Iliad,* the events of the last year of the war, from the funeral of Hector to the death of Achilles, the eventual sack of Troy, the return of the Greek heroes, and the final years of Odysseus' life, after his return to Ithaca. These poems clearly presuppose the existence of the *Iliad* and the *Odyssey* substantially as we have them and were therefore intended to complement Homer by recording the whole body of the Trojan cycle of legend. Though they are poems and their themes are still mythological, they are quasi-historical. They fill a certain kind of historical need which the dramatic poems of Homer had not filled. They show the developing interest in collecting and recording the mass of varied legends which has circulated for centuries in oral form.

The real impetus to historical research came later with the rise of rationalistic thought, which beginning in Ionia towards the end of the seventh century carried into the sixth and fifth centuries B.C. The rationalistic spirit found expression in a great variety of ways. In its attempt to discover the underlying principles which determined the nature of the universe, it turned its attention in every direction, and its exuberant energy led to many astonishing discoveries. A comprehensive study of Greek historiography should include a detailed analysis of the various strands of intellectual thought of this period, for each thinker, or "philosopher," had his share in posing questions and hypotheses which bear on later historical writing. Such a full analysis is impossible here; let us note the two principal directions of the intellectual movement of the period.

One direction was that of speculative thought, represented by those who are commonly called the natural philosophers. These philosophers, like Thales and Anaximander, formulated hypotheses concerning the origins and nature of the world. Their thought is both scientific and philosophic, for a separation between pure science and pure philosophy or metaphysics, is anachronistic at this early date. They are scientific in their rejection of received opinions and in their attempt to penetrate to the hidden physical laws governing the manifold changes and appearances of visible phenomena. They exemplify the necessary qualities of true scientists: a sense of detachment, a disinterested belief in logical thought, and acute observation. Their weakness as scientists lay in their neglect of the principle of experimentation. Their discoveries startle us by their modernity, but it is even more startling when we realize that they are, for the most part, purely theoretical hypotheses. These are not theories deduced from a process of trial and error but, in fact, dogmatic assertions, unproved and, at that time, mostly unprovable, about the nature of the world. For this reason it is right to call them philosophers rather than scientists. They were more preoccupied with the ultimate and abstract causes than with the minutiae of experimental data.

These natural philosophers were no longer satisfied with the traditional interpretations of life and the world, enshrined in the mythological poetic documents of Homer and Hesiod. Their search for new explanations became an attack on poetry, for they began to perceive that the poetic tradition represented a kind of dogmatism. It was not the dogmatism of theology but rather the dogmatism of a prevailing outlook on life which inhibited questioning; it was the unquestioning acceptance of the kind of interpretation which an oral culture formulates for itself. From this time there emerges a conflict between poets and philosophers which became progressively more strident. Some later philosophers in this rationalistic tradition express outright scorn for poets and the claims made, both by the poets themselves and by others, for the value of their poetry. Xenophanes, for example, is contemptuous of the current ideas of the gods which have been hallowed by the authority of Homer. His criticism is that Homer exerted a deleterious influence in sanctioning either ridiculous or immoral attributes of the gods. Heraclitus, another philosopher in this tradition, was even more caustic. He derided the pretensions of poets, not only of lesser and more modern poets but also of the greatest and most authoritative poets, Homer and Hesiod. Poets are accepted as teachers, says Heraclitus, but they are false teachers. Knowledge of many things does not lead to understanding, he says, in another place, or it would have given the poet Hesiod understanding. "Away with Homer," he says in one fragment (fr. 42).

In the attacks on poets the various philosophers are united in their scorn for the poet's claims to knowledge, or wisdom, that is to *sophia*. The poet's technical proficiency in creating a tale, a *mythos*, and the spell of his words, had established him as an exemplar of *sophia* in general. He was thought to be a man of understanding. His skill in one particular art had become all-embracing, until he became accepted as expert in all arts. The philosophers were attacking this spurious wisdom, together with the theological premise of such wisdom. They are creating a new kind of *sophia*, a human *sophia*, a *sophia* no longer dependent on divine revelation but based on human reason. They are making wisdom and reason human attributes, and this is a revolution. They were no longer content to accept an explanation merely because it had been hallowed by poetic tradition. They demanded the right to question and to apply new critical principles to old traditions. This attack on the poet's exclusive right to wisdom and understanding reaches its highest pitch in Plato. In several dialogues, but particularly in the *Republic*, he carries the attack beyond the mere name-calling of the earlier philosophers, to make the most searching criticism of the nature of poetry, of its effect on its audience, and of the debilitating influence of an art which is directed at the emotional rather than at the rational elements of the soul.

The importance of the role of the early philosophers in laying the groundwork of Greek historiography lies in their challenge to the poets' traditional authority as guardians and expositors of the truth. Their criticisms of the absurdities and naïveté of the poets' myths are, in fact, the first step in the formulation of the idea of truth. The concept of truth in history was anachronistic before the philosophers. It was an idea which was neither necessary nor possible in an age when oral legends abounded in variant forms and contradicted each other. By assailing the credibility of the poets' tales the philosophers created a new abstraction which had hitherto been irrelevant. Poetic authority and charm were no longer sufficient to establish one's veracity. Truth was now something to be ascertained by critical investigation and rational processes of thought.

The delineation of a new concept of scientific and rational truth was a necessary preliminary to historical thought. The philosophers, however, stopped short of genuine historical thought because of their neglect of empirical data. For this failure two factors are primarily responsible. First, in their opposition to the poets the philosophers repudiated the poetic myths *en masse*. Once having noted the obvious incongruities in the poets' tales, they quickly concluded that all the myths of the poets were equally false. In their counteroffensive against the poets' authority they were not willing to grant any concessions. The philosophers did not proceed to what might seem now the next logical step, that is, analyzing the Homeric narrative to separate history from myth or to determine the sociological origins of myth. For this failure we can hardly censure them. It was not until the nineteenth century that such an analysis of myth from an historical and anthropological perspective was begun and even today such analysis of the Homeric poems is still rudimentary.

The other reason for the philosophers' failure to achieve historical thought is that, despite their condemnation of poets, they were themselves poets. The apparent incongruity that the first philosophers should have been poets disappears when we understand that in a predominantly oral culture thinkers could have emerged only from the class of poets, for poets were those who were preeminently gifted with the power of the word. Only poets could have used the medium of words to exert any influence on others. Social conditions, therefore, made it necessary that poet and philosopher should have been originally one and the same man.

The philosophers were attempting to break the passive dependence of the Greeks on their authoritative poets, Homer and Hesiod, in order to create a new mode of thinking. And yet we must now admit that the philosophers were instituting their own kind of poetry which was to them more truthful than Homer's myths. Scholars have remarked that underlying all the cosmological speculations of the early philosophers was what almost amounted to an emotional obsession to find a structure, a system of order governing the phenomena of existence. The philosophers were determined to impose a rational order on the visible flux and chaos. The idea of a rational order in the world corresponding to the rational processes of a human intelligence is, of course, a poetic rather than a scientific idea. Scholars have also shown that the cosmogonies which the early philosophers postulated were, in fact, a more abstract and rationalized interpretation of the old poetic cosmogonies, inherited through Hesiod from their oriental neighbors. The philosophers were borrowing from the poets even as they attacked them.

Revolutionary as they now seem to be, in relationship to their times, the early philosophers yet remained closer to poetry than to science. Their thought was couched in poetic metaphor, and several actually wrote in verse rather than in prose. Poetic metaphor was more than the verbal medium in which they expressed their ideas. Their most abstract thought was itself a poetic metaphor, poetry carried to its highest levels. Moreover, many of the early philosophers were of priestly and aristocratic families. Their language betrays this affiliation. It is hieratic in style, exhibiting many of the features to be found in the language of mystery religions. It often has an oracular obscurity, indulges in mystical paradoxes, and borrows from the language of secret religious rites. It addresses itself to initiates, to those who have entered into the secrets of knowledge. The philosophers' language expresses their disdain for the uninitiated, for those men who lack understanding, who cannot distinguish illusion from reality, who prefer to walk in error rather than in true knowledge. This aristocratic and religious disdain is reflected also in the realm of empirical data. The philosophers were not technicians or artisans, forced to confront the practical aspects of nature; nor were they court engineers, paid to solve practical and technical problems. As aristocrats they could afford to direct their thought to the realm of purely abstract speculation. Thus the philosophers whose critical spirit led them to reject Homer as a creator of fantasies became in their turn mythmakers, transforming old myths and creating new ones.

Not all philosophical thought, however, had been as theoretical. The critical spirit which had begun to appear in the sixth century had been directed impartially toward cosmological speculation and the concrete facts of physical phenomena. The early philosophers were also scientists. A man like Anaximander not only posited abstract theories about the nature of the world but turned his attention to the very practical business of making a map. In time philosophy and science began to diverge into separate disciplines, but in the initial stages the dichotomy had not appeared. Historiography is more directly descended from this second line of early speculations, that is, from the more strictly scientific aspect of intellectual research, and it is to this direction that we must turn.

The Greeks were not given to scientific experimentation, but they were observant and curious. The Greeks who lived on the coast of Asia Minor had the appreciable advantage over their fellow Greeks in mainland Greece of having their observation sharpened by their proximity to the totally different cultures of the Persians. As seafaring traders they had direct contact with the Egyptians and Assyrians and brought back home reports of still other cultures farther inland. The coast of Asia Minor was a highly cosmopolitan part of the world. It was there that much philosophical speculation had its beginnings and many revolutionary ideas were introduced among the Greeks. It was the Ionian Greeks, for example, who borrowed the idea of coinage from their eastern neighbors and the system of writing from the Phoenicians—two inventions which had enormous economic and technological effect. The Ionian Greeks were thus exposed to a wealth of political systems, religious beliefs, myths, social customs. This exposure to various cultures forced the Ionian Greeks to a consciousness of their own ethnic identity. They were led to formulate and discuss the particular ideas which formed the basis of the Greek way of life. They were led, too, to speculate on the physical and sociological causes behind the differentiation of the various cultural traditions which could be observed in Ionia.

It is from this polyglot milieu that the early Greek histories sprang. The Greek word *historia* had originally no connection with the study of the past; it meant "establishing"—i.e., the establishing of truth. It signified investigation or "research." The first histories were just that: researches of any kind. They were not so much studies, in the sense of modern scholarly monographs, but collections of information, perhaps interspersed with the author's opinions and observations. Their subjects were at times historical, but they covered a wider range. They were geographical reports and ethnographic and mythographic, with no clear distinction between the separate fields.

These early histories are a reflection of the growing influence of literacy. They seem to be the direct product of the Greeks' new invention of writing. Suddenly this new invention had made preservation of records possible. The early historians were thus collectors of records. Since the origin of Greek historiography followed closely after the invention of writing, it is only natural that what the early prose writers collected was not written records—which, if they existed at all, must have been very few—but oral reports. Whether their subject was the history of a particular city from its founding to the present day or the customs of a particular culture, these writers were reporting what they could glean from oral accounts. Today we would call them compilers rather than historians. The story, the traditional oral tale, remained an important element in their work, for that was precisely what they were in search of. They were storytellers in prose.

When we see the result of this kind of investigation in Herodotus we are tempted to dismiss him as totally devoid of critical principles. He gives almost as much place in his histories to obviously mythical stories as to historical fact, and in his myths he is pleased to be able to record the small variants in the tale as told in one city or another. When Herodotus tells, for example, the story of Arion being borne through the sea on the back of a dolphin with almost as much care for detail as he might show in describing a major battle in the Persian Wars, we may think that he is totally indiscriminate in his attitude towards myth and history. This is to mistake his purpose. A principal object of Herodotus' histories is to collect the stories, the *logoi*. Herodotus' emphasis, twice repeated, in the story of Arion and the dolphin on the Corinthian and Lesbian sources of the story shows his attitude quite clearly. He is interested in his story and its source. His one opinion on the probability of the story can be only of secondary interest. As one scholar has noted, it is because Herodotus "respects the Story so much that every variant is important to him."* As a faithful reporter he is concerned for his accuracy in the smallest detail.

These early prose writers were called *logopoioi,* creators of stories, and later *logographoi,* writers of stories. Herodotus himself refers to such writers as *logioi.* All these words, built up on the simple *logos,* show that at first the principal subject of such writings was the *logos,* the story. These immediate predecessors of Herodotus, logographers as they are now generally called, brought their own critical standards to the writing of history. The philosophers had created the abstract idea of truth, which they had pursued assiduously in their own researches. The standard of the logographers was far different but equally important. They had created the idea of accuracy in reporting. It has been said that while the philosophers were "looking for the truth, Herodotus is looking for the evidence."** This observation may be applied, perhaps to a somewhat lesser degree, to Herodotus' predecessors also. Their intent was to record the traditions as faithfully as they could, to make them permanent. In spite of their limitations they have the genuinely historical spirit because in their care for the preservation of tradition and in their attempt to record the variant traditions without bias they show the first awakening of what can be called a true historical sense.

The best history will try, of course, to combine as far as possible the abstract Truth of the philosopher with the more concrete truth, or accuracy, of the logographers. The two streams, the philosophic and the scientific, must merge into one. At its zenith Greek historiography achieved this synthesis of the concrete and the abstract, but the achievement was as rare in Greece as it probably is today. The synthesis is an ideal, but it was an ideal first perceived and attempted by the Greeks.

THE LOGOGRAPHERS

The works of the logographers have come to us in only a fragmentary state. No manuscript has survived with a complete

* J. A. K. Thomson, *The Art of the Logos* (London, 1935), p. 30.
** Thomson, *op. cit.* 237, note 13.

text of any of their writings and our only knowledge is based on what can be gleaned from references to them or from quotations from their works in later writers. Reconstructions of the scope, purpose, and methods of these historians is therefore frankly speculative. For a better understanding of Herodotus and Thucydides, however, it is worthwhile to attempt some analysis of their work, however tentative the effort must be.*

HECATAEUS

HECATAEUS is mentioned four times by Herodotus, who refers to him as "Hecataeus the *logopoios*." According to Herodotus' stories, Hecataeus was a figure of some importance about 500 B.C. at Miletus in Asia Minor. We may date him, therefore, to about the end of the sixth century and into the fifth. His name was linked with that of Anaximander, who drew up the first map of the known world, and it is reasonable to assume that Hecataeus was caught up in the fervor of philosophical and scientific speculations in Ionia at that time. His works were probably two in number: one, a mythographical work, called *Genealogies* or *Histories* ("histories" being here used in the original sense of investigations), and a geographical work called *Periegesis*, literally "Circular Tour." In the absence of other concrete evidence, we may assume that Hecataeus was the first prose writer in the fields of mythography and geography. He was described in later times as a widely traveled man, and according to Herodotus' story, Hecataeus had visited Egypt. Undoubtedly Hecataeus had visited many of the cities which he described in his *Periegesis*, but whether he relied mainly on his personal observations or on accounts from others is not something we can now determine.

The *Genealogies* are less well represented in the surviving fragments than his *Periegesis*. This may attest to the greater popularity of his geographical and social descriptions over his mythological themes. The *Periegesis* seems to have been constructed as a travel around the Mediterranean, beginning in the west at the Pillars of

---

* For the details of the lives and works of the logographers I acknowledge a great debt to Lionel Pearson, *Early Ionian Historians* (Oxford, 1939).

Hercules, proceeding eastward through Europe, and then westward back along the coast of Africa. In the course of the journey he included topographical descriptions, ethnic traditions and customs.

It is difficult to assess the importance of Hecataeus. Herodotus certainly owes him a considerable debt for the plan of the geographical and ethnographic part of his work and was probably indebted too for much of his information. When Herodotus tells the story of how the priests in Egypt had shown him the same 345 statues of the high priests which they had shown to Hecataeus it sounds as if Herodotus had followed in Hecataeus' footsteps, retracing the ground Hecataeus had already covered, perhaps in an attempt to check on the truthfulness of Hecataeus' accounts. The Greek historians had no compunction about borrowing from another writer without naming their source, and we have really no way of knowing to what extent Herodotus and later writers drew from Hecataeus. It is a reasonable assumption, however, that Hecataeus laid the foundation of a new kind of writing—the descriptive account in prose of societies, their origins, their physical appearance, their contemporary practices, and their myths. Hecataeus was part historian, part mythographer, part physical and social anthropologist.

Later writers, when mentioning Hecataeus by name, generally do so disparagingly. Heraclitus includes him in his list of men who had learning of many things but were without *nous* (i.e., intelligence or understanding). His later reputation suggests that Hecataeus presented a conglomerate array of facts, legends, tall tales, extravagant explanations, without much discrimination. But the judgment of a man like Heraclitus reflects his own critical and rational standards which would find the mere collection of facts and reports, without a unifying rationale, to be a trivial occupation. Moreover, later criticisms of Hecataeus were applying to him a more rigid differentiation between myth and history than was possible in Hecataeus' own day. His statement of purpose is a significant document in historiography. He prefaces his *Genealogies* with the words: "Hecataeus the Milesian narrates the following. These things I write as they seem to me to be true, for the stories of the Greeks are numerous and, in my opinion, ridiculous." Noteworthy in this statement is the emphasis on the author's identity and personal opinions (and he is an author, not a poet, as he shows by his choice of the word "write"). Some of the themes which he treats may seem purely mythical to us, but at least Hecataeus is subjecting these traditional myths to his personal scrutiny and accepting personal responsibility for his conclusions. Hecataeus is asserting his own independent judgment. What his critical principles were the surviving fragments do not permit us to say. Certainly they would not have been considered acceptable historical principles in a later age. But at least Hecataeus shows us the beginning of the principle of selection and discrimination. He will accept certain stories as genuine and reject others. More interesting than the grounds for his choice is the emergence of such a guiding principle of selectivity in his writings.

Hecataeus stands midway between the epic poets and Herodotus. The poet Hesiod had stated that the Muses could tell false stories as well as true, and had called on his Muses to help him separate one from the other. Hesiod, still writing in the formulaic language of the epic poets, had been a mythographer in verse, who had begun the work of systematization of the conflicting oral traditions. He had tried to bring coherence into the confusion. Hecataeus continued Hesiod's systematization in his *Genealogies,* but he carried the process one step further by rationalizing some of the myths and by dropping the poetic pose of dependence on the Muses. However much an artistic fiction Hesiod's Muses may have been, Hesiod still chose to support his work by an appeal to their authority. Hecataeus, however, has entirely dispensed with divine authority. With the publishing of Hecataeus' *Genealogies* history, as investigation of the past, was clearly demarcated as a province of human thought.

Other logographers have suffered an even worse fate than Hecataeus. XANTHUS, who was perhaps a slightly older contemporary of Herodotus, was praised in antiquity (though by a literary scholar who lived several centuries after Xanthus) for the sound knowledge of history which he displayed in his *Lydiaca,* his historical work on his own country, Lydia. He is credited with having established the history of Lydia and with having provided Herodotus with inspiration or a model for his own work. We must assume that Xanthus had written a work in the tradition of Hecataeus, but had narrowed his scope to a single country, whose topography and historical traditions he has investigated and recorded. Of CHARON of Lampsacus we know even less. From references in later writers Charon evidently lived during the fifth century and had included at least some contemporary history in his *Persica,* a work probably similar to Xanthus' *Lydica,* which had included historical, mythological and geographical descriptions.

HELLANICUS is likewise another shadowy figure today, but an interesting one because he is the only earlier historian mentioned by name by Thucydides. He too was an Ionian, from the city of Mytilene. His dates are uncertain, but from Thucydides' comment we know that he had included in his works at least certain historical events after the Persian Wars and even incidents in the Peloponnesian War. He was probably a slightly older contemporary of Thucydides, and lived to the very end of the fifth century. His reputation must have been soundly established before Thucydides came to write his *History*. According to later writers he was a prolific author, with a total of perhaps twenty works to his credit. In these works he treated the migrations of the Greek peoples to Asia Minor, the histories of certain Greek cities in Asia Minor, and the chronological problems of early mythical periods. He wrote also a history of Attica from its origins to his own day, and a work called *Persica,* historical and mythical, which probably handled the history of Persia from the mythical origins to the Persian defeat by the Greeks at the Battle of Salamis in 480 B.C. He seems to have devoted much attention to tracing the origins of cities and peoples, and to bringing chronological order into the confusion of mythological traditions. In order to give a greater plausibility to the chronology of the lists of generations from the mythical times to his present day he apparently resorted to the device of duplicating certain legendary names or introducing new names into the lists, thereby adding a few generations as seemed necessary.

Our interest is aroused because Hellanicus had included certain events of the Persian Wars and perhaps the Peloponnesian War in his *Histories,* thus overlapping the periods treated by Herodotus and Thucydides. Unfortunately nothing but the barest references exist to his historical studies, so that we cannot compare his method with that of the two historians who superseded him. Thucydides, in his only reference to Hellanicus, disparages his chronological method in his treatment of the period between the Persian and Peloponnesian Wars. It is noteworthy to compare the methods of the two historians in this respect. Thucydides had apparently introduced a more exact method of dating events than Hellanicus had used, but Thucydides is far from exact by our standards and cumbersome. Chronological problems were too complex for even the best historians of that period.

What is remarkable about the fate of Hellanicus' work is that his historical studies declined almost into oblivion. We should have considered his work a most valuable additional source against which to weigh the accounts of Thucydides and Herodotus, but in antiquity he was remembered not for his contemporary historical accounts but for his mythological studies and observations. For the Alexandrian mythographer Apollodorus, Hellanicus was an important source for early mythological traditions, but no one seems to have been much interested in his importance as an historical source. Though he had written a history of Athens there is no surviving fragment of his works which refers to any of the figures who played an important part in Athenian history, such as Solon or the members of the Peisistratid family. His historical works were entirely eclipsed by the works of Thucydides and later fourth-century historians. In the fate of Hellanicus' work we see yet another instance of that curious Greek indifference to verification and corroboration of evidence and their ready acceptance of a single authoritative account.

Limited as our knowledge is, we can draw a few general conclusions about the primary concerns of these early historians and of their influence on later antiquity. Their interests ranged widely from mythology to current traditions to history to geography. Their works are rationalistic only to a degree. These historians were not highly analytical, and in later times were often condemned for their credulity in accepting preposterous stories and hypotheses. Their interest in establishing a chronological continuity between the mythical past and their own times is on one hand an attempt to attach the present to the past, to support present customs by derivation from the past, but it is, on the other hand, also the expression of a desire to detach themselves from the past. These historians are beginning to assert their present as something logically a consequence of the past but yet discrete from the past. The present is becoming something worthy of commemoration in its own right. No longer are the Ionians willing to be subsumed into the mythical past. The Homeric poems are no longer accepted as an adequate document of the Greek identity. The line between myth and history is still only faintly drawn, but the logographers' contribution is to assert the existence of such a line.

HERODOTUS

FOR the few reliable facts which can be given about the life of Herodotus we must rely almost totally on the few references in his own writings. An Ionian, he was born in the city of Halicarnassus early in the fifth century B.C. Some time about the middle of the century he was banished by Lygdamis, the tyrant of Halicarnassus, and traveled to Samos and thence to Athens, where he seems to have taken up residence. In 443 B.C. he went with a group of Athenians to establish the new Athenian colony at Thurii in Italy. Certain references in his narrative imply that he lived at least until the beginning of the Peloponnesian War in 431 B.C. During the course of his lifetime he traveled extensively around the Eastern Mediterranean, certainly visiting the Black Sea, Babylon, Phoenicia, and Egypt.

His *Histories* is the story of the rise of Persian power, the growing friction between Greece and Persia, and the decisive battles between the Greeks and the Persians at Marathon, Thermopylae, and Salamis. He carries his account down to the capture of the city of Sestos in 478 B.C. His story is, therefore, the historical record of events almost contemporaneous and even contemporaneous with his own lifetime. But Herodotus does not limit his narrative only to those nearly contemporaneous events. He uses them as the springboard from which to move into the far past. His mention of the conflict between Greece and Persia takes him back to the origins of the Persian hegemony. He first relates the reigns of Cyrus and Cambyses, then devotes a large section of his work to the reign of Darius, saving for the final section the climactic story of the decisive defeat of the Persian power in Greece. It is a story which reaches far into the past and slowly moves to its climax in the heroic stand of the small Greek states against the great Persian juggernaut.

Such is the skeletal outline, but it gives no idea of the varied subjects which are included in the *Histories,* nothing of the author's panoramic vision. Herodotus does not restrict himself to the Persians and Greeks, but casts his net wide to catch the history, geography, legends and customs of many countries of the Mediterranean, such as Egypt and Scythia. Herodotus has incorporated the observations and notes made on his various travels into the work, and used those legends and curiosities as the background against which to set the great struggle of the Greeks and Persians. Herodotus' *Histories* is a large tapestry of the eastern Mediterranean world of the sixth century B.C. into which are woven, along with genuinely historical material, sociological observations, sceptical considerations on early mythology and modern miracles, dialogues between Greeks and Persians on political theory, scientific hypotheses, folktales—some amusing, some perverse—legends associated with historical figures, and some backstairs gossip. It is a crowded and animated tapestry, ingenious and artfully woven. It is, among many things, the first comprehensive folklore study in European letters.

Herodotus fascinates us with his quiet irony, his amused tolerance, his wide range of interests. Yet when we compare him with other writers and thinkers in Greece who are his contemporaries, or even his predecessors, our first reaction is to dismiss Herodotus as a naïf, charming certainly, but out of the mainstream of serious intellectual thought. Beside the startling scientific hypotheses or the pregnant intellectual assertions of the philosophers and natural scientists, or the psychological explorations of myth in the dramas of the Athenian tragedians, the ideas and style of Herodotus seem artless and superficial. Had we no information about Herodotus, we might assume him to be the product of an earlier century in Greece or perhaps of a culture less intensely intellectual than that of Greece in the fifth century B.C. Herodotus frequently expresses his scepticism. "I record what I have heard," he says, "but I do not have to believe it. You may take this as my principle throughout my work."

In spite of this *caveat*, Herodotus' attitude towards miraculous events in his own time or towards historical causation is often not appreciably superior to the attitudes of folk religion. Divine manifestations in the form of oracles and omens cross the pages of his narrative without apology. Divine jealousy which exacts its catastrophic penalty from any man who reaches an eminence is so frequent a theme in his work that history virtually becomes a catalogue of examples of hybris and retribution. Fate plays its important part in the dramas of the Athenian tragedians too, but the difference between Sophocles and Herodotus is enormous. Beside the psychological probing of fate and character in *Oedipus Rex*, Herodotus' idea of Fate seems simplistic indeed. The very idea of Destiny which Herodotus assumes so uncritically Sophocles subjects to an agonized analysis, thereby raising it to a higher level of intellectual and psychological maturity. No such introspection is found in Herodotus; yet we cannot dismiss him, as ancient writers often did and as scholars in certain periods have done, without doing a great injustice to his real contribution to historiography and to the wider field of humanistic thought.

Herodotus is not only the first European historian whose work we possess; he is also the first literary artist in prose. Both aspects of his contribution entitle him to respect and serious study. Cicero had called Herodotus the Father of History. If the works of the earlier logographers existed we might have to modify that title; yet we suspect that any new discoveries of their works would still show Herodotus to be as superior to them in his conception of history as Thucydides was later to be superior to Herodotus.

Herodotus has much in common with the earlier logographers. Like Hecataeus he prefaces his work by identifying himself and calling his work *historiae*. His work is to be, like that of his predecessors, the record of personal research stamped with the author's authority and credibility. He too is a logographer in the literal sense, i.e., a collector of stories. His *Histories* is an encyclopedia of various stories from all over the Mediterranean, from Greek and non-Greek sources. His interest is not restricted to the purely historical. In the second half of his work, when he is dealing with historical events, Herodotus adheres to a stricter principle of historical relevance, but the first half of his work is under no such restriction. Some of his stories are historical, others legendary. Some are amusing or bizarre folktales. Others are aetiological myths which people tell to explain the existence of a local phenomenon or monument. Others deal with local customs, superstitions or religious observances. The word *history* still carries no connotation about the study of the past; its meaning is still "research," of whatever kind. Herodotus' *Histories* is, therefore, a mine of information in many fields which would today be considered separate disciplines, with no rigid distinctions between one interest and another. Herodotus is geographer, mythographer, ethnographer and historian all in one.

The stories which Herodotus collects are of necessity, like those of his predecessors, stories which have been preserved by oral tradition. His researches are not those of the modern historian. They are not the inspection and comparison of written documents, nor do they draw on the silent testimony of epigraphical or numismatic evidence. There were, of course, available at the time of Herodotus' writing the works of earlier logographers, and these Herodotus certainly consulted and even borrowed from, but we cannot determine to what extent Herodotus is dependent on them. By his time there was also undoubtedly something resembling public archives (though "archives" is probably too grandiose a name for the rudimentary records) in many of the Greek cities, in which lists of various public magistrates were recorded. Herodotus may have drawn on these for certain chronological sequences but he is still too much a native of the oral culture to be interested in the kind of chronicle that can be strung together from official archives or even to be fully aware of the value of such documentation. Herodotus' account of his conversation with the priests in Egypt gives an example of the kind of archives he would find interesting: the long corridors lined with the statues of successive priests provided the graphic kind of documentation which he and his listeners could appreciate. The visible monument and the stories which might be told in connection with such a monument, these are what catch his eye and ear.

Even where Herodotus is recording historical events, for which some documentation might be available, his method is the same. He avoids documenting his facts and prefers instead to hold his listeners' attention with the drama of the story. This is by no means to imply that Herodotus was indifferent to factual accuracy. Far from it. But he would have considered documentary facts a dull weight to impose upon the drama.

Because one of his principal interests is to record and preserve oral traditions, Herodotus discriminates little between the historical and the mythical, between the probable and the improbable. Occasionally he notifies us that he is excluding a story or an explanation for some event because of its palpable absurdity or because its inclusion would violate his sense of propriety but apart from a few such discretions he is the most catholic of writers. Not only is every kind of tale welcome in his pages but variants of the same tale are frequently included, with the evaluation left to the reader. Certain myths, such as the one of Heracles, intrigue him, and he tracks them down where he can. In later times he was to be severely censured for his catholicity. He was called a *mythopoios,* when the word had become derogatory, when the word *myth* had come to mean not any kind of story, but a false or improbable story.

This accusation was unfair but an understandable one. When the distinction between factual truth and myth had been more rigorously drawn, when history had been established as a category separate from mythology and folklore, later writers saw Herodotus' catholicity as indicative of either a gullible intelligence or a rather base willingness to sacrifice truth in the interests of popular entertainment. Modern scholarship has rehabilitated Herodotus' reputation. Some of his apparently extravagant anthropological tales we now see had some basis in truth, and in much of his genuinely historical record he has often surprised his critics by his accuracy. We can better understand the extent to which Herodotus' kind of research was inevitably dictated by the conditions of his time.

Because his sources, even in his more historical sections, are largely oral reports, Herodotus places much emphasis on the authority of his personal intelligence and integrity. His information is not the kind which can be easily verified by others. The famous battles of Marathon and Salamis were not written up in generals' memoirs or by the local press. There may have been written accounts of the chief events in reigns of the Persian kings, Darius and Xerxes, but it is doubtful whether Herodotus would have had access to such records. Certain historical facts he may have drawn from references in the poets or the logographers, but a handful of such facts does not make a sustained historical narrative. Herodotus, therefore, must assure us that he has taken pains in his personal research, and that he has maintained his objectivity in collecting and comparing the various accounts of a single event. He emphasizes the personal observation, experience, and intelligent reflection which he has brought to his study. In the absence of other corroborating evidence the only test of veracity is the author's powers of observation and intelligent discrimination.

This emphasis on the intelligence and reliability of the author is a feature to be found in Hecataeus' work, as presumably also in the writings of the other logographers. They were all men who were attempting to bring the spirit of rational inquiry to the myths and historical legends of the Greeks. They were contradicting received opinions about myths and miracles not so much with new data as on the basis of intelligent surmise. The personal credibility of the author in their writings was, therefore, necessary and commendable. It remained, however, a salient feature of all ancient historiography, not always to the advantage of historical studies. Thucydides, for example, asserts the thoroughness of his research and his objectivity as strongly as Herodotus and is contemptuous of his predecessors' lack of such care and objectivity. What is so admirable in Herodotus becomes much less admirable in Thucydides because Thucydides' research is into the facts, not merely the reports, and the facts which he relates can be more easily documented from inscriptions of decrees, assessments of tribute, civic archives, and other historical writings. The most convincing proof of the credibility of a history which relies on written documents is the actual citation of sources rather than the author's insistence on his mental acumen. The author's affirmation of his objectivity, therefore, is in Herodotus an important advance in historiography, but becomes a weakness in later historians who rely on it to the exclusion of available documentation.

For all his obvious affinity to the logographers, Herodotus is in one important respect quite different from them. His introductory words reveal the difference quite clearly. Herodotus states that his purpose is to record the deeds of the Greeks and the Persians so that their glory may not be lost to posterity. His central theme is to be the magnificent achievements of the Greeks and the barbarians. This is not the language of a logographer or even of an historian, but of a poet. To commemorate and immortalize great men is the attitude governing Homeric poetry. Herodotus is frankly following in Homer's footsteps in commemorating the achievements of his own day. Modern historians are not wholly free from the touch of the poet who would commemorate glorious deeds, but few historians today would admit that their primary motive was commemoration of the past. Responsible historians concentrate less on the glory and more on the aspects of the past which significantly affect the conditions of the present. But history had not become separated from poetry in Herodotus' day. History now concerns itself with the questions, how and why, but Herodotus is less interested in tracing abstract causes and more in the drama of unfolding events.

The memorable events which Herodotus chooses to relate were the Persian Wars which took place in the early part of the fifth century. His theme at once calls to mind Homer's theme: heroism in war. Herodotus not only imitates Homer; he competes with him. He gives the Greeks a new epic, an epic of the present which can stand beside the great epic of the past. He invests the present with a heroic significance which had hitherto been the exclusive property of the primeval past. If we can separate the facts of the Persian Wars from Herodotus' treatment of those wars, we can see how successful he was in heroizing the present. His evaluation of the wars is a gross exaggeration of their significance, but it is an evaluation which has prevailed through antiquity even to this day.

It is a misnomer to refer, as we do, to the conflict between the Greeks and the Persians as the "Persian Wars." As Thucydides later noted, the issues were decided in only three isolated battles, fought over a ten-year period, with little loss of life or destruction of property on the Greek side. There was more, it is true, to the confrontation between Persia and Greece than those few battles. There had been political machinations over a period of years, subventions, intrigue, and power plays between the Greeks of Asia Minor and various Persian satraps, but the "wars" were of limited scope and influence. Herodotus, however, with his eye on the epic proportions of the Trojan War in the *Iliad,* has created a national and even a universal epic by the inclusion of much material which is not strictly germane to the conflict between the two countries. That conflict comes as the climax of his work, and he has further enhanced its importance by his long and circuitous discussion of the most varied subjects. By including as the preamble to his main theme the history, geography, and ethnography of Egypt, Lydia, Scythia, and Mediterranean countries, and only slowly centering his attention on Greece and, within Greece, on Athens, he has made the Greeks' resistance to the Persian invader a momentous event in world history.

A momentous event it is still considered to be, but it is not at all certain that the course of European history would have been significantly altered if Darius or Xerxes had succeeded and had sailed back leaving their satraps as governors in Sparta and Athens. There were, after all, Greeks in the cities of Asia Minor who owed allegiance to the Persian king but they proved to be fractious subjects. The Great King's power over the Greek cities of Asia Minor was more nominal than real. How much less would he have been able to exert any effective control over the cities of mainland Greece far away across the sea. No, Hellas prostrate in chains at the feet of the Persian king was an image closer to the apocalyptic vision of tragedy than to political realities.

After the Persians suffered their disastrous defeat in Greece it was natural that national patriotism and relief that the danger had been averted should give rise to the belief among the Greeks that civilization had beaten back the forces of barbarism. The Athenians, furthermore, found the cry to be an expedient one as they set about creating their own hegemony to substitute for the Persian hegemony which had threatened Greece. Herodotus reflects this Hellenic and particularly Athenian pride and has his share in magnifying it. The wars are so elevated by his poetic and dramatic skill that we might almost suppose that the world shuddered and its denizens gaped with bated breath as Europe and Asia glared at each other, one afternoon, across a small plain in an obscure corner of the Balkans. Thucydides was later to criticize earlier writers (Herodotus?) for magnifying the Persian Wars entirely out of proper proportion and to claim that they were in fact trivial in comparison with the cataclysmic effects of the Peloponnesian War. In recent times some scholars have come to Herodotus' defense, but surely Thucydides was right. By any standards, whether the cost of the destruction of life or property or the political issues at stake, the Persian Wars were not of momentous significance. The Greek victory over the Persians certainly gave a dynamic impetus to art, commerce, and political thought at Athens and to a lesser degree elsewhere, but it was not so much the victory itself as the idea of the triumphant stand of small city-states against the massive power of the Persian king which triggered the release of that energy which we look at in amazement even today.

Herodotus' primary purpose, then, was to do for a contemporary event what Homer had done for the Trojan War. He chose a heroic theme, the confrontation of Greece and Persia, then proceeded to make of it something even more epic—the confrontation of two continents and two ideologies: Europe and Asia, freedom and slavery, democracy and tyranny. What was in fact a fairly straightforward military conflict became a War of Ideas, the heroic struggle of civilization against barbarism. It is fair to say that these issues were projected back into the conflict after the event. No such momentous issues were recognized during the event, or if they were, they were not governing motives in the behavior of the Greeks during the crisis. The oracle of Apollo at Delphi, that panHellenic shrine, had, after all, inclined more to the Persian side than to the Greek, and many other Greek cities either followed its example or exhibited a lukewarm enthusiasm at best for the defense of Greece.

The idea that civilization itself was at stake in the Persian Wars was undoubtedly largely a creation of the Athenians after Salamis as they set about building a navy and erecting magnificent temples on their Acropolis with their allies' money. If Herodotus did not formulate the idea, his epic treatment of the conflict is largely responsible for perpetuating that idea.

It was not, however, only in his choice of theme and in his vision of his theme that Herodotus showed himself to be more poet than historian. In his style, his vocabulary, his arrangement of the parts within the whole, Herodotus often recalls Homer. He has the same directness, the same delight in a story, the same pleasure in the peripheral detail. The structure of the whole work consciously looks back to the dramatic narrative form of Homeric epic. It is probable that the researches into geography, ethnography, and mythology which make up the first half of his work were originally intended as a separate work rather along the lines of the historical researches of the other logographers. But at some point Herodotus saw as his unifying theme the conflict between Greece and Persia, and then incorporated his earlier logographic researches into his more strictly factual history of the battles which now forms the latter half of his work.

The folkways of the Egyptians and Lydians have little to do with the battles of Marathon or Salamis, and a modern historian would consider them extraneous to the central theme. But dramatically they are highly satisfying. In their comprehensive range and their punctilious detail they create a dense, vivid milieu for the drama of the Persian Wars. The whole of the Mediterranean becomes a single canvas in the foreground of which the Persian Wars take their prominent place. But the background is crowded with figures vigorously pursuing their own ends and fulfilling their roles in their own dramas of passion and hybris. In each miniature tableau the figures are drawn with as much care as the larger figures in the foreground.

It is easy to overlook the enormous skill of Herodotus in the creation of his world and his contribution as a prose stylist. Verse had been the literary vehicle until shortly before Herodotus' time and the art of prose was still in its infancy when Herodotus set himself to write. The logographers had written their researches in prose but it was in his hands that the art of prose narrative came of age. In the whole of the classical period Herodotus has few rivals as a stylist.

Herodotus, then, found it natural to look to Homer as his model and in doing so created a new art form. Sometimes the artist in Herodotus militates against the historian. He is a storyteller rather than an analytic historian. He will follow his threads where they lead, and his eye is alert for the graphic, the dramatic, the unexpected. The dramatist in him may lead him at times to sacrifice historical accuracy in the interests of a moral tale, as when he has the Persian king debating the merits of various forms of government. It is possible that the Persians were interested in political theory, but the political debate seems more Greek than Persian, and even perhaps more post-Salamis than pre-Salamis. There are other discussions in Herodotus, on religion or culture, which are put in the mouths of the barbarians, though they sound more appropriate to the emerging analytic consciousness of the Greeks. But perhaps such issues were in fact debated by the more speculative barbarians who had caught the intellectual fever from the Greeks in Asia Minor. We may remain sceptical about some parts of Herodotus' record, but it has proved dangerous to condemn Herodotus for outright falsification. He has often surprised his critics by his accuracy.

The dramatist in Herodotus also led him to emphasize the supernatural element more than a modern historian could find acceptable. He accepts and incorporates the reports of oracles and omens, mostly without critical evaluation. Such instances of supernatural intervention are highly dramatic and have enormous popular appeal, but Herodotus' concentration on them distracts from more serious consideration of human motivation. An analysis which relies on the supernatural obscures rather than forwards our understanding of historical causation.

Quite valid objections, therefore, can be made to Herodotus' kind of historiography. We can appreciate his subtle wit and his lively narrative, but regret that he emphasizes engaging narrative to the virtual exclusion of serious analysis. We regret that he did not carry his scepticism further, that he did not probe deeper into psychology and historical causation. We must regret, too, the exaggerated weight which he attaches to the authority of his own observation and intelligence. Even though the sources available to Herodotus are different from those available to a modern historian, he could have been more precise. He could have given us better opportunity to exercise our own judgement. When he tells us, for example, that he talked with the priests in Egypt, many questions immediately occur to us. Did he converse in their language, or did he speak through an interpreter? If through an interpreter, was the interpreter Greek or Egyptian? Was he one of the priests or an outsider? What priests did Herodotus talk to, novices or high priests? Such details, and many others, we should consider essential for a true estimation of the accuracy and reliability of the information. Perhaps, we may think, Herodotus misunderstood the priests, or perhaps the priests misinformed him or even deliberately humored him with invented stories. Herodotus trusts his own powers of discrimination, and it does not occur to him that we should be less confident.

Similarly with other stories and facts. For some Herodotus merely says that this is the version which is current in a certain city. "This is the story which the Corinthians tell," he says in concluding his story of Arion and the dolphin, "and the Lesbians tell the same story." At other times his sources are even more anonymous. A story is told simply as Herodotus heard it; of the original narrator we know nothing. On still other occasions he acknowledges no sources at all. Almost certainly much of the ethnographic information in the first half of his work is garnered from the works of his predecessors. He may rely on them for topics or places which he has not personally investigated, but he does not think it necessary to inform us when and to what extent he draws on their researches. Plagiarism had not yet become the worst of scholastic vices. Similarly, even in his description of historic events, such as the battles at Marathon and Salamis, Herodotus gives us little or no information about his sources. We are left to deduce the identity of his informants from Herodotus' own narrative or from data which we may glean from outside his work. It is here, when he is dealing with important historical events, that Herodotus' failure to give us the means to estimate the relative value of his facts is particularly distressing. We find it regrettable that he should make his selection among the various accounts at his disposal without divulging the grounds for his selection.

For this failing, however, Herodotus cannot be altogether dismissed. The idea that objectivity of the observer may be ultimately impossible is a very recent development in historiography. It may well be universally accepted now among historians that any historical study must inevitably be colored by the personal bias of the historian. In sister disciplines the question of the objectivity of the observer is still one to raise blood counts and adrenalin levels. To compensate for the inherent parallax of vision the modern researcher bolsters his arguments wherever possible with incontrovertible facts, references to accessible documents, and discussions of previous studies on the same topic. Merely to state his case is not sufficient for the modern historian. He must persuade. His footnotes are the rhetoric of scientific persuasion. The impossibility of objectivity was a question never raised in antiquity. In this respect Herodotus is no more guilty than Thucydides, Tacitus, Sallust, or any other ancient historian. An historian might take issue with an earlier historian and give what he thought was a truer account of a particular event. He might question the objectivity of his predecessor; he might accuse his predecessor of bias; but that he himself or his sources might be equally biased was not a thought an ancient historian ever entertained. Critical as they frequently were of their predecessors' facts or interpretations, the ancient historians, from Herodotus to Polybius, were supremely confident of the impartiality of their own intellects. Not one ever feels it necessary, even when drawing information from a written document, to cite the document verbatim. The personal integrity or good faith of the historian was considered sufficient assurance of veracity.

Even the criticisms which the historians leveled at their predecessors are rarely directed to the directly historical parts of their works, to the facts or to the interpretation of those facts. Herodotus was accused of partiality at a later time, but the most contemptuous criticisms were directed at his apparently absurd fables and tall tales. When critics called him *fabulosus,* i.e., a writer of fictions, it was not his historical narrative which they were calling in question, but his willing acceptance of the supernatural and of the improbable tales which he picked up in his travels. Even Thucydides, who seems to be aiming his criticisms at Herodotus, although never mentioning him by name, does not attempt a new account of the battles of the Persian Wars, or even any new interpretation of the wars, although in the course of his own investigations he must have collected many facts which Herodotus had not included in his work. What he criticizes in his predecessors is the mythical element in their work, their faulty systems of chronology, their methods, and their scope.

When it came to philosophical ideas the Greeks were willing to engage in passionate debate. But with their disdain for facts they would have thought it a thankless task indeed to check those which another had already collected. The modern researcher must carefully sift through the minutest and most fragmentary kinds of data to check the facts in Herodotus' account. Thucydides, though he was not interested in rewriting Herodotus' account, had many more documents and traditions available to him than we have today with which to substantiate or to attack Herodotus' historical narrative. Thucydides even criticizes his predecessors for their inaccuracies on occasion; yet he does not bother to set the record straight himself. He was more interested in proposing a new method, a new kind of historiography, than in rewriting earlier history.

In spite of the obvious limitations in Herodotus' historical method and in his analytic powers, in spite of the dramatist in Herodotus who has his eye on the unexpected coincidences and the fulfillment of ominous oracles and who amplifies his theme in the manner of the poets, Herodotus is indubitably an historian. The ideas which pervade his work are genuinely historiographic. These ideas were to be defined more precisely by Thucydides, and still later by modern historians, but Herodotus' significance lies in his formulation of those ideas and in his commitment to them.

Herodotus' work is the record of actual events in the present and the result of his personal investigation into the accounts of those events. If an historian's duty is, in von Ranke's words, "to tell what actually happened," then Herodotus is certainly an historian. A common idiom in Herodotus' pages is the expression "the things which are," and this idiom well expresses Herodotus' ideal. He will tell "the things which are." The difference between Herodotus and von Ranke's modern historian is that the modern historian is in search of the facts while Herodotus is in search of the traditions of what happened. His documents will be the stories circulating by word of mouth in the various cities. Herodotus stakes his reputation not so much on the truth of an event as on the accuracy of his reporting of the traditions relating to the event. Herodotus was little interested in the lifeless chronicle to be extracted from mere catalogues, whether of kings or civic officials or of athletic victors. His history is the history of living oral traditions corrected by his personal observation and comparison. The constant presence of the author throughout his work, sympathetic and curious, weighing conflicting stories, examining monuments, questioning local inhabitants, tracing down a vagrant tradition, offering rationalizing hypotheses, calls attention to Herodotus' ideal of truth—not truth as a metaphysical abstraction, but truth as something more elementary, more concrete, and closer to the truth of science than of philosophy. If we understand the concrete nature of Herodotus' kind of truth, we shall understand that he has every right to be considered an historian. His emphasis on personal investigation of the traditions and his commitment to exactitude in his reporting mark Herodotus' truly scientific spirit.

Modern scholarship has tended to vindicate Herodotus' accuracy and to find his respect for facts to be far greater than was generally assumed in antiquity. Herodotus, in actuality, shows himself in his respect for facts considerably superior to his contemporaries and indeed to most later historians in antiquity. His garrulous style and relaxed manner hide the painstaking study behind the writing and obscure the fact, which modern scholarship is beginning to reveal, that in his pursuit of accuracy Herodotus set an ideal which few ancient historians were able to realize. Though Herodotus does not elaborate on the sources of his information as much as we would desire, he is often a great deal more explicit about his sources than later historians who frequently synthesized several traditions into a single account without a word of warning to their readers. Such is Herodotus' respect for the differing traditions that he often records variant versions of the same story, or at least informs us that the version he has recorded is but one of several which were current. His respect for the multitudinous variety of oral traditions is opposed to any narrow principle of selection. Any historian must select and edit his facts but Herodotus is more reluctant than most to do so. He wants to be exhaustive, encyclopedic. We have, furthermore, Herodotus' word that he retraced the steps of his predecessor Hecataeus in order to check the latter's facts and theories. To what extent Herodotus' journey around the Mediterranean was a replica of Hecataeus' earlier travels, or to what extent he has lifted passages from Hecataeus' accounts, we cannot tell. But we do know that Herodotus, as he traveled, was testing Hecataeus' account, and published his version of the facts as an improvement on Hecataeus. This perseverance in checking facts which another writer had already published was an admirable characteristic, and showed a spirit of critical inquiry which was rare among historians in antiquity.

It comes as a surprise to us today to hear that there was in antiquity considerable animosity against Herodotus. Even Cicero can in the same sentence call Herodotus the Father of History and a teller of myths and fables (*fabulosus*). One accusation which was particularly strong was that of partiality toward the Athenians in Herodotus' account. Plutarch, whose idea of history was a collection of legendary anecdotes which could be woven into biographical romances convenient to his own moral didacticism, this same Plutarch gave the stamp of literary authority to the charge of Herodotus' partiality. That Herodotus was writing for an Athenian audience is a reasonable assumption from the internal evidence. There is also no doubt as to where his sympathies lie in his comparisons of Greek and barbarian mores and institutions. As we read him today, however, we are struck not by his partiality towards Athens or Greece but by the very opposite characteristic. The degree of his impartiality would be a credit to any modern historian. Not only are both Spartans and Athenians given their due, but barbarians too are treated with sympathy and objectivity.

Herodotus' *Histories* is certainly a panegyric on Greek ideals and Greek accomplishments, but Herodotus' own purpose was, as he himself states, "to prevent the great deeds of the Greeks and the barbarians from losing the glory which is their due." He amply fulfilled his purpose. His whole work is distinguished by its tone of dispassionate objectivity.* He may at times be sceptical or quietly amused by some tale, but he is never scandalized. He may even be misinformed at times, but he is never patently unfair. Later historians such as Thucydides were to attempt an even more resolute impartiality than they thought Herodotus had achieved. Thucydides' intentions are admirable, but yet Thucydides' rigidity is also his weakness. He has an even greater confidence in his own objectivity than Herodotus, and his confidence leads him to eliminate any information which his own judgement finds irrelevant. As a result his work is sparser in facts and we are necessarily more dependent on his particular judgement and interpretation of events. Herodotus too asks us to take his word for the facts, but his impartiality is intellectually humbler than Thucydides', with the result that his work is far richer in sheer factual data. Herodotus is not disconcerted by the possible irrelevance of a story, and in his irrelevance lies not only much of his charm, but also, what is more important, much of his value. He reports even where he does not believe. And he is willing, even if not as consistently or as fully as we would wish, to identify his sources, whereas Thucydides ignores such a practice altogether. As a thinker Thucydides is more profound, but for our knowledge of the Greeks and their neighbors in the sixth and fifth centuries B.C. Herodotus' flexibility and his humility are more helpful.

But Herodotus is more than a convenient source book of facts. He is more than an antiquarian. His claim to be Europe's first historian still stands true, despite the vagaries of his narrative and the limitations of his analytical powers. With his impar-

* On this point see the excellent article "Truth and Politics" by Hannah Arendt in *The New Yorker,* XLIII (February 25, 1967), 49–88.

tiality and his dedication to accurate reporting he created not only a new genre in literature but also a new concept which we today call history. Even the discursiveness of his narrative is more than merely entertaining or informative. His concept of history is closely bound up with that discursiveness and catholicity. In his own way he created the idea of a universal history, one in which events do not happen in isolation but are all part of one unified drama. There had been chroniclers before Herodotus who had written the isolated histories of individual cities or of special events, but Herodotus was the first to take a contemporary event as the basis on which to create a unified study of a single period out of the complexities and diversities of cultural traditions. Later historians might make more searching explorations into the interdependence of events of disparate periods and places but it was Herodotus who first saw that history cannot be parochial, that history is something other than mere local annals. Herodotus thus gave to Europe a new intellectual concept and a new ideal. An in the execution of his work he came as close to realizing the ideal which he had created as any historian in antiquity. There are even those who will argue that historiography took a step backwards after Herodotus.

THUCYDIDES

To move from Herodotus to Thucydides seems, on first impression, a move not merely from one century to another but from antiquity to modern times. In spite of the obvious differences between the Greek city-states and modern nations in their institutions, their size, their character, Thucydides' world seems familiar and contemporary while Herodotus' does not. Herodotus and Thucydides, however, were near contemporaries. They were living within and viewing the same social conditions. It is, therefore, not the quality of the institutions which has altered so radically between the first historian and his successor as the temper of the individual. The mind of Thucydides is something radically new and his perception of that same world which Hereodotus inhabited is in consequence entirely different.

Herodotus' perspective is essentially that of the sixth century B.C. rather than of the fifth. It is not merely that his account is of events of a previous generation or a previous age. Even his scepticism, his rationalism, his formulation of theoretical questions on the merits of various political systems seem more at home in archaic Greece before the fifth century. In his theodicy too he is closer to a man like Hesiod, the cosmogonist, than to Sophocles.

But Thucydides' mind has assimilated the intellectual ideas of the fifth century. He sees the panorama of events through the filter of entirely new concepts. He does more than merely interpret the world in the light of these concepts. His mind wrestles with them and impels them in directions in which no one had yet taken them.

Thucydides is not a man who merely borrows from current intellectual movements. They have become a part of his very being; they define his particular vision. He sees in them possibilities of thought and analysis hitherto unknown. In reading Thucydides we are made aware of a mind in the process of creating such new categories and concepts.

It is this creative analytic intelligence in Thucydides which distinguishes him as a modern rather than an archaic writer. Conditions of modern times have become vastly different from those of his time. Yet, Thucydides' kind of analysis is modern, even if modern historians have discovered other categories which Thucydides did not sufficiently perceive or comprehend. So contemporary does his kind of analysis seem that it has been an easy error to project the similarity in the historiographic intent of Thucydides and modern historians into the world of actual events. When Thucydides writes of power politics, of the two political Colossi of the Greek world confronting each other, of class struggle, of political hysteria, of libertarian ideals used in justification of repressive autocracy, his world seems much more modern than it really is. Analogies are there, of course, but Thucydides' modern tone may make us miss the crucial distinctions.

Thucydides' active commitment to ideas and his attempt to subject history to an analysis based on ideas gives to his work, paradoxical as it may seem, a vividness and an impact more direct than we find even in Herodotus. Thucydides' kind of realism has a particularly modern ring. Thucydides' history is marked by a high level of intellectual abstraction. Where Herodotus tells the story Thucydides must also analyze in abstract categories. And yet Thucydides' account is more realistic not in spite of his abstractions but because of them. They are the observations of an intelligence which sees events from the inside rather than from the outside. Herodotus' account is the report from the outsider. The world he portrays is real enough, vivid and dynamic. People reveal their passions, their vanities, perversions, ambitions. Human will thwarts human will, to be thwarted in turn by the Divine Will. Men's highest ambitions are betrayed by trivial errors in their own judgment or by the innocent indiscretions of a young child. It is a world vividly alive and full of drama, but ultimately a superficial world. Herodotus sees events from a distance; he does not enter in them as does Thucydides.

It is true that Herodotus is recording many events of which he was not an eyewitness. He gives us the stories he has collected of times past or of alien cultures, and his primary interest is in the story. Thucydides, on the other hand, records events of his own lifetime, in which he personally participated. But it is a mistake to explain the immediacy of Thucydides' narrative as the result of his eyewitness observation and personal participation. As Herodotus was growing up when the Persian Wars were still of the immediate past he had as much opportunity to consult actual participants in those events of his early childhood as Thucydides had for the events of his *History*. He had grown up in centers such as Halicarnassus and Athens which were alive with philosophical speculation, with political debate and political machinations. He had lived to see the Delian League become an imperialist institution to render Athenian hegemony more secure. He had probably attended the tragedies in Athens, had talked with poets, philosophers, politicians. All the advantages, in short, which accrued to Thucydides by his residence in Athens, the boisterous commercial, intellectual and political crossroads of Greece, were available to Herodotus also. Then, too, Thucydides records many events at which he had not been present. He, too, must rely on other witnesses, some of whom may have been leaders who played decisive roles, others probably ordinary hoplites who hardly even understood the events which Thucydides asked them to recall for him.

The difference between the two is that Herodotus is the traveler, an observant traveler but still a traveler, in search of the curious. Thucydides has nothing in common with the guidebook mentality. He is, rather, a man who is compelled to enter, by a deliberate act of imagination, as fully as possible into events in order to analyze them from within. He had brought all his intellect and concentration to bear on the political activity of his own city and had thus analyzed and experienced them as a participant who understood the issues and personalities involved. He then projected this participant's kind of observation into events which he had not witnessed in other cities. It is because he has, mentally if not physically, entered into the political arena at Athens that he can make the mental leap to the internal politics in Corinth or elsewhere and to the intercity politics which dominate his accounts.

It is not only in political debate that Thucydides shows this empathetic understanding. Even his factual narratives, such as his account of the military affair at Pylos between the Athenians and the Spartans or his account of the Athenians' disastrous expedition to Syracuse, read like the reports of a man who was on the scene and also on a high enough level of command to see the pattern of the whole. When, for example, Thucydides describes the fighting at Pylos as a sea battle fought from the land and a land battle fought on the sea, this kind of observation strikes us as one made by Thucydides to himself as he listened to various accounts and visualized the scene for himself. He has created the whole scene down to its last details in his own mind and then tries to project that same visual accuracy into his narrative. Thucydides restricts his narrative to far fewer events than Herodotus does, but in the events which he chooses to relate he is far more concerned about detail than Herodotus. Where Herodotus may single out one dramatic or picturesque detail, Thucydides approaches the event as a scientist classifying a new species. All details are important. Minor inaccuracies in certain details may indicate that Thucydides was not a participant in a particular event, but such inaccuracies, as the proof of his absence from the scene, only increase our admiration for his painstaking reconstruction of the event from the accounts of others and for his imaginative grasp of the situation in its complexity. Thucydides' analysis of politics is perceptive and lively, not solely because he was more active in politics than Herodotus, though he perhaps was so. It is a reflection of his insistence on accuracy in all details and of his ability to project himself, with greater empathy, into the very center of any situation.

Accuracy is, indeed, the theme of Thucydides' statement of purpose. His chief criticism of his predecessors is directed at their inaccuracies. Hellanicus, who had written a history of Athens from the end of the Persian Wars down to the time of the Peloponnesian Wars, is the only historian whom Thucydides identifies by name, and he identifies Hellanicus only to criticize his factual errors and his chronological confusions. His other predecessors Thucydides criticizes in more general terms. In a passage which concludes Thucydides' analysis of past history Thucydides sets forth his method and principles directly, and in doing so disparages the efforts of earlier historians. He claims that his evidence is better than that of poets or of logographers "who are less interested in telling the truth than in catching the attention of the public, whose authorities cannot be checked, and whose subject matter, owing to the passage of time, is mostly lost in the unreliable streams of mythology." "We claim instead," he continues, "to have used only the plainest evidence and to have reached conclusions which are reasonably accurate" (Warner trans). He continues by stating that it has been his principle not to write down the first story that he heard or to rely only on his own impressions, but to check the accounts of various witnesses, and to collate them into a single coherent account. He concludes by apologizing for the "absence of the storytelling element" in his work, but claims that his work was designed not for the "taste of an immediate public but as a possession to last forever."

Thucydides here criticizes his predecessors on two counts: their motives, which allowed them to pander to popular taste for entertainment, and their indifference towards accuracy. Their work is *mythodes,* given to *mythoi.* By this word he probably means not only the romantic element of their tales, but the whole divine apparatus of oracles, omens, and epiphanies—all the implausible and unverifiable details which earlier historians had freely incorporated into their writings. Clearly, Herodotus is here being indicted though he is not by any means the sole object of Thucydides' barbs. Thucydides is criticizing a method of historiography which was in general practice and instituting a more rigorous, more scientific method which, he confesses, may seem less entertaining.

Entertaining Herodotus' *Histories* certainly is, and entertaining Herodotus meant it to be. Thucydides seems not to appreciate, however, the different scope and method of Herodotus' kind of history, its encyclopedic preservation of oral traditions. Nor could Thucydides have appreciated that in the fragmentary state of our knowledge of Greece we should find Herodotus' encyclopedia of inestimable value, that Herodotus' *Histories* also was to become a possession forever. Thucydides, disparaging the possible value of Herodotus' kind of research, limits his objective to recording only those events which he can himself verify, with occasional intelligent guesses about events before his time. His verification must be by personal experience and observation, by comparison and evaluation of conflicting evidence and by written documents.

Written documents, in particular, assume an importance in his writing which marks a new stage in ancient historiography. He seems to have been the first historian to understand the importance of such documents and to utilize them as corroborative evidence. He used the official archives of cities such as Athens to date his events, and on occasion he seems to quote verbatim the text of important inscriptions, though he does not tell us that he is quoting. Thucydides thus extended Herodotus' conception of accuracy one step further. Now it is not accuracy in reporting, but the accuracy of the event itself which must be established. Thucydides gave to fact, i.e., to what actually happened, a preeminence which it had not previously enjoyed and created a new ideal, that of factual Truth.

It is interesting to watch Thucydides' struggle for factual accuracy in one sphere of his work, viz., chronology. An accurate chronology has become so elementary for us that we can easily overlook the complexities with which Thucydides had to labor. Any event occurring anywhere in the world can now be dated and timed with scientific precision, but it was no such easy matter in Greece where each city had its own calendar. Each calendar, being lunar, needed periodic intercalations to bring it back into conformity with the solar year. The names of the months varied from city to city; calendar years began at various seasons in the various years, and the method of intercalation was by our standards only approximate and commanded, it seems, little interest even within each city. Time reckoning was, in the Greek world, highly idiosyncratic.

In his attempt to reduce the chronological chaos to order, Thucydides gives an absolute time for the beginning of the War by a system of cross-dating. In order to fix the moment exactly he resorts to four chronological systems and a seasonal reference in Book II:2: "In the fifteenth year of the truce; i.e., in the 48th year of the priestess-ship of Chrysis at Argos, the year when Aenesias was ephor at Sparta, when the archonship of Pythodorus at Athens had still two months to run at the beginning of spring, a Theban force made an armed entry into Plataea." Cumbersome as this cross-referencing was, in comparison to a simple and precise date like our November 11, 1918, it by no means ends Thucydides' difficulties.

The problems of the Greek calendars were really too complex for Thucydides to settle satisfactorily. But his system has the merit of establishing a fairly exact absolute chronology which was meaningful beyond merely local chronologies. It further enables him to number the years of the war consecutively. He then can place events within those years by references to the season. In spite of the obvious limitations of such a method and some inevitable inaccuracies, Thucydides achieves in a complex work dealing with events widely separated geographically and chronologically an exactitude which was, it seems, unique in Greece. If they did nothing else, his efforts dramatized the awkwardness of the Greek calendar systems. Yet succeeding generations of Greeks seem to have shown little interest in the problems. Chronological accuracy might be valued among the Greeks for certain commercial or religious reasons, where it was a matter of payment of debts or celebrations of festivals, but it must have seemed otiose to achieve such punctilious accuracy in historical writing. Thucydides' achievement went largely ignored.

Thucydides' insistence on accuracy and on verifiable data leads him to exclude anything that he would consider irrelevant to the scope of his *History*. His subject is the Peloponnesian War, and except for a digression on Greek prehistory and another on the period between the Persian and the Peloponnesian Wars, he remains strictly within his chosen theme. He is not interested in other people's conjectures or in oral traditions. From the abundance of conflicting accounts he ascertains what he believes is the truth and then gives only his synthesized version of what happened. This makes for a leaner, more intense narrative. Our attention is not allowed to wander down pleasant byways.

Thucydides' restriction of his *History* to his own time brings two important ideas to historiography: the emphasis on what is verifiable, what can be known; the recognition of the present as something discrete from the past and intrinsically important. Thucydides was not, of course, entirely original in his recognition of the present. We can see in the earlier historians and in Herodotus an increasing awareness of and interest in the present. Herodotus himself had tried to present the Persian Wars, a contemporary event, as a worthy rival of the legendary Trojan War. There is in Greek literature a piece of political analysis which goes by the name of the Old Oligarch in which there is the attempt at an analysis of present political conditions such as we find in Thucydides. But these writers seem to be groping towards an awareness which becomes in Thucydides an unshakable conviction. With Thucydides the present comes into its own as something more worthy of interest than the past.

It has, in all periods, been difficult for men to analyze their present conditions. The past has always seemed more ordered, more inevitable even, while the present has been a confusion. It has been natural for men to look towards the past where they thought they could find an order which was lacking in the present. The optimism of the nineteenth century, however, and the idea of scientific progress have given us a new bias. This bias has given us an admiration and even an obsession with the present which was almost totally absent in ancient Greece. The modern analytical method has made analysis of the present even a popular form of entertainment. We are all too familiar with surveys and critical investigations of every aspect of our daily lives, undertaken by foundations, government subcommittees, university research teams. Every newspaper columnist feels himself entitled to speculate on our politics, our religion, our shifting sexual mores. With our obsession for analysis of the present and predictions of the future we find it hard to appreciate Thucydides' innovation and even his lonely position as a thinker. What Thucydides achieved was a totally new orientation in perspective. The present is no longer merely a replica of the past or an ephemeral and even irrelevant intrusion upon the heroic vision of the past but the only subject worthy of intelligent investigation.

In his digression into prehistory, which scholars have called his Archaeology, Thucydides makes one venture into the past, but even there his orientation towards the present is obvious. Thucydides uses the observable conditions of the present as a control to measure past events. He applies to the past the same principles which he has abstracted from his analysis of the present. The logographers and philosophers had done this to some extent. They had rejected the myths of the gods in Homer as being incompatible with their more scientific and philosophical concepts of the universe. They had made a critique of Homer along theological and moral lines, but the human situation they had accepted as Homer told it. Thucydides makes an important advance on their work by bringing his analytic investigation to bear on the human and political situation in Homer. He still accepts or seems to accept Homer's account of the Trojan War as the historical account of an historical event, but for that he can hardly be censured when Priam's Troy is still as much a historical reality for modern scholars as for ancient Greeks. But Thucydides is not primarily concerned with the historicity of the Trojan War. He gives us enough warnings that no event in the poetic past is a reliable certainty. His purpose is rather to use the Trojan War in support of his argument that the present events which he has chosen to narrate are superior in their importance and their effects to the events of the past.

The Trojan War was considered the greatest war of the past,

the one in which the united forces of Greece were engaged, and yet in comparison to the present conflict (the Peloponnesian War) it was not of outstanding magnitude. All traditions about the past are highly suspect, says Thucydides, but even if we accept Homer's account we must agree that the Trojan War was of lesser significance than the present war. Homer and the other poets of the Homeric legends were the documents in which were enshrined the glories of an heroic past. Thucydides' sensible but quite revolutionary tactic was to use those documents as the firmest evidence of the nonheroic character of the past. Far from being heroic superhumans, Agamemnon and his allies were little more than marauding pirates who had scarcely the resources to wage a war at all. As the natural philosophers had trimmed Homer's theology, Thucydides trims Homer's heroes and their superhuman feats down to realistic nonheroic scale. One can understand why Thucydides should expect his work to be unpopular. Greek iconoclasm had not yet touched the national heroes. The Greeks were readier to sacrifice on the altar of scientific rationalism Zeus and his fellow Olympians than Achilles and Ajax. The gods might be naïve myths, but the Homeric heroes were reflections of the Greeks themselves, the expression of the highest national ideals. Plato was later to attack Homer's heroes for their unseemly lapses from heroic standards to show that they were hardly worthy objects of admiration. Thucydides attacked the whole Golden Age of the heroes as being a mirage absurdly inflated by the rhetoric of poets and the blind adulation of successive centuries. Ultimately, Thucydides' method of attack, if he had pursued it, could have been far more destructive to the traditional reverence accorded to Homer than Plato's method. While Plato merely censured the heroes for particular lapses from the heroic code Thucydides found the idea of heroism in Homer's primitive feudal society ludicrous.

His whole archaeology section is highly interesting for what it reveals of Thucydides' deductive principles. Archaeology is something of a misnomer since his analysis is not the result of any genuine excavation or fieldwork. It is rather the intelligent guess about the past, as Thucydides himself acknowledges, based on the same criteria with which he examines the relative power of the

Greek states in his own time. "Pre-history" would give a more exact indication of the scope of this section. The deflation of the age of heroes is but one aspect of Thucydides' achievement here. Another achievement, and one which has received more recognition, is his sketch of the social evolution of the Greek people from pre-Homeric times to his own day. It is commonly said that the idea of progress was not held by the ancient Greeks. Thucydides is a clear exception to this generalization. In his view Greece had progressed from a number of nomadic tribes living in isolation to a cooperative alliance under a single powerful man like Agamemnon to the present hegemony of two powerful states. From nomads to federated tribes to nation is the evolutionary course he describes.

The cause of this development, according to Thucydides, was more than anything else the growth of capital. Again Thucydides refutes his critics who consider him lacking in the modern tools of historical investigation. Economics is, to Thucydides, not merely one important factor but the most important factor in social change. His analysis of the economic difficulties suffered by the Greeks at Troy because of their lack of money is a model of an historian's incisive explication of what documentary evidence is available. It is obvious enough to us now as we read Homer that his heroes knew nothing of a money economy, but Thucydides was the first to point this out. Furthermore, he was the first to understand how the absence of a monetary system inevitably determined the size of the Greek army, the nature of the fighting at Troy, and the duration of the Trojan War. Whatever Homer's factual accuracy, the economic situation portrayed in the *Iliad* is as Thucydides perceived it. The Greeks clearly did not take vast supplies with them to Troy, nor could they have brought the monetary resources to purchase such supplies from friendly tribes. They must, therefore, have devoted much of their time and their forces to obtaining the daily necessities by piracy up and down the coast. And, as Thucydides observed, it is unlikely that a force which was encamped on hostile territory for ten full years, and dependent for its survival on the success of piratical expeditions could have been a very large one. Several centuries later Xerxes was to attempt such a vast expedition to Greece, and his supplies were probably far more abundant than Agamemnon's were, but unless he had won an immediate and absolute victory, he could not have maintained his army in Greece for more than a few weeks. Undoubtedly Thucydides had Xerxes' fate in mind when he thought of Agamemnon and his ten-year siege of Troy.

In his Archaeology Thucydides also lays great emphasis on naval power as another important factor in the growth of states. But the navies which he considers, both past and present, are really nothing but further developments dependent on the increase of capital. The earliest inhabitants of Greece, says Thucydides, had a primitive and precarious economy. They could produce barely enough to satisfy their daily needs and were unable to store up a surplus. But as tribes were slowly able to accumulate a surplus they were able to establish themselves in more stable communities, with walls built to protect them from less prosperous neighbors. In time a man like Minos of Crete was sufficiently wealthy to organize a navy to protect and increase his revenues. As seafaring became safer, commerce developed between the cities, and cities became more oriented towards the sea. As the process continued, the cities which could maintain a viable commerce by sea and offer protection against piracy to weaker cities became more powerful while their allies became proportionately more dependent. The progression is clear: originally a primitive agrarian economy in which a gradual accumulation of a surplus in produce leads to commerce. Commerce leads in its turn to the accumulation of capital which leads to the financing of navies which then accelerate the process even more towards capitalism and imperialism.

Clearly Thucydides has his eye on the development of the Athenian empire and has interpreted the past empires in the light of that development. It was easy to notice how important for Athens' imperial advance was her accumulation of capital. Thucydides could have reasoned that the power of Minos or Agamemnon must have advanced in a similar way. What is remarkable in Thucydides' sketch, however, is his ability to trace the role of economics back to a time far before the heyday of commercial prosperity, to the state of primitive agrarian culture before capital was even possible. By an intuitive leap Thucydides discovered the genesis and nature of capitalism.

Thucydides' conjectural reconstruction of the past is thus a notable document in the history of Greek thought. If only that piece of his work had survived, it would have revealed a man of shrewd observation and creative intelligence. But it is only a digression made in support of his claim that the present moment is far more significant than anything which has hitherto happened. And so it is to the rest of his *History* that we must look for the full display of his intellectual powers. The rest of his work we find, as we should expect, to be characterized by the same analytic perspicacity.

Though Thucydides shows a scientific devotion to facts and details, it is not because of the intrinsic interest of the facts, or because all facts are for him equally important, but rather because he is searching for the hidden causes to which the facts may give the clue. His predominant interest is in causes, but causes in the realm of human action, and so it is to human nature and the human environment that he looks. Not content with historical causation alone, he attempts to distinguish between causes and to arrange them in order of priority. There are real causes and alleged causes for an event; there are pretexts and ulterior motives left unspoken; there are true but unobserved causes which contrast with supposed causes. Modern scholars may not be altogether satisfied with Thucydides' categories but they generally acknowledge his contribution to categorical analysis of human motivation and behavior.

Thucydides' theme, according to the words of his introduction, is the conflict among the Greek states which we now call the Peloponnesian War. At the end of his introduction, when he has discussed the relative insignificance of past wars and has stated his principles of research, he proceeds to announce the grievances between Athens and Sparta which led to the outbreak of hostilities. Immediately before listing these grievances, however, Thucydides adds a personal opinion, hardly more than a parenthetical note: "But the real reason, in my opinion, was the growth of Athenian power and the fear which this caused in Sparta." Immediately there follow the reasons for the declaration of war as they were asserted by each side. We could find in Herodotus a similar kind of personal hypothesis set beside the current explanations of an event, but what distinguished Thucydides' personal parenthesis is that this is, in fact, the true theme of the whole of his *History*. He will be interested in the reasons which the participants in any action may give for their behavior, but he will be far more interested in the causes lying far outside the participants' explanations, causes which the participants themselves may scarcely perceive. Of these less recognized causes, the most important for Thucydides is the effect which the growth of power has both on its possessor and on those who feel its threat on their own independence.

Thucydides has sometimes been called a political analyst rather than an historian, or, if an historian, primarily a political historian. Certainly politics, and more particularly power politics, dominate his account. His story is the story of how Athens gradually extended her sphere of influence until the majority of Greek cities had become *de facto* subject states, how this increasing access of power altered the political and moral climate in Athens, and how the growing arrogance and obstinacy of the Athenians led to political excesses and to increasing hostility and resistance throughout the Greek world. The events which took place in the fifty years between the Persian and the Peloponnesian Wars are treated summarily in a few pages in Book I, and there are a few other minor digressions included to explain some event during the War or to support some point Thucydides makes. Apart from these few ventures into the past Thucydides' *History* keeps strictly to the events of the War, which it reports in chronological sequence. Yet Thucydides is able to convey through his digression on the events before the war and through the speeches which he has characters utter not only descriptions of the progress of Athens' power but also reflections made by Athenians and others on the nature and prerogatives of power. In the course of his narrative Thucydides explores this theme of the nature of power on many levels. There is for Thucydides a politics of power, an economics of power and a psychology of power. All the aspects of power together combine to create a self-perpetuation of power and a self-aggrandizement which in turn create a reaction in those who feel threatened by such power. Thucydides sees something like a chain reaction which is set in motion by power, until the possessor of power becomes as much a victim of his power as those whom he would subject to it. Thucydides' *History* is the story of the great city of Athens slowly falling victim to its own greatness.

Thucydides has much to say about international, or more accurately, intercity politics. He has much to say too about intracity politics, and many of his observations there are equally acute. His most famous description of internal civil strife is in Book III, chapters 82 ff., where Thucydides describes the rise of the political parties in the Corinthian colony of Corcyra. Thucydides does not elaborate on the civil strife in other cities but, as he notes, the disorder which first erupted in Corcyra was to be repeated throughout the Hellenic world so that he does not find it necessary to give much space to similar internal situations as they occurred elsewhere. His description of the politics in Corcyra is sufficient to stand as an epitome of the general social upheaval which was devastating Greece.

Thucydides has been rightly called a historian of the class struggle, and it is common to take his analysis of the factional strife at Corcyra as proof of his perception. The truth is that he explicitly denies that the turmoil at Corcyra was a genuine class struggle. In his analysis of the evolution of societies from the primitive agrarian state to imperialistic mercantile state that he exhibits a better understanding of the disruption which the rise of capital effects on a society. What was happening in Corcyra was indeed a class struggle; it was the disruption caused by the increase of capital within a city, but Thucydides seems to understand the effects which the rise of capitalism had in the relations between cities better than the effects within cities. He admits that Corcyra had split into two parties, an oligarchic and a democratic party, and that the political platform of the one was government by the aristocracy and of the other equality for the masses, but Thucydides considers these platforms as little more than slogans seized upon by individuals who were promoting their own interests. It is an ideological rather than a class struggle which Thucydides sees taking place. As party lines hardened, and under the increased tensions of war, men pursued their private interests with ever increasing disregard for political unity or for the interests of others. A city like Corcyra was split into two ideological factions, says Thucydides, and loyalties to the party took precedence over loyalty to the city or even to the family. So divisive was this party conflict that men of each party were willing to invite outside interference, whether from the Athenians or from the Spartans, if by doing so they could frustrate the ambitions of the other party.

Thucydides, in his vivid description of the deterioration of character caused by passions given full vent in the civil war at Corcyra, loses his own tone of cool appraisal and becomes himself an impassioned defendant of the conventions of civilized life. He is impartial in this only, that he attributes the blame equally to men of both the democratic and oligarchic parties. He unequivocally censures both parties for their destructive actions. Undoubtedly the vicious effects on character which Thucydides catalogues were to be seen. In a general social upheaval there is little place for moderate and conciliatory men. Radical movements are inevitably acrimonious. But it is curious that Thucydides, who is elsewhere so astute in his observations on the decisive effect of economic and technological change on society, should see in the civil war at Corcyra only the desperate ambitions of irresponsible individuals. Thucydides sees here the symptoms rather than the cause. That there were real grievances underlying the civil strife, even if the grievances were exploited and manipulated by men driven by personal ambition, Thucydides seems reluctant to acknowledge.

Perhaps the explanation for Thucydides' limitation here lies in the general confusion caused by the wide inter-city war. Had the civil war occurred in a period of universal peace, Thucydides could have studied it as an isolated and purely internal phenomenon. But since it occurred during a total Hellenic war, Thucydides saw the civil strife not as a separate condition influenced by the war, but rather as yet another of the destructive consequences of the war, a deliberate exploitation of the conditions of war by men who saw opportunities for personal aggrandizement. The psychology of war, which exhibited itself first in the deterioration of relations between cities, later spread to factions within cities. The contagion which brutalized the behavior of one city towards another spread until it brutalized the behavior between citizen and fellow-citizen, until finally the war became not only a struggle for power between cities, ruinous as that was, but a struggle for power between rival factions and individuals within the same city. We should consider the civil war as dependent on many factors and merely exacerbated by the wider war, whereas for Thucydides the internal disruptions are the direct consequence of the general war. Whatever reservations we may have about Thucydides' explanation or lack of explanation, it is to Thucydides' credit that he recognized the importance of the social phenomenon of civil strife and has described its symptoms with such sensitivity that modern scholars have been able to use his description as an important document in their study of the evolution of social institutions in antiquity.

Thucydides' description of the body politic reminds us also of that other incisive description, the description of the plague which attacked Athens shortly after the beginning of the Peloponnesian War. In both passages Thucydides attempts a rigorous exactitude in description. The care with which Thucydides details the course of the disease and its various symptoms shows Thucydides' affinity to the Hippocratic school of medicine. In the fifth century this school on the island of Cos had published several tracts on various diseases and prescriptions for a general physical regimen. It has been said that Hippocrates and his followers were the true scientists of Greece, for they were the only men who adhered strictly to the principle of empiricism without recourse to rational abstractions. In their hands medicine came close to being the only empirical science in Greece. Thucydides has clearly been influenced by their method. It seems certain that he has detailed the symptoms of the Plague as fully and accurately as possible in order to provide a useful document for researchers of a later time who might some day discover the remedy. Medical science was powerless at the time when the disease occurred but Thucydides writes his diagnosis, as he himself says, to help in the identification of the disease if it should occur again. As to theorizing about the origins of the disease,

Thucydides leaves that, with what seems a slight note of contempt, to others "with or without medical experience." Thucydides will restrict himself solely to the observable facts; let others theorize. And though Thucydides himself was a victim of the disease, his description is as disinterested as humanly possible.

We can scarcely avoid the conclusion that Thucydides' description of the symptoms of the Plague is paradigmatic for Thucydides' method in the whole of his *History*. We can see the same clinical analysis of symptoms in his description of the party struggle in Corcyra and throughout the work. In his *History* he attempts to bring the same clinical detachment and exactitude to the study of the social organism as the Hippocratic school had brought to the study of the physical organism. This is why he prides himself on the value of his work for future generations. It will be, he says, a possession for ever and the reason for his belief is that his *History* is more than a document of facts but a diagnosis, a case history of a political struggle to which future thinkers and political scientists will refer.

Perhaps Thucydides' kinship with the medical scientists dictates his severe impartiality. Some scholars have considered Thucydides to be completely amoral in his observation of the growth of Athenian imperialism and the increasing brutality of Athens towards her subjects. They have even found it slightly monstrous that Thucydides could have recorded the Athenian policy with such equanimity. It is true that Thucydides rarely allows his personal judgments to intrude into his historical descriptions, but he is far from detached in his emotional response. There is no doubt that the ideal of Athens, as presented by Pericles in the Funeral Oration in Book II, is for Thucydides the glory of Athens. Athens indeed could and should be the school of Hellas. But it is equally certain that Thucydides shows through historical facts and through speeches made by men of other cities and by Athenians themselves that Athens again and again betrays her finest ideals. Whether Thucydides accepts unreservedly the legitimacy of the Athenian empire is problematic, but it is certain that Thucydides is dismayed at the Athenians' arrogant use of their power. They become rigid when they should be flexible, oppressive when they should be magnanimous. By his selection of facts, by the juxtaposition of certain events, and by the Sophistic kind of arguments in the speeches, Thucydides leads us to the inevitable conclusion that Athens is pursuing a ruinous course. The whole of Thucydides' *History* is a heavy indictment of Athens. The eulogistic passages, Pericles' Funeral Oration in particular, only strengthen the case against Athens. People expect Sparta to be ponderous, intractable, and lacking in political sophistication. People expect more from the city of Aeschylus and Sophocles, the city which has made a passionate commitment to the ideal of freedom, the city, in other words, which Pericles describes in his Funeral Oration. Thucydides is far from detached. He was no more detached about the political events, in which he himself participated, than he was about the Plague which he had himself suffered (and who knows how many of his relatives and friends were casualties of the same disease?). His tone of detachment is maintained only by an act of will. The apparent scientific detachment in his writing serves to emphasize the horror of the catastrophe in which the Greek world was engulfed.

For all his contribution to the scientific study of human affairs, however, Thucydides remains an artist. This fact has an important bearing on the kind of work he wrote. Thucydides is famous for his almost excessive use of rhetorical devices, of at times labored parallelisms and antitheses in his vocabulary and phrasing. But his artistry is more than a rhetorical finish spread over the work. The whole *History* is a work of art, even a prose poem we might say, though Thucydides would probably raise strong objection to such a classification. Some scholars have taken the extreme view that Thucydides was not scientific in the least, but a tragedian, and have asserted that his *History* is the tragedy of the fall of Athens. We do not have to deny all scientific principles in Thucydides, however, to admit that he saw the Peloponnesian War as a great human drama on an even vaster scale than the mythical dramas of Troy and Thebes, and the impending fall of Athens as a catastrophe of epic proportions. The subject itself of Thucydides' *History* called for both the artist and the scientist in Thucydides, but more than that, the poetic perspective of the Greek mind was still so strongly operative that Thucydides could scarcely eradicate it from his mind even if he had wished to. Just as the natural philosophers, while scoffing at the absurdities of popular religion, used the religious conceptions of the world as the foundation of their new philosophical systems and drew on the old religious imagery to convey their new abstract ideas, so Thucydides, while scoffing at the nonfactual myths of the poets, drew on the conceptions of the poets for his dramatic narrative.

Thucydides was undoubtedly influenced by the Athenian tragedies but it was not merely his seeing the performances of tragedies which gave him the idea for the form of his work. Rather, both Thucydides and the tragedians were expressing themselves inevitably in a common idiom. However much Thucydides attempted to dissociate himself from the poets, he was as much an heir of Homer's epic and dramatic vision as they were. The idea of a prose narrative was still something new, and Thucydides, like Herodotus, is standing at the point of transition to discursive prose. What Thucydides did was to create a new *mythos,* the *mythos* of Athens, but he would have claimed the superiority of his *mythos* over those of the poets. Theirs were fictional or largely fictional, but his was based on a recognized reality.

Thucydides is, therefore, both poet and scientist, and outstanding as both. Where there are weaknesses in his *History,* however, they are generally the result of his ambivalent perspective. By modern standards Thucydides is far too casual about his sources. We would expect a historian to cite his authorities in more detail and to document his facts with whatever evidence is available. Thucydides' choice for the inclusion or omission of certain events is arbitrary. He includes only what he considers germane, and his somewhat rigid idea of relevance has put a severe limitation of his work. Other evidence, epigraphical or literary, has revealed events or facts of great significance for the history of the War which Thucydides has ignored altogether. Thucydides has also been criticized for his use of the dramatic device of the speeches which he has composed for certain climactic points in the narrative. Thucydides admits that these speeches are not verbatim transcripts but assures us that they convey the general sense of what was said on a given occasion, as he himself recalled it or was told by others, or that they give the kind of argument which was appropriate to the particular occasion which he has recorded. But in spite of his assurance that he has written no entirely fictional speech but has recreated, if somewhat freely, a speech which was actually uttered, his method is open to much criticism. It has been one of the most notorious problems in Thucydidean scholarship. We simply cannot be certain of the veracity of the speeches and at times we are tempted to think that Thucydides used the speeches as the medium through which to express the theoretical principles, such as the relative claims of morality versus expediency, underlying any particular source of action. We may also be inclined to wonder whether Thucydides used the device to create the formal arguments which might have been uttered rather than those which were actually given by the various leaders or ambassadors. A modern historian would not have resorted to such an ambiguous device; for him only verbatim transcripts would be acceptable.

But these faults of omission and the lapse, in the speeches, from the otherwise rigid insistence on accuracy are symptomatic of the struggle in which Thucydides was engaged to separate history and political analysis from the sphere of poetry into the sphere of science. Thucydides still has the vision of the poet, and the poet's pride in the truth of his vision, but he has transposed his vision to the sphere of contemporary events. His truth, therefore, has become a factual rather than a poetic truth. Thucydides assiduously pursues factual truth, with a supreme confidence in the facts as he has ascertained him. After the assurances he gives on his own detachment and the emphasis he lays on his careful sifting of the evidence, he would probably be astonished that others might dispute his facts or his interpretation. To question his facts is to question his personal, even his scientific integrity. A modern historian has a little more humility in the face of the complexity of human events. Personal integrity is necessary but the modern historian does not identify his personal integrity so closely with the truth. He acknowledges that honest and scrupulous use of the evidence are not enough to compensate for the idiosyncrasy of a single perspective.

By modern standards, therefore, Thucydides can be criticized on several counts, and sometimes severely criticized. By the standards of ancient historiography, however, his work is a monumental achievement. He had attempted to humanize the old heroic epics and pre-historical legends, to analyze them for what they might reveal of political and social conditions of an earlier age. That in itself, obvious enough as it seems now, was a remarkable innovation. But his enduring achievement was his attempt at strict factual accuracy and his acute political analysis of the most significant event of his time. He gave to historiography an ideal which was rarely attempted and even less rarely realized until the rise of modern scientific thought. Thucydides has some claim to being the most modern of ancient writers.

GREEK HISTORIOGRAPHY AFTER THUCYDIDES

HISTORY as a true intellectual discipline withered in Greece after Thucydides and virtually disappeared altogether. Not that the Greeks stopped writing histories and chronicles. On the contrary, historical writing was a popular form of literary exercise in the fourth and third centuries B.C. There was a great antiquarian interest in the Hellenistic period, and men derived pleasure from scholarly researches into the obscurity of the past. Athens, in particular, was fortunate to have many men who devoted themselves to research into various aspects of her past. The studies of these scholars on chronology, on official decrees, on the lists of magistrates and the like, though they have not come down to us *verbatim*, were incorporated into later compilations and have given us in this way valuable information to supplement Thucydides' account of the fifth century. Nevertheless, in spite of the abundance of antiquarian curiosity and the industriousness of Hellenistic scholars, the qualities which so distinguished Thucydides' work were gone: his critical spirit, his recognition of the relative value of documents, and his powers of political and sociological analysis.

Historical writing came increasingly under the influence of rhetoric in the fourth century B.C. and thereafter. Rhetoric had grown to importance as a formal educational discipline under the encouragement of the Sophists in the fifth century, but had come under a severe attack by Plato as being not only non-philosophical but positively contrary to philosophy and true education. Its cause was championed anew in the fourth century by the orator and writer Isocrates. He succeeded in making the study and practice of rhetoric eminently respectable, eminently moral and edifying. So successful was he that rhetoric became firmly established as the core of the educational curriculum. No man could be considered an educated gentleman who was not thoroughly finished in all the theories and techniques of forensic persuasion. The chief dangers to which literature was liable when under the influence of rhetoric were the excesses of a florid style which increasingly took precedence over content, and the simplistic moral viewpoint rhetoricians, following Isocrates' example, insisted upon in order to assure themselves that rhetoric was not necessarily a charlatan's bag of tricks.

History was particularly susceptible to the deleterious influence of rhetoric. Thucydides had achieved the synthesis which is the ideal of the historian: the scholar's attention to factual detail and the thinker's analysis of the abstract causes of events. But after him history disintegrated into two separate forms. Scholars made their investigations into the facts, and others of a more philosophic than scientific temperament, who were trained in the practice of rhetoric, drew on such detailed studies to offer their general interpretative histories. The interpretative historians moved steadily further from any contact with real historical investigation, and gave themselves more to theorizing and moralizing. History inevitably moved with them progressively further from the ideals of accuracy and analysis based on observation and fact, which Herodotus and Thucydides had established, towards an altogether different genre, one closer to essay-writing than to what Thucydides would have recognized as history. History became less scientific as it became progressively more *belles lettres*. The interpretative historians were, for the most part, little interested in original research and relied instead on whatever authorities were already available to them, showing, often, little discrimination between their various authorities. History became in their hands compilations from the accepted authorities with the writer's occasional animadversion on the bias or the defects of the older historians who were being thus excerpted. Rarely were these later historical writings serious new examinations of the facts.

Perhaps Herodotus and Thucydides, by hiding the traces of their own scholarship so carefully and presenting to the public only their finished products in a highly artistic form, were partly to blame for this deterioration. Had they supported their emphatic assertions of personal research with the modern kind of scholarly apparatus of footnotes and transcribed documents, the historians of a later age would perhaps have better understood exactly what standards Herodotus and Thucydides had set for historiography. Instead, the highly dramatic form of their finished works obscured the distance which Herodotus and Thucydides had in fact travelled from pure drama. Later historians perhaps saw the ideal in the dramatic form rather than in the research and analysis which lay behind that artistic form.

Three historians, XENOPHON, THEOPOMPUS, and EPHORUS, carried on, in the fourth century, the history of Greece from the point where Thucydides had left off. Of these three Xenophon, though the evidence has led some scholars to believe he may have been the least critical, enjoyed the greatest popularity; in consequence his work has survived in its entirety while the writings of the others are known to us only through the use made of them by later writers. The popularity and survival of Xenophon's work gives us some idea of what the popular preference was, and is therefore a good indication of the trends in historiography which were most likely to win favor.

Xenophon's one strictly historical work was the *Hellenica* which continued the history of Greece down to the fall of the Theban supremacy in 362 B.C. Books I and II of the *Hellenica,* which Xenophon modelled closely after Thucydides, are superior to the rest of the work, but it is probable that the survival of the whole work is due less to its historical interest or merits than to the great popularity of certain other works of Xenophon's. His *Memorabilia,* which gave his memories of Socrates, his *Anabasis,* which was his account of the march, in which Xenophon had participated, of the Greek mercenaries under Cyrus the Younger in 399 B.C., and his

Cyropaedia had an immediate appeal, both because of their subjects and because of Xenophon's lucid prose. The *Memorabilia* and the *Anabasis* are historical works, but hardly history in the Thucydidean sense. They are the personal recollections of one individual rather than serious attempts to ascertain factual truth by the study of documents. The *Cyropaedia* is even less historical. It purports to be an historical record of the education of Cyrus the Elder, but is in fact a thinly veiled tract on the ideal education of the ideal ruler. It is a fictional treatment of an historical personality presented for didactic purposes. Such a didactic and fictional portrait commands little interest today but the question of the education of the benevolent monarch was a popular topic in the days of the Roman Empire and again in the Renaissance. Xenophon's kind of moralizing portraiture could count on a perennial audience until fairly modern times, when the idea of monarchy began to lose its force. We dismiss Xenophon today as an historian, but it is well to remember that through antiquity, through the Middle Ages and the Renaissance, Xenophon was ranked close to, or even on a level with, Herodotus and Thucydides. Most probably Xenophon was more widely read than either of them and his influence on men's ideas of classical antiquity and classical historiography was far greater than theirs.*

Ephorus is notable for his attempt to write a "universal history;" i.e., a history of the Greek world from the time of the settlement of the Dorians down to his own day in the mid-fourth century. It was an ambitious work which is now lost to us, but it became one of the principal authorities for later compilers. Through the borrowings of the later historian Diodorus Ephorus remains almost our only source for the history of Greece in the period between the Persian and Peloponnesian Wars, except for Thucydides' brief excursus. What we can surmise about Ephorus, however, indicates a man of superficial observation, whose work was vitiated by a lack of discrimination and by ready moralizing. Nevertheless, his name was linked with that of Thucydides, and he was held in high repute for

---

* It is indicative of Xenophon's influence that when Machiavelli comes to write his treatise on the prerogatives of the ruler he cites Xenophon alone among ancient Greek authors for his discussions of the same subject in his *Cyropaedia* and his fictional dialogue *Hiero*.

centuries. This esteem is indicative of how little antiquity had learned from Thucydides' kind of historiography. It suggests also that Thucydides was praised but little read. Thucydides was universally acknowledged as one of the greatest historians, but for their actual knowledge of the past men probably preferred to turn to the less demanding efforts of such compilers as Ephorus. The high reputation of Ephorus is but another indication of how ready people were to accept compilations and epitomes in preference to original research and documentation.

There is one Greek historian who stands out as a man who resisted the prevailing trend towards dependence on the compilations of others, towards the ready moralizing and the rhetorical excesses. The life of POLYBIUS covered the greater part of the second century B.C. He was among the Greeks taken as hostages to Rome after the victory of the Romans over the Greeks at the battle of Pydna in 168 B.C. During the many years of his residence in Rome he came deeply under the influence of the ideals of the Roman political system and decided to write a history of the growth of Roman power in the Mediterranean from the time of the Second Punic War (220 B.C.) to the conquest of Macedonia in 168 B.C. He later extended his History to embrace the final destruction of Carthage and the subjugation of Greece in 146 B.C.

Polybius too, like Ephorus, was attempting a universal history, but there was a greater cogency to the idea of a universal history in his day than there had been before. It was not merely an academic concept. Before the time at which his History begins, says Polybius, events which had happened in various parts of the world had little effect on each other. But at the moment when his History opens the Mediterranean is indeed a single interdependent community. Roman, African, Greek and Asian affairs are directly and conspicuously related. The unity of history is no longer a dramatic fiction but an evident political reality.

Polybius' work was a *magnum opus* running to some forty books. Unfortunately the parts of his work in which he was recounting the events contemporaneous with his own lifetime are now lost to us so that we cannot make an accurate judgement on how well his personal investigations measured up to his avowed critical principles. For his critical principles were admirably high. In what has survived he shows no acquaintance with Thucydides but like Thucydides he lays great emphasis on personal research, on verification of the facts, on the use and critical evaluation of primary documents. He is interested in the problem of historical causation, and concerned to distinguish true causes from apparent causes or mere pretexts. He is prone to speculation and theorizing, but it is a theorizing which is built on the foundation of accuracy in detail. His is a valiant effort to raise history once again to the level of a serious study of the past, but an effort, the evidence seems to indicate, which was doomed to be a solitary cry. He was the last of the Greeks of antiquity to attempt to make of history a discipline both scientific and philosophic.

In PLUTARCH we see a return to the trends of historiography made popular by Xenophon in the fourth century. Plutarch, in fact, well represents the culmination of those trends. Plutarch was a learned citizen of the rather insignificant little town of Chaeronea whose lifetime spanned the second half of the first century A.D. and well into the second century. He studied at Athens, traveled to Rome, held various political offices, and was a priest of Apollo at Delphi. Most of his life was spent in the modest surroundings of Chaeronea, where he, in his good library of the ancient authors, wrote essays on a wide variety of subjects, antiquarian, literary, historical and ethical. The best known of his works today are the *Parallel Lives* in which he set side by side one Greek and one Roman historical figure in order to develop the salient aspects of the character of each.

Plutarch creates a reaction which is uncomfortably ambivalent in modern scholars. Plutarch himself confesses that his *Lives* were not history, and most scholars, when discussing ancient historiography, are prompt to take him at his word and ignore him. On the other hand, almost any study of an historical problem in antiquity will make repeated references to Plutarch's *Lives*. He is accepted as a source by modern scholars and at the same time denied any place as an historian. To illustrate this ambivalence, J. B. Bury's *Ancient Greek Historians* gives Plutarch not a single page and only cites his name a couple of times. But A. W. Gomme, in his exhaustive

Commentary on Thucydides, feels it necessary to devote a full thirty pages of his introduction to an examination of Plutarch as a source for the history of fifth-century Greece. Practically, historians find Plutarch indispensable as a source book, but his historiographic principles they find a distinct embarrassment.

The difficulty lies in Plutarch's own concept of the kind of biography he was writing and of the value of such biography. "I am writing not histories but lives," he states at the beginning of his *Alexander.* He goes on to say that his interest is not in exhaustive biography but in the *ethos,* the character of a man. That character, he believes, is often to be discovered in the chance actions or words of a man rather than in his most conspicuous achievements. Just as a painter concentrates on a subject's face and the facial expressions which most reveal character, while disregarding the rest of the body, so Plutarch will attempt, he says, to be the portrait painter of a man's soul, concentrating on those manifestations in the man's behavior which are the most definitive expressions of the man's inner ethic.

This is not history as Thucydides would recognize it, nor even biography in the ordinary sense of the word, but character study, and character study of a particular kind, one oriented towards a man's virtues and vices. Plutarch is an essayist and a moralist, and is frank enough to admit as much to us. Generally Plutarch's words "not history but lives" have been sufficient to excuse him in the eyes of scholars from the demands of the historian's discipline. Since he did not claim to be an historian, it is argued, why should we expect an historian's accuracy from him? A man is as much entitled to write moral essays as historical studies. The fallacy in Plutarch's argument, however, is that he has chosen historical persons as the subjects of his moral essays, and the pronouncements he may make on the character of each man are only as good as the facts on which such pronouncements are based. It is all very well to say "I am not writing history," but if this means that the writer is indifferent to historical accuracy, then he could just as soon write on mythical or purely fictitious persons as on historical ones. Why not Achilles rather than Themistocles, Aeneas rather than Caesar? The truth is, Plutarch has chosen historical personalities precisely because the moral arguments he may make gain their cogency from the historical reality of the men whom he describes. Plutarch may claim he is not writing history, but he is far from suggesting that he expects us to accept his studies as fictions, since the value of his moral judgements rests on the factual accuracy of his biographies.

Plutarch is, therefore, whether he admits it or not, writing history. His method seems to have been to select his facts from the various historians whose works were available to him in his personal library. He relied heavily on the accepted authorities such as Thucydides but felt himself at liberty to draw on the anecdotal material and even gossip which someone like Thucydides studiously avoided. He often gives us no indication of his sources but the diligent sleuthing of modern scholars has done much to detect the eclectic nature of his studies. In some of his *Lives,* where his authority is principally Thucydides, his record is reliably accurate, but in others an indiscriminately collated mélange of good and bad sources. In certain of his *Lives* he has synthesized one favorable and another unfavorable source with little thought for the possible contradictions which such a method may produce. He is useful because our sources are so scanty, but scholars must pick their way through his material with the greatest caution.

Were Plutarch merely an essayist among a host of excellent historians we could read him for his charm and his anecdotes, but turn to the historians for more accurate information. But Plutarch, in spite of his disclaimer, was really using the methods which were considered adequate in historiography. The difference between his work and historical studies, he seems to suggest, is that history is the tale of the distinguished and significant acts of great men in the political and social sphere while his is the study of the character, the essence of the individual. Plutarch will not belabor the historical events because those have been recorded by others; instead, he will use their records as the basis of his psychological and moral interpretations.

But psychological biography, as Plutarch was writing it, was already what history had become. The methods which Plutarch used—the eclectic compilation of data from literary sources, dictated by personal tastes and bias—were the methods prevalent in historical writing. The rather superficial examination of the sources which we find in Plutarch, the interest in the psychology and the morals of notable men, the somewhat simplistic didacticism with its emphasis on virtues and vices, the indifference towards personal research into the facts, all these are in the main characteristic of the interpretative kind of historical study. It was just this kind of interpretative and didactic history which held the field over the exacting antiquarian researches.

It is illustrative of the new attitude towards history and of the news standards of historiography that Plutarch's *Lives*, whatever their author's disclaimers, were accepted as authoritative history not only in his own day but for centuries afterwards. Plutarch's kind of psychological biography led the way directly to the archetypal kind of perspective with which the Middle Ages viewed the past. Thucydides' kind of factual accuracy and personal research was of little interest to men of the Middle Ages who found in Plutarch's moral picture gallery lessons of eternal truth. In the Renaissance, too, with the revival of classical learning, it was to writers like Xenophon and Plutarch that men turned for their knowledge of classical antiquity rather than to Thucydides or Herodotus. It is probably safe to say that what Europeans from the Renaissance to the eighteenth century knew about Greece was gathered more from the pages of Plutarch and Xenophon than from all the other ancient Greek writers combined. Plutarch endured for centuries as the most popular and the most informative of classical authors just because his idea of history corresponded so appropriately with the prevalent idea of history through those centuries. It was only with the rise of the idea of scientific history in the nineteenth century that Plutarch's authority began to fall into disrepute. It is significant that the corpus of Plutarch's work is one of the largest which has survived from classical antiquity. Plutarch was a prolific writer, but many others were equally prolific and their works have been sadly decimated in transmission over the centuries. It is no accident that Plutarch's works escaped the catastrophic attrition which the works of Aeschylus and Sophocles suffered.

Scholars today prefer to ignore Plutarch, even though often betraying themselves by the frequency of their citations of his works.

This prejudice against him is only of very recent vintage. No study of ancient historiography can afford to ignore him for Plutarch's *Lives* were certainly history for his contemporaries and for successive centuries. His biographical essays exemplify what historiography had become in antiquity; his approach to History became now the accepted one.

There were other Greek historians after Plutarch; notably APPIAN and ARRIAN, who lived through the greater part of the second century A.D., in the age of the Antonines. Appian wrote a *History of Rome* in some twenty-four books, covering the events of the city from the earliest legendary past down to the Civil Wars at the end of the Republic. Appian is an important source for the student of Roman history because for certain periods his works are our only extant historical source. In this respect the first book of his *Civil Wars* is particularly valuable. Arrian wrote several works of various kinds, but the only work which has been preserved is his *Anabasis of Alexander,* modeled on the *Anabasis* by Xenophon, an author whom he much admired and emulated.

The paucity of historical records from antiquity makes both historians valuable, but yet both were compilers, writing several centuries after the events which they narrated. Appian mentions several earlier sources and undoubtedly had access to records which are no longer available. Neither writer, however, shows evidence of a keen analytical intelligence. Theirs is not so much an attempt to offer new critical interpretations of the past based on their personal examination and evaluation of the old documentary evidence as to draw together earlier historical writings into a single comprehensive narrative. They offer us useful information at many points and often help us in tracing the variant historical traditions, but they show themselves susceptible to the weaknesses which mar the work of the later historians. Though their style is for the most part unpretentious they enjoy indulging in some rhetorical flourish and in composing speeches to be put in the mouth of an historical character at some decisive moment—speeches of varying degrees of probability and reliability—and they are too ready to accept earlier historical narratives, whether good or bad, biased or unbiased, to the exclusion of other kinds of corroborative evidence.

These later historians mark the end of serious historical researches in ancient Greece. Plutarch is a representative of the culmination of the movement away from personal investigation of factual evidence towards the exploitation of past historical accounts in support of personal moral judgments. The pendulum has, with Plutarch, come full swing, back to the kind of History which Herodotus and the logographers had tried to destroy with their personal investigations into facts. History has with Plutarch again become myth, and the historian a new kind of *mythopoios,* a maker of myths which can suitably embody moral lessons. Plutarch's myths, being based on written documents, some of which are of unimpeachable reliability, are perhaps closer to the truth than the myths handed down by the poets in the oral tradition before the days of Herodotus. But, given the essential difference in sources and media, Plutarch's method is not so very different from that of the oral poets of Greece. History has become once again a body of legend from which one is free to draw as one pleases for paradigmatic lessons and which, furthermore, one is also free to embellish as one pleases. The sustained popularity of Plutarch's *Lives* suggests its own moral lesson: the historiographic ideals which both Herodotus and Thucydides had tried to institute are perhaps too austere ever to be the universal norm. The kind of history which will continue to be taught in the schools or enjoyed by the general reader will probably be closer to Plutarch's standards than to those of his more rigorous predecessors.

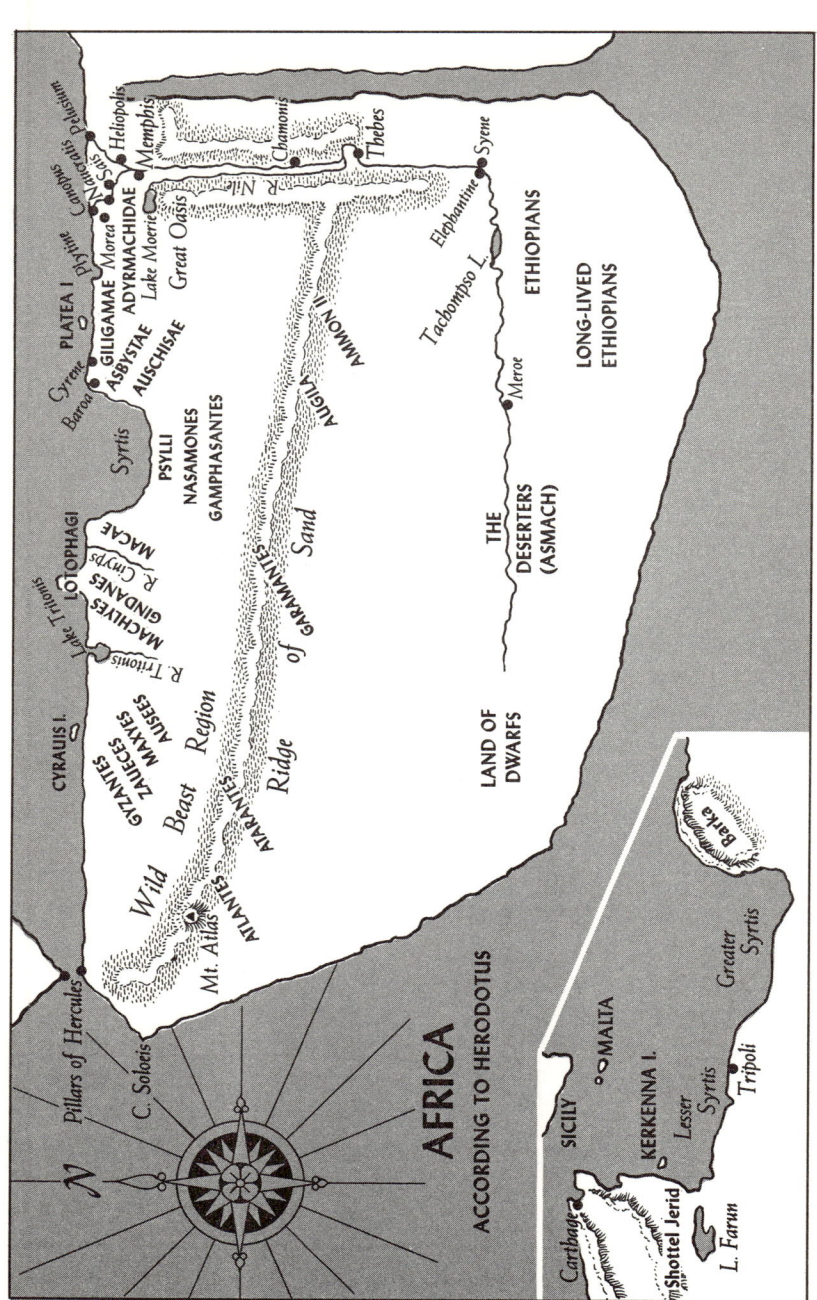

Map of Africa according to Herodotus

HERODOTUS · THE HISTORIES*

Book I:1–13

THESE ARE the researches of Herodotus of Halicarnassus, which he publishes, in the hope of thereby preserving from decay the remembrance of what men have done, and of preventing the great and wonderful actions of the Greeks and the Barbarians from losing their due meed of glory; and withal to put on record what were their grounds of feud.

1. According to the Persians best informed in history, the Phoenicians began the quarrel. This people, who had formerly dwelt on the shores of the Erythraean Sea, having migrated to the Mediterranean and settled in the parts which they now inhabit, began at once, they say, to adventure on long voyages, freighting their vessels with the wares of Egypt and Assyria. They landed at many places on the coast, and among the rest at Argos, which was then pre-eminent above all the states included now under the common name of Hellas. Here they exposed their merchandise, and traded with the natives for five or six days; at the end of which time, when almost everything was sold, there came down to the beach a number of women, and among them the daughter of the king, who was, they say, agreeing in this with the Greeks, Io, the child of Inachus. The women were standing by the stern of the ship intent upon their purchases, when the Phoenicians, with a general shout, rushed upon them. The greater part made their escape, but some were seized and carried off. Io herself was among the captives. The Phoenicians put the women on board their vessel and set sail for Egypt. Thus did Io pass into Egypt, according to the Persian story,

---
* Selections from Herodotus, *The Persian Wars*, translated by George Rawlinson, ed. F. R. B. Godolphin (New York: Modern Library, 1942).

which differs widely from the Phoenician; and thus commenced, according to their authors, the series of outrages.

2. At a later period, certain Greeks, with whose name they are unacquainted, but who would probably be Cretans, made a landing at Tyre, on the Phoenician coast, and bore off the king's daughter, Europé. In this they only retaliated; but afterwards the Greeks, they say, were guilty of a second violence. They manned a ship of war, and sailed to Æa, a city of Colchis, on the river Phasis; from whence, after despatching the rest of the business on which they had come, they carried off Medea, the daughter of the king of the land. The monarch sent a herald into Greece to demand reparation of the wrong, and the restitution of his child; but the Greeks made answer, that having received no reparation of the wrong done them in the seizure of Io the Argive, they should give none in this instance.

3. In the next generation afterwards, according to the same authorities, Alexander the son of Priam, bearing these events in mind, resolved to procure himself a wife out of Greece by violence, fully persuaded, that as the Greeks had not given satisfaction for their outrages, so neither would he be forced to make any for his. Accordingly he made prize of Helen; upon which the Greeks decided that, before resorting to other measures, they would send envoys to reclaim the princess and require reparation of the wrong. Their demands were met by a reference to the violence which had been offered to Medea, and they were asked with what face they could now require satisfaction, when they had formerly rejected all demands for either reparation or restitution addressed to them.

4. Hitherto the injuries on either side had been mere acts of common violence; but in what followed the Persians consider that the Greeks were greatly to blame, since before any attack had been made on Europé, they led an army into Asia. Now as for the carrying off of women, it is the deed, they say, of a rogue; but to make a stir about such as are carried off, argues a man a fool. Men of sense care nothing for such women, since it is plain that without their own consent they would never be forced away. The Asiatics, when the Greeks ran off with their women, never troubled themselves about the matter; but the Greeks, for the sake of a single

Lacedaemonian girl, collected a vast armament, invaded Asia, and destroyed the kingdom of Priam. Henceforth they ever looked upon the Greeks as their open enemies. For Asia, with all the various tribes of barbarians that inhabit it, is regarded by the Persians as their own; but Europe and the Greek race they look on as distinct and separate.

5. Such is the account which the Persians give of these matters. They trace to the attack upon Troy their ancient enmity towards the Greeks. The Phoenicians, however, as regards Io, vary from the Persian statements. They deny that they used any violence to remove her into Egypt; she herself, they say, having formed an intimacy with the captain, while his vessel lay at Argos, and perceiving herself to be with child, of her own freewill accompanied the Phoenicians on their leaving the shore, to escape the shame of detection and the reproaches of her parents. Whether this latter account be true, or whether the matter happened otherwise, I shall not discuss further. I shall proceed at once to point out the person who first within my own knowledge inflicted injury on the Greeks, after which I shall go forward with my history, describing equally the greater and the lesser cities. For the cities which were formerly great, have most of them become insignificant; and such as are at present powerful, were weak in the olden time. I shall therefore discourse equally of both, convinced that human happiness never continues long in one stay.

6. Croesus, son of Alyattes, by birth a Lydian, was lord of all the nations to the west of the river Halys. This stream, which separates Syria from Paphlagonia, runs with a course from south to north, and finally falls into the Euxine. So far as our knowledge goes, he was the first of the barbarians who had dealings with the Greeks, forcing some of them to become his tributaries, and entering into alliance with others. He conquered the Æolians, Ionians, and Dorians of Asia, and made a treaty with the Lacedaemonians. Up to that time all Greeks had been free. For the Cimmerian attack upon Ionia, which was earlier than Croesus, was not a conquest of the cities, but only an inroad for plundering.

7. The sovereignty of Lydia, which had belonged to the Heraclides, passed into the family of Croesus, who were called the

Mermnadae, in the manner which I will now relate. There was a certain king of Sardis, Candaules by name, whom the Greeks called Myrsilus. He was a descendant of Alcaeus, son of Hercules. The first king of this dynasty was Agron, son of Ninus, grandson of Belus, and great-grandson of Alcaeus; Candaules, son of Myrsus, was the last. The kings who reigned before Agron sprang from Lydus, son of Atys, from whom the people of the land, called previously Meonians, received the name of Lydians. The Heraclides, descended from Hercules and the slavegirl of Jardanus, having been entrusted by these princes with the management of affairs, obtained the kingdom by an oracle. Their rule endured for twenty-two generations of men, a space of 505 years, during the whole of which period, from Agron to Candaules, the crown descended in the direct line from father to son.

8. Now it happened that this Candaules was in love with his own wife; and not only so, but thought her the fairest woman in the whole world. This fancy had strange consequences. There was in his bodyguard a man whom he specially favoured, Gyges, the son of Dascylus. All affairs of greatest moment were entrusted by Candaules to this person, and to him he was wont to extol the surpassing beauty of his wife. So matters went on for a while. At length, one day, Candaules, for he was fated to end ill, thus addressed his follower, "I see you do not credit what I tell you of my lady's loveliness; but come now, since men's ears are less credulous than their eyes, contrive some means whereby you may behold her naked." At this the other loudly exclaimed saying, "What most unwise speech is this, master, which you have uttered? Would you have me behold my mistress when she is naked? Remember that a woman, with her clothes, puts off her bashfulness. Our fathers, in time past, distinguished right and wrong plainly enough, and it is our wisdom to submit to be taught by them. There is an old saying, 'Let each look on his own.' I hold your wife for the fairest of all womankind. Only, I beseech you, ask me not to do wickedly."

9. Gyges thus endeavoured to decline the king's proposal, trembling lest some dreadful evil should befall him through it. But the king replied to him, "Courage, friend; suspect me not of the design to prove you by this discourse; nor dread your mistress, lest mischief

befall you at her hands. Be sure I will so manage that she shall not even know that you have looked upon her. I will place you behind the open door of the chamber in which we sleep. When I enter to go to rest she will follow me. There stands a chair close to the entrance, on which she will lay her clothes one by one as she takes them off. You will be able thus at your leisure to peruse her person. Then, when she is moving from the chair towards the bed, and her back is turned on you, be it your care that she see you not as you pass through the door-way."

10. Gyges, unable to escape, could but declare his readiness. Then Candaules, when night came, led Gyges into his sleeping-chamber, and a moment after the queen followed. She came in, and laid her garments on the chair, and Gyges gazed on her. After a while she moved towards the bed, and her back being then turned, he glided stealthily from the apartment. As he was passing out, however, she saw him, and instantly divining what had happened, she neither screamed as her shame impelled her, nor even appeared to have noticed anything, purposing to take vengeance upon the husband who had so affronted her. For among the Lydians, and indeed among the barbarians generally, it is reckoned a deep disgrace, even to a man, to be seen naked.

11. No sound or sign of intelligence escaped her at the time. But in the morning, as soon as day broke, she hastened to choose from among her retinue, such as she knew to be most faithful to her, and preparing them for what was to ensue, summoned Gyges into her presence. Now it had often happened before that the queen had desired to confer with him, and he was accustomed to come to her at her call. He therefore obeyed the summons, not suspecting that she knew what had occurred. Then she addressed these words to him, "Take your choice, Gyges, of two courses which are open to you. Slay Candaules, and thereby become my lord, and obtain the Lydian throne, or die this moment in his room. So you will not again, obeying all behests of your master, behold what is not lawful for you. It must needs be, that either he perish by whose counsel this thing was done, or you, who saw me naked, and so did break our usages." At these words Gyges stood awhile in mute astonishment; recovering after a time, he earnestly besought the queen that

she would not compel him to so hard a choice. But finding he implored in vain, and that necessity was indeed laid on him to kill or to be killed, he made choice of life for himself, and replied by this inquiry, "If it must be so, and you compel me against my will to put my lord to death, come, let me hear how you will have me set on him." "Let him be attacked," she answered, "on that spot where I was by him shown naked to you, and let the assault be made when he is asleep."

12. All was then prepared for the attack, and when night fell, Gyges, seeing that he had no retreat or escape, but must absolutely either slay Candaules, or himself be slain, followed his mistress into the sleeping-room. She placed a dagger in his hand, and hid him carefully behind the self-same door. Then Gyges, when the king was fallen asleep, entered privily into the chamber and struck him dead. Thus did the wife and kingdom of Candaules pass into the possession of his follower Gyges, of whom Archilochus the Parian, who lived about the same time, made mention in a poem written in Iambic trimeter verse.

13. Gyges was afterwards confirmed in the possession of the throne by an answer of the Delphic oracle. Enraged at the murder of their king, the people flew to arms, but after a while the partisans of Gyges came to terms with them, and it was agreed that if the Delphic oracle declared him king of the Lydians, he should reign; if otherwise, he should yield the throne to the Heraclidae. As the oracle was given in his favour he became king. The Pythian priestess, however, added that, in the fifth generation from Gyges, vengeance should come for the Heraclidae; a prophecy of which neither the Lydians nor their princes took any account till it was fulfilled. Such was the way in which the Mermnadae deposed the Heraclidae, and themselves obtained the sovereignty.

Descriptive Digression on Egypt
Book I:35–96

35. CONCERNING EGYPT ITSELF I shall extend my remarks to a great length, because there is no country that possesses so many wonders, nor any that has such a number of works which defy

description. Not only is the climate different from that of the rest of the world, and the rivers unlike any other rivers, but the people also, in most of their manners and customs, exactly reverse the common practice of mankind. The women attend the markets and trade, while the men sit at home at the loom; and here, while the rest of the world works the woof up the warp, the Egyptians work it down; the women likewise carry burthens upon their shoulders, while the men carry them upon their heads. They eat their food out of doors in the streets, but retire for private purposes to their houses, giving as a reason that what is unseemly, but necessary, ought to be done in secret, but what has nothing unseemly about it, should be done openly. A woman cannot serve the priestly office, either for god or goddess, but men are priests to both; sons need not support their parents unless they choose, but daughters must, whether they choose or no.

36. In other countries the priests have long hair, in Egypt their heads are shaven; elsewhere it is customary, in mourning, for near relations to cut their hair close; the Egyptians, who wear no hair at any other time, when they lose a relative, let their beards and the hair of their heads grow long. All other men pass their lives separate from animals, the Egyptians have animals always living with them; others make barley and wheat their food; it is a disgrace to do so in Egypt, where the grain they live on is spelt, which some call *zea*. Dough they knead with their feet; but they mix mud, and even take up dirt, with their hands. They are the only people in the world—they at least, and such as have learnt the practice from them—who use circumcision. Their men wear two garments apiece, their women but one. They put on the rings and fasten the ropes to sails inside; others put them outside. When they write or calculate, instead of going, like the Greeks, from left to right, they move their hand from right to left; and they insist, notwithstanding, that it is they who go to the right, and the Greeks who go to the left. They have two quite different kinds of writing, one of which is called sacred, the other common.

37. They are religious to excess, far beyond any other race of men, and use the following ceremonies: They drink out of brazen cups, which they scour every day: there is no exception to this

practice. They wear linen garments, which they are specially careful to have always fresh washed. They practise circumcision for the sake of cleanliness, considering it better to be cleanly than comely. The priests shave their whole body every other day, that no lice or other impure thing may adhere to them when they are engaged in the service of the gods. Their dress is entirely of linen, and their shoes of the papyrus plant: it is not lawful for them to wear either dress or shoes of any other material. They bathe twice every day in cold water, and twice each night; besides which they observe, so to speak, thousands of ceremonies. They enjoy, however, not a few advantages. They consume none of their own property, and are at no expense for anything; but every day bread is baked for them of the sacred corn, and a plentiful supply of beef and of goose's flesh is assigned to each, and also a portion of wine made from the grape. Fish they are not allowed to eat; and beans,—which none of the Egyptians ever sow, or eat, if they come up of their own accord, either raw or boiled—the priests will not even endure to look on, since they consider it an unclean kind of pulse. Instead of a single priest, each god has the attendance of a college, at the head of which is a chief priest; when one of these dies, his son is appointed in his room.

38. Male kine are reckoned to belong to Epaphus, and are therefore tested in the following manner: One of the priests appointed for the purpose searches to see if there is a single black hair on the whole body, since in that case the beast is unclean. He examines him all over, standing on his legs, and again laid upon his back; after which he takes the tongue out of his mouth, to see if it be clean in respect of the prescribed marks (what they are I will mention elsewhere); he also inspects the hairs of the tail, to observe if they grow naturally. If the animal is pronounced clean in all these various points, the priest marks him by twisting a piece of papyrus round his horns, and attaching thereto some sealing-clay, which he then stamps with his own signet-ring. After this the beast is led away; and it is forbidden, under the penalty of death, to sacrifice an animal which has not been marked in this way.

39. The following is their manner of sacrifice: They lead the victim, marked with their signet, to the altar where they are about

to offer it, and setting the wood alight, pour a libation of wine upon the altar in front of the victim, and at the same time invoke the god. Then they slay the animal, and cutting off his head, proceed to flay the body. Next they take the head, and heaping imprecations on it, if there is a market-place and a body of Greek traders in the city, they carry it there and sell it instantly; if, however, there are no Greeks among them, they throw the head into the river. The imprecation is to this effect: They pray that if any evil is impending either over those who sacrifice, or over universal Egypt, it may be made to fall upon that head. These practices, the imprecations upon the heads, and the libations of wine, prevail all over Egypt, and extend to victims of all sorts; and hence the Egyptians will never eat the head of any animal.

40. The disembowelling and burning are, however, different in different sacrifices. I will mention the mode in use with respect to the goddess whom they regard as the greatest, and honour with the chiefest festival. When they have flayed their steer they pray, and when their prayer is ended they take the paunch of the animal out entire, leaving the intestines and the fat inside the body; they then cut off the legs, the ends of the loins, the shoulders, and the neck; and having so done, they fill the body of the steer with clean bread, honey, raisins, figs, frankincense, myrrh, and other aromatics. Thus filled, they burn the body, pouring over it great quantities of oil. Before offering the sacrifice they fast, and while the bodies of the victims are being consumed they beat themselves. Afterwards, when they have concluded this part of the ceremony, they have the other parts of the victim served up to them for a repast.

41. The male kine, therefore, if clean, and the male calves, are used for sacrifice by the Egyptians universally; but the females they are not allowed to sacrifice, since they are sacred to Isis. The statue of this goddess has the form of a woman but with horns like a cow, resembling thus the Greek representations of Io; and the Egyptians, one and all, venerate cows much more highly than any other animal. This is the reason why no native of Egypt, whether man or woman, will give a Greek a kiss, or use the knife of a Greek, or his spit, or his cauldron, or taste the flesh of an ox, known to be pure, if it has been cut with a Greek knife. When kine die, the following is

the manner of their sepulture: The females are thrown into the river; the males are buried in the suburbs of the towns, with one or both of their horns appearing above the surface of the ground to mark the place. When the bodies are decayed, a boat comes, at an appointed time, from the island called Prosôpitis,—which is a portion of the Delta, nine schoenes in circumference,—and calls at the several cities in turn to collect the bones of the oxen. Prosôpitis is a district containing several cities; the name of that from which the boats come is Atarbêchis. Venus has a temple there of much sanctity. Great numbers of men go forth from this city and proceed to the other towns, where they dig up the bones, which they take away with them and bury together in one place. The same practice prevails with respect to the interment of all other cattle—the law so determining; they do not slaughter any of them.

42. Such Egyptians as possess a temple of the Theban Jove, or live in the Thebaïc canton, offer no sheep in sacrifice, but only goats; for the Egyptians do not all worship the same gods, excepting Isis and Osiris, the latter of whom they say is the Grecian Bacchus. Those, on the contrary, who possess a temple dedicated to Mendes, or belong to the Mendesian canton, abstain from offering goats, and sacrifice sheep instead. The Thebans, and such as imitate them in their practice, give the following account of the origin of the custom: "Hercules," they say, "wished of all things to see Jove, but Jove did not choose to be seen of him. At length, when Hercules persisted, Jove hit on a device—to flay a ram, and, cutting off his head, hold the head before him, and cover himself with the fleece. In this guise he showed himself to Hercules." Therefore the Egyptians give their statues of Jupiter the face of a ram; and from them the practice has passed to the Ammonians, who are a joint colony of Egyptians and Ethiopians, speaking a language between the two; hence also, in my opinion, the latter people took their name of Ammonians, since the Egyptian name for Jupiter is Amun. Such, then, is the reason why the Thebans do not sacrifice rams, but consider them sacred animals. Upon one day in the year, however, at the festival of Jupiter, they slay a single ram, and stripping off the fleece, cover with it the statue of that god, as he once covered

himself, and then bring up to the statue of Jove an image of Hercules. When this has been done, the whole assembly beat their breasts in mourning for the ram, and afterwards bury him in a holy sepulchre.

43. The account which I received of this Hercules makes him one of the twelve gods. Of the other Hercules, with whom the Greeks are familiar, I could hear nothing in any part of Egypt. That the Greeks, however (those I mean who gave the son of Amphitryon that name), took the name from the Egyptians, and not the Egyptians from the Greeks, is I think clearly proved, among other arguments, by the fact that both the parents of Hercules, Amphitryon as well as Alcmêna, were of Egyptian origin. Again, the Egyptians disclaim all knowledge of the names of Neptune and the Dioscûri, and do not include them in the number of their gods; but had they adopted the name of any god from the Greeks, these would have been the likeliest to obtain notice, since the Egyptians, as I am well convinced, practised navigation at that time, and the Greeks also were some of them mariners; so that they would have been more likely to know the names of these gods than that of Hercules. But the Egyptian Hercules is one of their ancient gods. Seventeen thousand years before the reign of Amasis, the twelve gods were, they affirm, produced from the eight: and of these twelve, Hercules is one.

44. In the wish to get the best information that I could on these matters, I made a voyage to Tyre in Phoenicia, hearing there was a temple of Hercules at that place, very highly venerated. I visited the temple, and found it richly adorned with a number of offerings, among which were two pillars, one of pure gold, the other of emerald, shining with great brilliancy at night. In a conversation which I held with the priests, I inquired how long their temple had been built, and found by their answer that they, too, differed from the Greeks. They said that the temple was built at the same time that the city was founded, and that the foundation of the city took place two thousand three hundred years ago. In Tyre I remarked another temple where the same god was worshipped as the Thasian Hercules. So I went on to Thasos, where I found a temple of

Hercules which had been built by the Phoenicians who colonised that island when they sailed in search of Europa. Even this was five generations earlier than the time when Hercules, son of Amphitryon, was born in Greece. These researches show plainly that there is an ancient god Hercules; and my own opinion is, that those Greeks act most wisely who build and maintain two temples of Hercules, in the one of which the Hercules worshipped is known by the name of Olympian, and has sacrifice offered to him as an immortal, while in the other the honours paid are such as are due to a hero.

45. The Greeks tell many tales without due investigation, and among them the following silly fable respecting Hercules: "Hercules," they say, "went once to Egypt, and there the inhabitants took him, and putting a chaplet on his head, led him out in solemn procession, intending to offer him a sacrifice to Jupiter. For a while he submitted quietly; but when they led him up to the altar and began the ceremonies, he put forth his strength and slew them all." Now to me it seems that such a story proves the Greeks to be utterly ignorant of the character and customs of the people. The Egyptians do not think it allowable even to sacrifice cattle, excepting sheep and the male kine and calves, provided they be pure, and also geese. How, then, can it be believed that they would sacrifice men? And again, how would it have been possible for Hercules alone, and, as they confess, a mere mortal, to destroy so many thousands? In saying thus much concerning these matters, may I incur no displeasure either of god or hero!

46. I mentioned above that some of the Egyptians abstain from sacrificing goats, either male or female. The reason is the following: These Egyptians, who are the Mendesians, consider Pan to be one of the eight gods who existed before the twelve, and Pan is represented in Egypt by the painters and the sculptors, just as he is in Greece, with the face and legs of a goat. They do not, however, believe this to be his shape, or consider him in any respect unlike the other gods; but they represent him thus for a reason which I prefer not to relate. The Mendesians hold all goats in veneration, but the male more than the female, giving the goatherds of the males especial honour. One is venerated more highly than all the

rest, and when he dies there is a great mourning throughout all the Mendesian canton. In Egyptian, the goat and Pan are both called Mendes.

47. The pig is regarded among them as an unclean animal, so much so that if a man in passing accidentally touch a pig, he instantly hurries to the river, and plunges in with all his clothes on. Hence, too, the swineherds, notwithstanding that they are of pure Egyptian blood, are forbidden to enter into any of the temples, which are open to all other Egyptians; and further, no one will give his daughter in marriage to a swineherd, or take a wife from among them, so that the swineherds are forced to intermarry among themselves. They do not offer swine in sacrifice to any of their gods, excepting Bacchus and the Moon, whom they honour in this way at the same time, sacrificing pigs to both of them at the same full moon, and afterwards eating of the flesh. There is a reason alleged by them for their detestation of swine at all other seasons, and their use of them at this festival, with which I am well acquainted, but which I do not think it proper to mention. The following is the mode in which they sacrifice the swine to the Moon: As soon as the victim is slain, the tip of the tail, the spleen, and the caul are put together, and having been covered with all the fat that has been found in the animal's belly, are straightway burnt. The remainder of the flesh is eaten on the same day that the sacrifice is offered, which is the day of the full moon: at any other time they would not so much as taste it. The poorer sort, who cannot afford live pigs, form pigs of dough, which they bake and offer in sacrifice.

48. To Bacchus, on the eve of his feast, every Egyptian sacrifices a hog before the door of his house, which is then given back to the swineherd by whom it was furnished, and by him carried away. In other respects the festival is celebrated almost exactly as Bacchic festivals are in Greece, excepting that the Egyptians have no choral dances. They also use, instead of phalli, another invention, consisting of images a cubit high, pulled by strings, which the women carry round to the villages. A piper goes in front; and the women follow, singing hymns in honour of Bacchus. They give a religious reason for the peculiarities of the image.

49. Melampus, the son of Amytheon, cannot (I think) have

been ignorant of this ceremony—nay, he must, I should conceive, have been well acquainted with it. He it was who introduced into Greece the name of Bacchus, the ceremonial of his worship, and the procession of the phallus. He did not, however, so completely apprehend the whole doctrine as to be able to communicate it entirely; but various sages since his time have carried out his teaching to greater perfection. Still it is certain that Melampus introduced the phallus, and that the Greeks learnt from him the ceremonies which they now practise. I therefore maintain that Melampus, who was a wise man, and had acquired the art of divination, having become acquainted with the worship of Bacchus through knowledge derived from Egypt, introduced it into Greece, with a few slight changes, at the same time that he brought in various other practices. For I can by no means allow that it is by mere coincidence that the Bacchic ceremonies in Greece are so nearly the same as the Egyptian—they would then have been more Greek in their character, and less recent in their origin. Much less can I admit that the Egyptians borrowed these customs, or any other, from the Greeks. My belief is that Melampus got his knowledge of them from Cadmus the Tyrian, and the followers whom he brought from Phoenicia into the country which is now called Boeotia.

50. Almost all the names of the gods came into Greece from Egypt. My inquiries prove that they were all derived from a foreign source; and my opinion is that Egypt furnished the greater number. For with the exception of Neptune and the Dioscûri, whom I mentioned above, and Juno, Vesta, Themis, the Graces, and the Nereids, the other gods have been known from time immemorial in Egypt. This I assert on the authority of the Egyptians themselves. The gods, with whose names they profess themselves unacquainted, the Greeks received, I believe, from the Pelasgi, except Neptune. Of him they got their knowledge from the Libyans, by whom he has been always honoured, and who were anciently the only people that had a god of the name. The Egyptians differ from the Greeks also in paying no divine honours to heroes.

51. Besides those which have been here mentioned, there are many other practices whereof I shall speak hereafter, which the

Greeks have borrowed from Egypt. The peculiarity, however, which they observe in the statues of Mercury they did not derive from the Egyptians, but from the Pelasgi; from them the Athenians first adopted it, and afterwards it passed from the Athenians to the other Greeks. For just at the time when the Athenians were entering into the Hellenic body, the Pelasgi came to live with them in their country, whence it was that the latter came first to be regarded as Greeks. Whoever has been initiated into the mysteries of the Cabiri will understand what I mean. The Samothracians received these mysteries from the Pelasgi, who, before they went to live in Attica, were dwellers in Samothrace, and imparted their religious ceremonies to the inhabitants. The Athenians, then, who were the first of all the Greeks to make their statues of Mercury in this way, learnt the practice from the Pelasgians; and by this people a religious account of the matter is given, which is explained in the Samothracian mysteries.

52. In early times the Pelasgi, as I know by information which I got at Dodôna, offered sacrifices of all kinds, and prayed to the gods, but had no distinct names or appellations for them, since they had never heard of any. They called them gods ($\theta\epsilon oi$, disposers), because they had disposed and arranged all things in such a beautiful order. After a long lapse of time the names of the gods came to Greece from Egypt, and the Pelasgi learnt them; only as yet they knew nothing of Bacchus, of whom they first heard at a much later date. Not long after the arrival of the names they sent to consult the oracle at Dodôna about them. This is the most ancient oracle in Greece, and at that time there was no other. To their question, "Whether they should adopt the names that had been imported from the foreigners?" the oracle replied by recommending their use. Thenceforth in their sacrifices the Pelasgi made use of the names of the gods, and from them the names passed afterwards to the Greeks.

53. Whence the gods severally sprang, whether or no they had all existed from eternity, what forms they bore—these are questions of which the Greeks knew nothing until the other day, so to speak. For Homer and Hesiod were the first to compose Theogonies, and give the gods their epithets, to allot them their several offices and

occupations, and describe their forms; and they lived but four hundred years before my time,* as I believe. As for the poets who are thought by some to be earlier than these, they are, in my judgment, decidedly later writers. In these matters I have the authority of the priestesses of Dodôna for the former portion of my statements; what I have said of Homer and Hesiod is my own opinion.

58. The Egyptians were also the first to introduce solemn assemblies, processions, and litanies to the gods; of all which the Greeks were taught the use by them. It seems to me a sufficient proof of this, that in Egypt these practices have been established from remote antiquity, while in Greece they are only recently known.

59. The Egyptians do not hold a single solemn assembly, but several in the course of the year. Of these the chief, which is better attended than any other, is held at the city of Bubastis in honour of Diana. The next in importance is that which takes place at Busiris, a city situated in the very middle of the Delta; it is in honour of Isis, who is called in the Greek tongue Demêter (Ceres). There is a third great festival in Saïs to Minerva, a fourth in Heliopolis to the Sun, a fifth in Buto to Latona, and a sixth in Paprêmis to Mars.

60. The following are the proceedings on occasion of the assembly at Bubastis: Men and women come sailing all together, vast numbers in each boat, many of the women with castanets, which they strike, while some of the men pipe during the whole time of the voyage; the remainder of the voyagers, male and female, sing the while, and make a clapping with their hands. When they arrive opposite any of the towns upon the banks of the stream, they approach the shore, and, while some of the women continue to play and sing, others call aloud to the females of the place and load them with abuse, while a certain number dance, and some standing up

---

* The date of Homer has been variously stated. It is plain from the expressions which Herodotus here uses that in his time the general belief assigned to Homer an earlier date than that which he considered the true one. His date would place the poet about B.C. 880–830, which is very nearly the mean between the earliest and the latest epochs that are assigned to him. The earliest date that can be exactly determined, is that of the author of the life of Homer usually published with the works of Herodotus, who places the birth of the poet 622 years before the invasion of Xerxes, or B.C. 1102.—tr.

uncover themselves. After proceeding in this way all along the river-course, they reach Bubastis, where they celebrate the feast with abundant sacrifices. More grape-wine is consumed at this festival than in all the rest of the year besides. The number of those who attend, counting only the men and women, and omitting the children, amounts, according to the native reports, to seven hundred thousand.

61. The ceremonies at the feast of Isis in the city of Busiris have been already spoken of. It is there that the whole multitude, both of men and women, many thousands in number, beat themselves at the close of the sacrifice, in honour of a god, whose name a religious scruple forbids me to mention. The Carian dwellers in Egypt proceed on this occasion to still greater lengths, even cutting their faces with their knives, whereby they let it be seen that they are not Egyptians, but foreigners.

62. At Sais, when the assembly takes place for the sacrifices, there is one night on which the inhabitants all burn a multitude of lights in the open air round their houses. They use lamps in the shape of flat saucers filled with a mixture of oil and salt, on the top of which the wick floats. These burn the whole night, and give to the festival the name of the Feast of Lamps. The Egyptians who are absent from the festival observe the night of the sacrifice, no less than the rest, by a general lighting of lamps; so that the illumination is not confined to the city of Saïs, but extends over the whole of Egypt. And there is a religious reason assigned for the special honour paid to this night, as well as for the illumination which accompanies it.

63. At Heliopolis and Buto the assemblies are merely for the purpose of sacrifice; but at Paprêmis, besides the sacrifices and other rites which are performed there as elsewhere, the following custom is observed: When the sun is getting low, a few only of the priests continue occupied about the image of the god, while the greater number, armed with wooden clubs, take their station at the portal of the temple. Opposite to them is drawn up a body of men, in number above a thousand, armed like the others with clubs, consisting of persons engaged in the performance of their vows. The image of the god, which is kept in a small wooden shrine covered

with plates of gold, is conveyed from the temple into a second sacred building the day before the festival begins. The few priests still in attendance upon the image place it, together with the shrine containing it, on a four-wheeled car, and begin to drag it along; the others, stationed at the gateway of the temple, oppose its admission. Then the votaries come forward to espouse the quarrel of the god, and set upon the opponents, who are sure to offer resistance. A sharp fight with clubs ensues, in which heads are commonly broken on both sides. Many, I am convinced, die of the wounds that they receive, though the Egyptians insist that no one is ever killed.

* * * *

65. Egypt, though it borders upon Libya, is not a region abounding in wild animals. The animals that do exist in the country, whether domesticated or otherwise, are all regarded as sacred. If I were to explain why they are consecrated to the several gods, I should be led to speak of religious matters, which I particularly shrink from mentioning; the points whereon I have touched slightly hitherto have all been introduced from sheer necessity. Their custom with respect to animals as follows:—For every kind there are appointed certain guardians, some male, some female, whose business it is to look after them; and this honour is made to descend from father to son. The inhabitants of the various cities, when they have made a vow to any god, pay it to his animals in the way which I will now explain. At the time of making the vow they shave the head of the child, cutting off all the hair, or else half, or sometimes a third part, which they then weigh in a balance against a sum of silver; and whatever sum the hair weighs is presented to the guardian of the animals, who thereupon cuts up some fish, and gives it to them for food—such being the stuff whereon they are fed. When a man has killed one of the sacred animals, if he did it with malice prepense, he is punished with death; if unwittingly, he has to pay such a fine as the priests choose to impose. When an ibis, however, or a hawk is killed, whether it was done by accident or on purpose, the man must die.

66. The number of domestic animals in Egypt is very great, and would be still greater were it not for what befalls the cats. As the

females, when they have kittened, no longer seek the company of the males, these last, to obtain once more their companionship, practise a curious artifice. They seize the kittens, carry them off, and kill them, but do not eat them afterwards. Upon this the females, being deprived of their young, and longing to supply their place, seek the males once more, since they are particularly fond of their offspring. On every occasion of a fire in Egypt the strangest prodigy occurs with the cats. The inhabitants allow the fire to rage as it pleases, while they stand about at intervals and watch these animals, which, slipping by the men or else leaping over them, rush headlong into the flames. When this happens, the Egyptians are in deep affliction. If a cat dies in a private house by a natural death, all the inmates of the house shave their eyebrows; on the death of a dog they shave the head and the whole of the body.

67. The cats on their decease are taken to the city of Bubastis, where they are embalmed, after which they are buried in certain sacred repositories. The dogs are interred in the cities to which they belong, also in sacred burial-places. The same practice obtains with respect to the ichneumons; the hawks and shrew-mice, on the contrary, are conveyed to the city of Buto for burial, and the ibises to Hermopolis. The bears, which are scarce in Egypt, and the wolves, which are not much bigger than foxes, they bury wherever they happen to find them lying.

68. The following are the peculiarities of the crocodile: During the four winter months they eat nothing: they are four-footed, and live indifferently on land or in the water. The female lays and hatches her eggs ashore, passing the greater portion of the day on dry land, but at night retiring to the river, the water of which is warmer than the night-air and the dew. Of all known animals this is the one which from the smallest size grows to be the greatest: for the egg of the crocodile is but little bigger than that of the goose, and the young crocodile is in proportion to the egg; yet when it is full grown, the animal measures frequently seventeen cubits and even more. It has the eyes of a pig, teeth large and tusk-like, of a size proportioned to its frame; unlike any other animal, it is without a tongue; it cannot move its under jaw, and in this repect too it is singular, being the only animal in the world which moves the

upper jaw but not the under. It has strong claws and a scaly skin, impenetrable upon the back. In the water it is blind, but on land it is very keen of sight. As it lives chiefly in the river, it has the inside of its mouth constantly covered with leeches; hence it happens that, while all the other birds and beasts avoid it, with the trochilus it lives at peace, since it owes much to that bird: for the crocodile, when he leaves the water and comes out upon the land, is in the habit of lying with its mouth wide open, facing the western breeze: at such times the trochilus goes into his mouth and devours the leeches. This benefits the crocodile, who is pleased, and takes care not to hurt the trochilus.

69. The crocodile is esteemed sacred by some of the Egyptians; by others he is treated as an enemy. Those who live near Thebes, and those who dwell around Lake Moeris, regard them with special veneration. In each of these places they keep one crocodile in particular, who is taught to be tame and tractable. They adorn his ears with ear-rings of molten stone or gold, and put bracelets on his fore-paws, giving him daily a set portion of bread, with a certain number of victims; and, after having thus treated him with the greatest possible attention while alive, they embalm him when he dies, and bury him in a sacred repository. The people of Elephantiné, on the other hand, are so far from considering these animals as sacred, that they even eat their flesh. In the Egyptian language they are not called crocodiles, but Champsae. The name of crocodiles was given them by the Ionians, who remarked their resemblance to the lizards, which in Ionia live in the walls, and are called crocodiles.

71. The hippopotamus, in the canton of Paprêmis, is a sacred animal, but not in any other part of Egypt. It may be thus described: It is a quadruped, cloven-footed, with hoofs like an ox, and a flat nose. It has the mane and tail of a horse, huge tusks which are very conspicuous, and a voice like a horse's neigh. In size it equals the biggest oxen, and its skin is so tough that when dried it is made into javelins.

73. They have also another sacred bird called the phoenix, which I myself have never seen, except in pictures. Indeed, it is a great rarity, even in Egypt, only coming there (according to the

accounts of the people of Heliopolis) once in five hundred years, when the old phoenix dies. Its size and appearance, if it is like the pictures, are as follows: The plumage is partly red, partly golden, while the general make and size are almost exactly that of the eagle. They tell a story of what this bird does, which does not seem to me to be credible: that he comes all the way from Arabia, and brings the parent bird, all plastered over with myrrh, to the temple of the Sun, and there buries the body. In order to bring him, they say, he first forms a ball of myrrh as big as he finds that he can carry; then he hollows out the ball, and puts his parent inside, after which he covers over the opening with fresh myrrh, and the ball is then of exactly the same weight as at first; so he brings it to Egypt, plastered over as I have said, and deposits it in the temple of the Sun. Such is the story they tell of the doings of this bird.

* * *

77. With respect to the Egyptians themselves, it is to be remarked that those who live in the corn country, devoting themselves, as they do, far more than any other people in the world, to the preservation of the memory of past actions, are the best skilled in history of any men that I have ever met. The following is the mode of life habitual to them: For three successive days in each month they purge the body by means of emetics and clysters, which is done out of a regard for their health, since they have a persuasion that every disease to which men are liable is occasioned by the substances whereon they feed. Apart from any such precautions, they are, I believe, next to the Libyans, the healthiest people in the world—an effect of their climate, in my opinion, which has no sudden changes. Diseases almost always attack men when they are exposed to a change, and never more than during changes of the weather. They live on bread made of spelt, which they form into loaves called in their own tongue cyllêstis. Their drink is a wine which they obtain from barley, as they have no vines in their country. Many kinds of fish they eat raw, either salted or dried in the sun. Quails also, and ducks and small birds, they eat uncooked, merely first salting them. All other birds and fishes, excepting those which are set apart as sacred, are eaten either roasted or boiled.

78. In social meetings among the rich, when the banquet is ended, a servant carries round to the several guests a coffin, in which there is a wooden image of a corpse, carved and painted to resemble nature as nearly as possible, about a cubit or two cubits in length. As he shows it to each guest in turn, the servant says, "Gaze here, and drink and be merry; for when you die, such will you be."

79. The Egyptians adhere to their own national customs, and adopt no foreign usages. Many of these customs are worthy of note: among others their song, the Linus, which is sung under various names not only in Egypt but in Phoenicia, in Cyprus, and in other places; and which seems to be exactly the same as that in use among the Greeks, and by them called Linus. There were very many things in Egypt which filled me with astonishment, and this was one of them. Whence could the Egyptians have got the Linus? It appears to have been sung by them from the very earliest times. For the Linus in Egyptian is called Manerôs; and they told me that Manerôs was the only son of their first king, and that on his untimely death he was honoured by the Egyptians with these dirge-like strains, and in this way they got their first and only melody.

80. There is another custom in which the Egyptians resemble a particular Greek people, namely the Lacedaemonians. Their young men, when they meet their elders in the streets, give way to them and step aside; and if an elder come in where young are present, these latter rise from their seats. In a third point they differ entirely from all the nations of Greece. Instead of speaking to each other when they meet in the streets, they make an obeisance, sinking the hand to the knee.

81. They wear a linen tunic fringed about the legs, and called *calasiris;* over this they have a white woollen garment thrown on afterwards. Nothing of woollen, however, is taken to their temples or buried with them, as their religion forbids it. Here their practice resembles the rites called Orphic and Bacchic, but which are in reality Egyptian and Pythagorean; for no one initiated in these mysteries can be buried in a woollen shroud, a religious reason being assigned for the observance.

82. The Egyptians likewise discovered to which of the gods each

month and day is sacred; and found out from the day of a man's birth, what he will meet with in the course of his life, and how he will end his days, and what sort of man he will be—discoveries whereof the Greeks engaged in poetry have made a use. The Egyptians have also discovered more prognostics than all the rest of mankind besides. Whenever a prodigy takes place, they watch and record the result; then, if anything similar ever happens again, they expect the same consequences.

83. With respect to divination, they hold that it is a gift which no mortal possesses, but only certain of the gods: thus they have an oracle of Hercules, one of Apollo, of Minerva, of Diana, of Mars, and of Jupiter. Besides these, there is the oracle of Latona at Buto, which is held in much higher repute than any of the rest. The mode of delivering the oracles is not uniform, but varies at the different shrines.

84. Medicine is practised among them on a plan of separation; each physician treats a single disorder, and no more: thus the country swarms with medical practitioners, some undertaking to cure diseases of the eye, others of the head, others again of the teeth, others of the intestines, and some those which are not local.

85. The following is the way in which they conduct their mournings, and their funerals: On the death in any house of a man of consequence, forthwith the women of the family beplaster their heads, and sometimes even their faces, with mud; and then, leaving the body indoors, sally forth and wander through the city, with their dress fastened by a band, and their bosoms bare, beating themselves as they walk. All the female relations join them and do the same. The men too, similarly begirt, beat their breasts separately. When these ceremonies are over, the body is carried away to be embalmed.

86. There are a set of men in Egypt who practise the art of embalming, and make it their proper business. These persons, when a body is brought to them, show the bearers various models of corpses, made in wood, and painted so as to resemble nature. The most perfect is said to be after the manner of him whom I do not think it religious to name in connection with such a matter; the second sort is inferior to the first, and less costly; the third is the

cheapest of all. All this the embalmers explain, and then ask in which way it is wished that the corpse should be prepared. The bearers tell them, and having concluded their bargain, take their departure, while the embalmers, left to themselves, proceed to their task. The mode of embalming, according to the most perfect process, is the following: They take first a crooked piece of iron, and with it draw out the brain through the nostrils, thus getting rid of a portion, while the skull is cleared of the rest by rinsing with drugs; next they make a cut along the flank with a sharp Ethiopian stone, and take out the whole contents of the abdomen, which they then cleanse, washing it thoroughly with palm wine, and again frequently with an infusion of pounded aromatics. After this they fill the cavity with the purest bruised myrrh, with cassia, and every sort of spicery except frankincense, and sew up the opening. Then the body is placed in natrum for seventy days, and covered entirely over. After the expiration of that space of time, which must not be exceeded, the body is washed, and wrapped round, from head to foot, with bandages of fine linen cloth, smeared over with gum, which is used generally by the Egyptians in the place of glue, and in this state it is given back to the relations, who enclose it in a wooden case which they have had made for the purpose, shaped into the figure of a man. Then fastening the case, they place it in a sepulchral chamber, upright against the wall. Such is the most costly way of embalming the dead.

87. If persons wish to avoid expense, and choose the second process, the following is the method pursued: Syringes are filled with oil made from the cedar-tree, which is then, without any incision or disembowelling, injected into the abdomen. The passage by which it might be likely to return is stopped, and the body laid in natrum the prescribed number of days. At the end of the time the cedar-oil is allowed to make its escape; and such is its power that it brings with it the whole stomach and intestines in a liquid state. The natrum meanwhile has dissolved the flesh, and so nothing is left of the dead body but the skin and the bones. It is returned in this condition to the relatives, without any further trouble being bestowed upon it.

88. The third method of embalming, which is practised in the

case of the poorer classes, is to clear out the intestines with a clyster, and let the body lie in natrum the seventy days, after which it is at once given to those who come to fetch it away.

89. The wives of men of rank are not given to be embalmed immediately after death, nor indeed are any of the more beautiful and valued women. It is not until they have been dead three or four days that they are carried to the embalmers. This is done to prevent indignities from being offered them. It is said that once a case of this kind occurred: the man was detected by the information of his fellow-workman.

90. Whenever any one, Egyptian or foreigner, has lost his life by falling a prey to a crocodile, or by drowning in the river, the law compels the inhabitants of the city near which the body is cast up to have it embalmed, and to bury it in one of the sacred repositories with all possible magnificence. No one may touch the corpse, not even any of the friends or relatives, but only the priests of the Nile, who prepare it for burial with their own hands—regarding it as something more than the mere body of a man—and themselves lay it in the tomb.

91. The Egyptians are averse to adopt Greek customs, or, in a word, those of any other nation. This feeling is almost universal among them. At Chemmis, however, which is a large city in the Thebaïc canton near Neapolis, there is a square enclosure sacred to Perseus, son of Danaë. Palm trees grow all round the place, which has a stone gateway of an unusual size, surmounted by two colossal statues, also in stone. Inside this precinct is a temple, and in the temple an image of Perseus. The people of Chemmis say that Perseus often appears to them, sometimes within the sacred enclosure, sometimes in the open country: one of the sandals which he has worn is frequently found—two cubits in length, as they affirm—and then all Egypt flourishes greatly. In the worship of Perseus Greek ceremonies are used; gymnastic games are celebrated in his honour, comprising every kind of contest, with prizes of cattle, cloaks, and skins. I made inquiries of the Chemites why it was that Perseus appeared to them and not elsewhere in Egypt, and how they came to celebrate gymnastic contests unlike the rest of the Egyptians: to which they answered, "that Perseus belonged to

their city by descent. Danaüs and Lynceus were Chemmites before they set sail for Greece, and from them Perseus was descended," they said, tracing the genealogy; "and he, when he came to Egypt for the purpose" (which the Greeks also assign) "of bringing away from Libya the Gorgon's head, paid them a visit, and acknowledged them for his kinsmen—he had heard the name of their city from his mother before he left Greece—he bade them institute a gymnastic contest in his honour, and that was the reason why they observed the practice."

92. The customs hitherto described are those of the Egyptians who live above the marsh-country. The inhabitants of the marshes have the same customs as the rest, as well in those matters which have been mentioned above as in respect of marriage, each Egyptian taking to himself, like the Greeks, a single wife; but for greater cheapness of living the marsh-men practise certain peculiar customs, such as these following. They gather the blossoms of a certain water-lily, which grows in great abundance all over the flat country at the time when the Nile rises and floods the regions along its banks—the Egyptians call it the lotus—they gather, I say, the blossoms of this plant and dry them in the sun, after which they extract from the centre of each blossom a substance like the head of a poppy, which they crush and make into bread. The root of the lotus is likewise eatable, and has a pleasant sweet taste: it is round, and about the size of an apple. There is also another species of the lily in Egypt, which grows, like the lotus, in the river, and resembles the rose. The fruit springs up side by side with the blossom, on a separate stalk, and has almost exactly the look of the comb made by wasps. It contains a number of seeds, about the size of an olive-stone, which are good to eat: and these are eaten both green and dried. The byblus (papyrus), which grows year after year in the marshes, they pull up, and cutting the plant in two, reserve the upper portion for other purposes, but take the lower, which is about a cubit long, and either eat it or else sell it. Such as wish to enjoy the byblus in full perfection bake it first in a closed vessel, heated to a glow. Some of these folk, however, live entirely on fish, which are gutted as soon as caught, and then hung up in the sun: when dry, they are used as food.

93. Gregarious fish are not found in any numbers in the rivers; they frequent the lagunes, whence, at the season of breeding, they proceed in shoals towards the sea. The males lead the way, and drop their milt as they go, while the females, following close behind, eagerly swallow it down. From this they conceive, and when, after passing some time in the sea, they begin to be in spawn, the whole shoal sets off on its return to its ancient haunts. Now, however, it is no longer the males, but the females, who take the lead: they swim in front in a body, and do exactly as the males did before, dropping, little by little, their grains of spawn as they go, while the males in the rear devour the grains, each one of which is a fish. A portion of the spawn escapes and is not swallowed by the males, and hence come the fishes which grow afterwards to maturity. When any of this sort of fish are taken on their passage to the sea, they are found to have the left side of the head scarred and bruised; while if taken on their return, the marks appear on the right. The reason is, that as they swim down the Nile seaward, they keep close to the bank of the river upon their left, and returning again up stream they still cling to the same side, hugging it and brushing against it constantly, to be sure that they miss not their road through the great force of the current. When the Nile begins to rise, the hollows in the land and the marshy spots near the river are flooded before any other places by the percolation of the water through the river-banks; and these, almost as soon as they become pools, are found to be full of numbers of little fishes. I think that I understand how it is this comes to pass. On the subsidence of the Nile the year before, though the fish retired with the retreating waters, they had first deposited their spawn in the mud upon the banks: and so, when at the usual season the water returns, small fry are rapidly engendered out of the spawn of the preceding year. So much concerning the fish.

94. The Egyptians who live in the marshes use for the anointing of their bodies an oil made from the fruit of the sillicyprium, which is known among them by the name of "kiki." To obtain this they plant the sillicyprium (which grows wild in Greece) along the banks of the rivers and by the sides of the lakes, where it produces fruit in great abundance, but with a very disagreeable

smell. This fruit is gathered, and then bruised and pressed, or else boiled down after roasting: the liquid which comes from it is collected and is found to be unctuous, and as well suited as olive-oil for lamps, only that it gives out an unpleasant odour.

95. The contrivances which they use against gnats, wherewith the country swarms, are the following: In the parts of Egypt above the marshes the inhabitants pass the night upon lofty towers, which are of great service, as the gnats are unable to fly to any height on account of the winds. In the marsh country, where there are no towers, each man possesses a net instead. By day it serves him to catch fish, while at night he spreads it over the bed in which he is to rest, and creeping in, goes to sleep underneath. The gnats, which, if he rolls himself up in his dress or in a piece of muslin, are sure to bite through the covering, do not so much as attempt to pass the net.

96. The vessels used in Egypt for the transport of merchandise are made of the Acantha (Thorn), a tree which in its growth is very like the Cyrenaïc lotus, and from which there exudes a gum. They cut a quantity of planks about two cubits in length from this tree, and then proceed to their ship-building, arranging the planks, like bricks, and attaching them by ties to a number of long stakes or poles till the hull is complete, when they lay the cross-planks on the top from side to side. They give the boats no ribs, but caulk the seams with papyrus on the inside. Each has a single rudder, which is driven straight through the keel. The mast is a piece of acantha-wood, and the sails are made of papyrus. These boats cannot make way against the current unless there is a brisk breeze; they are, therefore, towed up-stream from the shore: down-stream they are managed as follows: There is a raft belonging to each, made of the wood of the tamarisk, fastened together with a wattling of reeds; and also a stone bored through the middle, about two talents in weight. The raft is fastened to the vessels by a rope, and allowed to float down the stream in front, while the stone is attached by another rope astern. The result is that the raft, hurried forward by the current, goes rapidly down the river, and drags the "baris" (for so they call this sort of boat) after it; while the stone, which is pulled along in the wake of the vessel, and lies deep in the water, keeps

the boat straight. There are a vast number of these vessels in Egypt, and some of them are of many thousand talents' burthen.

Battle of Marathon and Excursus on the Alcmaeonid Family
Book VI: 102–125

102. THE PERSIANS, having thus brought Eretria into subjection, after waiting a few days, sailed for Attica, greatly straitening the Athenians as they approached, and thinking to deal with them as they had dealt with the people of Eretria. And because there was no place in all Attica so convenient for their horse as Marathon, and it lay moreover quite close to Eretria, . . . Hippias, the son of Pisistratus, conducted them thither.

103. When intelligence of this reached the Athenians, they likewise marched their troops to Marathon, and there stood on the defensive, having at their head ten generals, of whom one was Miltiades.

Now this man's father, Cimon, the son of Stesagoras, was banished from Athens by Pisistratus, the son of Hippocrates. In his banishment it was his fortune to win the four-horse chariot-race at Olympia, whereby he gained the very same honour which had before been carried off by Miltiades, his half-brother on the mother's side. At the next Olympiad he won the prize again with the same mares, upon which he caused Pisistratus to be proclaimed the winner, having made an agreement with him that on yielding him this honour he should be allowed to come back to his country. Afterwards, still with the same mares, he won the prize a third time, whereupon he was put to death by the sons of Pisistratus, whose father was no longer living. They set men to lie in wait for him secretly, and these men slew him near the town-hall in the night-time. He was buried outside the city, beyond what is called the Valley Road, and right opposite his tomb were buried the mares which had won the three prizes. The same success had likewise been achieved once previously, to wit, by the mares of Evagoras the Lacedaemonian, but never except by them. At the time of Cimon's death, Stesagoras, the elder of his two sons, was in the Chersonese, where he lived with Miltiades his uncle; the younger, who was called Miltiades after the founder of the Chersonite colony, was with his father in Athens.

104. It was this Miltiades who now commanded the Athenians, after escaping from the Chersonese, and twice nearly losing his life. First he was chased as far as Imbrus by the Phoenicians, who had a great desire to take him and carry him up to the king; and when he had avoided this danger, and, having reached his own country, thought himself to be altogether in safety, he found his enemies waiting for him, and was cited by them before a court and impeached for his tyranny in the Chersonese. But he came off victorious here likewise, and was thereupon made general of the Athenians by the free choice of the people.

105. And first, before they left the city, the generals sent off to Sparta a herald, one Philippides, who was by birth an Athenian, and by profession and practice a trained runner. This man, according to the account which he gave to the Athenians on his return, when he was near Mount Parthenium, above Tegea, fell in with the god Pan, who called him by his name, and bade him ask the Athenians, "Why they neglected him so entirely, when he was kindly disposed towards them, and had often helped them in times past, and would do so again in time to come?" The Athenians, entirely believing in the truth of this report, as soon as their affairs were once more in good order, set up a temple to Pan under the Acropolis, and, in return for the message which I have recorded, established in his honour yearly sacrifices and a torch-race.

106. On the occasion of which we speak, when Philippides was sent by the Athenian generals, and, according to his own account, saw Pan on his journey, he reached Sparta on the very next day after quitting the city of Athens. Upon his arrival he went before the rulers, and said:

"Men of Lacedaemon, the Athenians beseech you to hasten to their aid, and not allow that state, which is the most ancient in all Greece, to be enslaved by the barbarians. Eretria is already carried away captive, and Greece weakened by the loss of no mean city."

Thus did Philippides deliver the message committed to him. And the Spartans wished to help the Athenians, but were unable to give them any present aid, as they did not like to break their established law. It was the ninth day of the month, and they could not march out of Sparta on the ninth, when the moon had not reached the full. So they waited for the full of the moon.

107. The barbarians were conducted to Marathon by Hippias, the son of Pisistratus, who the night before had seen a strange vision in his sleep. He seemed to have intercourse with his mother, and conjectured the dream to mean that he would be restored to Athens, recover the power which he had lost, and afterwards live to a good old age in his native country. Such was the sense in which he interpreted the vision. He now proceeded to act as guide to the Persians, and in the first place he landed the prisoners taken from Eretria upon the island that is called Aegileia, belonging to the Styreans, after which he brought the fleet to anchor off Marathon, and marshalled the bands of the barbarians as they disembarked. As he was thus employed it chanced that he sneezed and at the same time coughed with more violence than was his wont. Now as he was a man advanced in years, and the greater number of his teeth were loose, it so happened that one of them was driven out with the force of the cough, and fell down into the sand. Hippias took all the pains he could to find it, but the tooth was nowhere to be seen; whereupon he fetched a deep sigh, and said to the bystanders, "After all the land is not ours, and we shall never be able to bring it under. All my share in it is the portion of which my tooth has possession."

So Hippias believed that this fulfilled his dream.

108. The Athenians were drawn up in order of battle in a precinct belonging to Heracles, when they were joined by the Plataeans, who came in full force to their aid. Some time before, the Plataeans had put themselves under the rule of the Athenians, and these last had already undertaken many labours on their behalf. The occasion of the surrender was the following. The Plataeans suffered grievous things at the hands of the men of Thebes; so, as it chanced that Cleomenes, the son of Anaxandridas, and the Lacedaemonians were in their neighbourhood, they first of all offered to surrender themselves to them. But the Lacedaemonians refused

to receive them, and said, "We dwell too far off from you, and ours would be but cold comfort. You might oftentimes be carried into slavery before one of us heard of it. We counsel you rather to give yourselves up to the Athenians, who are your next neighbours, and well able to shelter you."

This they said, not so much out of good will towards the Plataeans as because they wished to involve the Athenians in trouble by engaging them in wars with the Boeotians. The Plataeans, however, when the Lacedaemonians gave them this counsel, complied at once; and when the sacrifice to the Twelve Gods was being offered at Athens, they came and sat as suppliants about the altar, and gave themselves up to the Athenians. The Thebans no sooner learned what the Plataeans had done then instantly they marched out against them, while the Athenians sent troops to their aid. As the two armies were about to join battle, the Corinthians, who chanced to be at hand, would not allow them to engage; both sides consented to take them for arbitrators, whereupon they made up the quarrel, and fixed the boundary-line between the two states upon this condition: that if any of the Boeotians wished no longer to belong to Boeotia, the Thebans should allow them to follow their own inclinations. The Corinthians, when they had thus decreed, departed to their homes; the Athenians likewise set off on their return, but the Boeotians fell upon them during the march, and a battle was fought wherein they were worsted by the Athenians. Hereupon these last would not be bound by the line which the Corinthians had fixed, but advanced beyond those limits, and made the Asopus the boundary-line between the country of the Thebans and that of the Plataeans and Hysians. Under such circumstances did the Plataeans give themselves up to Athens; and now they were come to Marathon to aid the Athenians.

109. The Athenian generals were divided in their opinions; and some advised not to risk a battle, because they were too few to engage such a host as that of the Medes; while others were for fighting at once, and among these last was Miltiades. He therefore, seeing that opinions were thus divided, and that the less worthy counsel appeared likely to prevail, resolved to go to the Polemarch, and have a conference with him. For the man on whom the lot fell

to be polemarch,* at Athens was entitled to give his vote with the ten generals, since anciently the Athenians allowed him an equal right of voting with them. The Polemarch at this juncture was Callimachus of Aphidnae; to him therefore Miltiades went, and said:

"With you it rests, Callimachus, either to bring Athens to slavery, or, by securing her freedom, to leave behind to all future generations a memory beyond even Harmodius and Aristogeiton. For never since the time that the Athenians became a people were they in so great a danger as now. If they bow their necks beneath the yoke of the Medes, the woes which they will have to suffer when given into the power of Hippias are already determined on; if, on the other hand, they fight and overcome, Athens may rise to be the very first city in Greece. How it comes to pass that these things are likely to happen, and how the determining of them in some sort rests with you, I will now proceed to make clear. We generals are ten in number, and our votes are divided; half of us wish to engage, half to avoid a combat. Now, if we do not fight, I look to see a great disturbance at Athens which will shake men's resolutions, and then I fear they will submit themselves; but if we fight the battle before any unsoundness show itself among our citizens, let the gods but give us fair play, and we are well able to overcome the enemy. On you therefore we depend in this matter, which lies wholly in your own power. You have only to add your vote to my side and your country will be free, and not free only, but the first state in Greece. Or, if you prefer to give your vote to them who would decline the combat, then the reverse will follow."

110. Miltiades by these words gained Callimachus; and the addition of the polemarch's vote caused the decision to be in favor of fighting. Hereupon all those generals who had been desirous of hazarding a battle, when their turn came to command the army, gave up their right to Miltiades. He however, though he accepted

---

* The Polemarch, or War-Archon, was the third archon in dignity, and before the time of Cleisthenes had constitutionally the general superintendence of all military matters, having succeeded to the office of the kings as respected war. When Herodotus wrote, the polemarch had no military functions at all, but attended to the personal and family interests of the metics and foreigners.—tr.

their offers, nevertheless waited, and would not fight, until his own day of command arrived in due course.

111. Then at length, when his own turn was come, the Athenian battle was set in array, and this was the order of it. Callimachus the polemarch led the right wing, for it was at that time a rule with the Athenians to give the right wing to the polemarch. After this followed the tribes, according as they were numbered, in an unbroken line; while last of all came the Plataeans, forming the left wing. And ever since that day it has been a custom with the Athenians, in the sacrifices and assemblies held each fifth year at Athens, for the Athenian herald to implore the blessing of the gods on the Plataeans conjointly with the Athenians. Now as they marshalled the host upon the field of Marathon, in order that the Athenian front might be of equal length with the Median [Persian], the ranks of the centre were diminished, and it became the weakest part of the line, while the wings were both made strong with a depth of many ranks.

112. So when the battle was set in array, and the victims showed themselves favourable, instantly the Athenians, so soon as they were let go, charged the barbarians at a run. Now the distance between the two armies was little short of a mile. The Persians, therefore, when they saw the Greeks coming on at speed, made ready to receive them, although it seemed to them that the Athenians were bereft of their senses, and bent upon their own destruction; for they saw a mere handful of men coming on at a run without either horsemen or archers. Such was the opinion of the barbarians; but the Athenians in close array fell upon them, and fought in a manner worthy of being recorded. They were the first of the Greeks, so far as I know, who introduced the custom of charging the enemy at a run, and they were likewise the first who dared to look upon the Median garb, and to face men clad in that fashion. Until this time the very name of the Medes had been a terror to the Greeks to hear.

113. The two armies fought together on the plain of Marathon for a length of time; and in the mid battle, where the Persians themselves and the Sacae had their place, the barbarians were victorious, and broke and pursued the Greeks into the inner country;

but on the two wings the Athenians and the Plataeans defeated the enemy. Having so done, they suffered the routed barbarians to fly at their ease, and joining the two wings in one, fell upon those who had broken their own centre, and fought and conquered them. These likewise fled, and now the Athenians hung upon the runaways and cut them down, chasing them all the way to the shore, on reaching which they laid hold of the ships and called aloud for fire.

114. It was in the struggle here that Callimachus the polemarch, after greatly distinguishing himself, lost his life; Stesilaus too, the son of Thrasilaus, one of the generals, was slain; and Cynaegirus, the son of Euphorion, having seized on a vessel of the enemy's by the ornament at the stern, had his hand cut off by the blow of an axe, and so perished; as likewise did many other Athenians of note and name.

115. Nevertheless the Athenians secured in this way seven of the vessels, while with the remainder the barbarians pushed off, and taking aboard their Eretrian prisoners from the island where they had left them, doubled Cape Sunium, hoping to reach Athens before the return of the Athenians. The Alcmaeonidae were accused by their countrymen of suggesting this course to them; they had, it was said, an understanding with the Persians, and made a signal to them, by raising a shield, after they were embarked in their ships.

116. The Persians accordingly sailed round Sunium. But the Athenians with all possible speed marched away to the defence of their city, and succeeded in reaching Athens before the appearance of the barbarians; and as their camp at Marathon had been pitched in a precinct of Heracles, so now they encamped in another precinct of the same god at Cynosarges. The barbarian fleet arrived, and lay to off Phalerum, which was at that time haven of Athens; but after resting awhile upon their oars, they departed and sailed away to Asia.

117. There fell in this battle of Marathon, on the side of the barbarians, about 6,400 men; on that of the Athenians, 192. Such was the number of the slain on the one side and the other. A strange prodigy likewise happened at this fight. Epizelus, the son of

Cuphagoras, an Athenian, was in the thick of the fray, and behaving himself as a brave man should, when suddenly he was stricken with blindness, without blow of sword or dart, and this blindness continued thenceforth during the whole of his after life. The following is the account which he himself, as I have heard, gave of the matter: he said that a gigantic warrior, with a huge beard, which shaded all his shield, stood over against him, but the ghostly semblance passed him by, and slew the man at his side. Such, as I understand, was the tale which Epizelus told.

118. Datis meanwhile was on his way back to Asia, and had reached Myconus, when he saw in his sleep a vision. What it was is not known; but no sooner was day come than he caused strict search to be made throughout the whole fleet, and finding on board a Phoenician vessel an image of Apollo overlaid with gold, he inquired from whence it had been taken, and learning to what temple it belonged, he took it with him in his own ship to Delos, and placed it in the temple there, enjoining the Delians, who had now come back to their island, to restore the image to the Theban Delium, which lies on the coast over against Chalcis. Having left these injunctions, he sailed away; but the Delians failed to restore the statue, and it was not till twenty years afterwards that the Thebans, warned by an oracle, themselves brought it back to Delium.

119. As for the Eretrians, whom Datis and Artaphernes had carried away captive, when the fleet reached Asia, they were taken up to Susa. Now king Darius, before they were made his prisoners, nourished a fierce anger against these men for having injured him without provocation; but now that he saw them brought into his presence, and become his subjects, he did them no other harm, but only settled them at one of his own stations in Cissia, a place called Ardericca, twenty-six miles distant from Susa, and five miles from the well which yields produce of three different kinds. For from this well they get bitumen, salt, and oil, procuring it in the way that I will now describe: they draw with a swipe, and instead of a bucket make use of the half of a wine-skin; with this the man dips, and after drawing, pours the liquid into a reservoir, wherefrom it passes into another, and there takes three different shapes. The salt

and the bitumen forthwith collect and harden, while the oil is drawn off into casks. It is called by the Persians rhadinace,* is black, and has an unpleasant smell. Here then king Darius established the Eretrians, and here they continued to my time, and still spoke their old language. So thus it fared with the Eretrians.

120. After the full of the moon 2,000 Lacedaemonians came to Athens. So eager had they been to arrive in time, that they took but three days to reach Attica from Sparta. They came, however, too late for the battle; yet, as they had a longing to behold the Medes, they continued their march to Marathon and there viewed the slain. Then, after giving the Athenians all praise for their achievement, they departed and returned home.

121. But it fills me with wonderment, and I cannot believe the report, that the Alcmaeonidae had an understanding with the Persians, and held them up a shield as a signal, wishing Athens to be brought under the yoke of the barbarians and of Hippias—the Alcmaeonidae, who have shown themselves at least as bitter haters of tyrants as was Callias, the son of Phaehippus, and father of Hipponicus. This Callias was the only person at Athens who, when the Pisistratidae were driven out, and their goods were exposed for sale by the vote of the people, had the courage to make purchases, and likewise in many other ways to display the strongest hostility. . . .

123. Now the Alcmaeonidae fell not a whit short of this person in their hatred of tyrants, so that I am astonished at the charge made against them, and cannot bring myself to believe that they held up a shield; for they were men who had remained in exile during the whole time that the tyranny lasted, and they even contrived the trick by which the Pisistratidae were deprived of their throne. Indeed I look upon them as the persons who in good truth gave Athens her freedom far more than Harmodius and Aristogeiton. For these last merely exasperated the other Pisistratidae by slaying Hipparchus, and were far from doing anything towards putting down the tyranny; whereas the Alcmaeonidae were manifestly the actual deliverers of Athens, if at least it be true that the

---

* Petroleum—tr.

priestess was prevailed upon by them to bid the Lacedaemonians set Athens free, as I have already related.

124. But perhaps they were offended with the people of Athens, and therefore betrayed their country. Nay, but on the contrary there were none of the Athenians who were held in such general esteem, or who were so laden with honours. So that it is not even reasonable to suppose that a shield was held up by them on this account. A shield was shown, no doubt; that cannot be gainsaid; but who it was that showed it I cannot any further determine.

125. Now the Alcmaeonidae were, even in days of yore, a family of note at Athens, but from the time of Alcmaeon, and again of Megacles, they rose to special eminence. The former of these two personages, Alcmaeon, the son of Megacles, when Croesus the Lydian sent men from Sardis to consult the Delphic oracle, gave aid gladly to his messengers, and assisted them to accomplish their task. Croesus, informed of Alcmaeon's kindnesses by the Lydians who from time to time conveyed his messages to the god, sent for him to Sardis, and, when he arrived, made him a present of as much gold as he should be able to carry at one time about his person. Finding that this was the gift assigned him, Alcmaeon took his measures, and prepared himself to receive it in the following way. He clothed himself in a loose tunic, which he made to bag greatly at the waist, and placing upon his feet the widest buskins that he could anywhere find, followed his guides into the treasure-house. Here he fell to upon a heap of gold-dust, and in the first place packed as much as he could inside his buskins, between them and his legs; after which he filled the breast of his tunic quite full of gold, and then sprinkling some among his hair, and taking some likewise in his mouth, he came forth from the treasure-house, scarcely able to drag his legs along, like anything rather than a man, with his mouth crammed full, and his bulk increased every way. On seeing him, Croesus burst into a laugh, and not only let him have all that he had taken, but gave him presents besides of fully equal worth. Thus this house became one of great wealth, and Alcmaeon was able to keep horses for the chariot-race, and won the prize at Olympia.

Herodotus compares Greek and Egyptian chronology and checks the account of the earlier logographer, Hecataeus. Book II: 142–146

142. THUS FAR I have spoken on the authority of the Egyptians and their priests. They declare that from their first king to this last-mentioned monarch, the priest of Vulcan, was a period of three hundred and forty-one generations; such, at least, they say, was the number both of their kings and of their high priests, during this interval. Now three hundred generations of men make ten thousand years, three generations filling up the century; and the remaining forty-one generations make thirteen hundred and forty years. Thus the whole number of years is eleven thousand, three hundred and forty; in which entire space, they said, no god had even appeared in a human form; nothing of this kind had happened either under the former or under the later Egyptian kings. The sun, however, had within this period of time, on four several occasions, moved from his wonted course, twice rising where he now sets, and twice setting where he now rises. Egypt was in no degree affected by these changes; the productions of the land, and of the river, remained the same; nor was there anything unusual either in the diseases or the deaths.

143. When Hecataeus the historian was at Thebes, and, discoursing of his genealogy, traced his descent to a god in the person of his sixteenth ancestor, the priests of Jupiter did to him exactly as they afterwards did to me, though I made no boast of my family. They led me into the inner sanctuary, which is a spacious chamber, and showed me a multitude of colossal statues, in wood, which they counted up, and found to amount to the exact number they had said; the custom being for every high priest during his lifetime to set up his statue in the temple. As they showed me the figures and reckoned them up, they assured me that each was the son of the one preceding him; and this they repeated throughout the whole line, beginning with the representation of the priest last deceased, and continuing till they had completed the series. When Hecataeus, in giving his genealogy, mentioned a god as his sixteenth

ancestor, the priests opposed their genealogy to his, going through this list, and refusing to allow that any man was ever born of a god. Their colossal figures were each, they said, a Pirômis, born of a Pirômis, and the number of them was three hundred and forty-five; through the whole series Pirômis followed Pirômis, and the line did not run up either to a god or a hero. The word *Piromis* may be rendered "gentleman."

144. Of such a nature were, they said, the beings represented by these images—they were very far indeed from being gods. However, in the times before them it was otherwise; then Egypt had gods for its rulers, who dwelt upon the earth with men, one being always supreme above the rest. The last of these was Horus, the son of Osiris, called by the Greeks Apollo. He deposed Typhon, and ruled over Egypt as its last god-king. Osiris is named Dionysus (Bacchus) by the Greeks.

145. The Greeks regard Hercules, Bacchus, and Pan as the youngest of the gods. With the Egyptians, on the other hand, Pan is exceedingly ancient, and belongs to those whom they call "the eight gods," who existed before the rest. Hercules is one of the gods of the second order, who are known as "the twelve"; and Bacchus belongs to the gods of the third order, whom the twelve produced. I have already mentioned how many years intervened according to the Egyptians between the birth of Hercules and the reign of Amasis. From Pan to this period they count a still longer time; and even from Bacchus, who is the youngest of the three, they reckon fifteen thousand years to the reign of that king. In these matters they say they cannot be mistaken, as they have always kept count of the years, and noted them in their registers. But from the present day to the time of Bacchus, the reputed son of Semelé, daughter of Cadmus, is a period of not more than sixteen hundred years; to that of Hercules, son of Alemêna, is about nine hundred; while to the time of Pan, son of Penelopé (Pan, according to the Greeks, was her child by Mercury), is a shorter space than to the Trojan war, eight hundred years or thereabouts.

146. It is open to all to receive whichever he may prefer of these two traditions; my own opinion about them has been already declared. If indeed these gods had been publicly known, and had

grown old in Greece, as was the case with Hercules, son of Amphitryon, Bacchus, son of Semelé, and Pan, son of Penelopé, it might have been said that the last-mentioned personages were men who bore the names of certain previously existing deities. But Bacchus, according to the Greek tradition, was no sooner born than he was sewn up in Jupiter's thigh, and carried off to Nysa, above Egypt, in Ethiopia; and as to Pan, they do not even profess to know what happened to him after his birth. To me, therefore, it is quite manifest that the names of these gods became known to the Greeks after those of their other deities, and that they count their birth from the time when they first acquired a knowledge of them. Thus far my narrative rests on the accounts given by the Egyptians.

Battle of Thermopylae
Book VII: 201–239

201. KING XERXES pitched his camp in the region of Malis called Trachinia, while on their side the Greeks occupied the straits. These straits the Greeks in general call Thermopylae (the Hot Gates); but the natives and those who dwell in the neighbourhood, call them Pylae (the Gates). Here then the two armies took their stand; the one master of all the region lying north of Trachis, the other of the country extending southward of that place to the verge of the continent.

202. The Greeks who at this spot awaited the coming of Xerxes were the following: From Sparta, 300 men-at-arms: from Arcadia, 1,000 Tegeans and Mantineans, 500 of each people; 120 Orchomenians, from the Arcadian Orchomenus; and 1,000 from other cities: from Corinth, 400 men: from Phlius, 200: and from Mycenae eighty. Such was the number from the Peloponnese. There were also present, from Boeotia, 700 Thespians and 400 Thebans.

203. Besides these troops, the Locrians of Opus and the Phocians had obeyed the call of their countrymen, and sent, the former all the force they had, the latter 1,000 men. For envoys had gone from the Greeks at Thermopylae among the Locrians and Phocians, to call on them for assistance, and to say, "They were themselves but the vanguard of the host, sent to precede the main body,

which might every day be expected to follow them. The sea was in good keeping, watched by the Athenians, and the Aeginetans, and the rest of the fleet. There was no cause why they should fear; for after all the invader was not a god but a man; and there never had been, and never would be, a man who was not liable to misfortunes from the very day of his birth, and those greater in proportion to his own greatness. The assailant therefore, being only a mortal, must needs fall from his glory." Thus urged, the Locrians and the Phocians had come with their troops to Trachis.

204. The various nations had each captains of their own under whom they served; but the one to whom all especially looked up, and who had the command of the entire force, was the Lacedaemonian, Leonidas. Now Leonidas was the son of Anaxandridas, who was the son of Leo, who was the son of Eurycratidas, who was the son of Anaxander, who was the son of Eurycrates, who was the son of Polydorus, who was the son of Alcamenes, who was the son of Telecles, who was the son of Archelaus, who was the son of Agesilaus, who was the son of Doryssus, who was the son of Labotas, who was the son of Echestratus, who was the son of Agis, who was the son of Eurysthenes, who was the son of Aristodemus, who was the son of Aristomachus, who was the son of Cleodaeus, who was the son of Hyllus, who was the son of Heracles.

Leonidas had come to be king of Sparta quite unexpectedly.

205. Having two elder brothers, Cleomenes and Dorieus, he had no thought of ever mounting the throne. However when Cleomenes died without male offspring, as Dorieus was likewise deceased, having perished in Sicily, the crown fell to Leonidas, who was older than Cleombrotus, the youngest of the sons of Anaxandridas, and, moreover, was married to the daughter of Cleomenes. He had now come to Thermophylae, accompanied by the 300 men which the law assigned him, whom he had himself chosen from among the citizens, and who were all of then fathers with sons living. On his way he had taken the troops from Thebes, whose number I have already mentioned, and who were under the command of Leontiades the son of Eurymachus. The reason why he made a point of taking troops from Thebes and Thebes only was, that the Thebans were strongly suspected of being well inclined to

the Medes. Leonidas therefore called on them to come with him to the war, wishing to see whether they would comply with his demand, or openly refuse, and disclaim the Greek alliance. They, however, though their wishes leant the other way, nevertheless sent the men.

206. The force with Leonidas was sent forward by the Spartans in advance of their main body, that the sight of them might encourage the allies to fight, and hinder them from going over to the Medes, as it was likely they might have done had they seen Sparta backward. They intended presently, when they had celebrated the Carneian festival, which was what now kept them at home, to leave a garrison in Sparta, and hasten in full force to join the army. The rest of the allies also intended to act similarly; for it happened that the Olympic festival fell exactly at this same period. None of them looked to see the contest at Thermopylae decided so speedily; wherefore they were content to send forward a mere advanced guard. Such accordingly were the intentions of the allies.

207. The Greek forces at Thermopylae, when the Persian army drew near to the entrance of the pass, were seized with fear, and a council was held to consider about a retreat. It was the wish of the Peloponnesians generally that the army should fall back upon the Peloponnese, and there guard the Isthmus. But Leonidas, who saw with what indignation the Phocians and Locrians heard of this plan, gave his voice for remaining where they were, while they sent envoys to the several cities to ask for help, since they were too few to make a stand against an army like that of the Medes.

208. While this debate was going on, Xerxes sent a mounted spy to observe the Greeks, and note how many they were, and what they were doing. He had heard, before he came out of Thessaly, that a few men were assembled at this place, and that at their head were certain Lacedaemonians, under Leonidas, a descendant of Heracles. The horseman rode up to the camp, and looked about him, but did not see the whole army; for such as were on the further side of the wall (which had been rebuilt and was now carefully guarded) it was not possible for him to behold; but he observed those on the outside, who were encamped in front of the rampart. It chanced that at this time the Lacedaemonians held the

outer guard, and were seen by the spy, some of them engaged in gymnastic exercises, others combing their long hair. At this the spy greatly marvelled, but he counted their number, and when he had taken accurate note of everything, he rode back quietly; for no one pursued after him, or paid any heed to his visit. So he returned, and told Xerxes all that he had seen.

209. Upon this, Xerxes, who had no means of surmising the truth—namely, that the Spartans were preparing to do or die manfully—but thought it laughable that they should be engaged in such employments, sent and called to his presence Demaratus the son of Ariston, who still remained with the army. When he appeared, Xerxes told him all that he had heard, and questioned him concerning the news, since he was anxious to understand the meaning of such behaviour on the part of the Spartans. Then Demaratus said, "I spoke to you, O King, concerning these men long since, when we had but just begun our march upon Greece; you, however, only laughed at my words, when I told you of all this, which I saw would come to pass. Earnestly do I struggle at all times to speak truth to you, sire; and now listen to it once more. These men have come to dispute the pass with us, and it is for this that they are now making ready. It is their custom, when they are about to hazard their lives, to adorn their heads with care. Be assured, however, that if you can subdue the men who are here and the Lacedaemonians who remain in Sparta, there is no other nation in all the world which will venture to lift a hand in their defence. You have now to deal with the first kingdom and town in Greece, and with the bravest men."

Then Xerxes, to whom what Demaratus said seemed altogether to surpass belief asked further, "How it was possible for so small an army to contend with his?"

"O King," Demaratus answered, "let me be treated as a liar, if matters fall not out as I say."

210. But Xerxes was not persuaded any the more. Four whole days he suffered to go by,* expecting that the Greeks would run away. When, however, he found on the fifth that they were not

---

* We may suppose that the Persian king looked at first to obtaining the cooperation of his fleet, and only began the attack when that hope failed him—tr.

gone, thinking that their firm stand was mere impudence and recklessness, he grew wroth, and sent against them the Medes and Cissians, with orders to take them alive and bring them into his presence. Then the Medes rushed forward and charged the Greeks, but fell in vast numbers: others however took the places of the slain, and would not be beaten off, though they suffered terrible losses. In this way it became clear to all, and especially to the king, that though he had plenty of combatants, he had but very few warriors. The struggle, however, continued during the whole day.

211. Then the Medes, having met so rough a reception, withdrew from the fight; and their place was taken by the band of Persians under Hydarnes, whom the king called his Immortals: they, it was thought, would soon finish the business. But when they joined battle with the Greeks, it was with no better success than the Median detachment—things went much as before—the two armies fighting in a narrow space, and the barbarians using shorter spears than the Greeks, and having no advantage from their numbers. The Lacedaemonians fought in a way worthy of note, and showed themselves far more skilful in fight than their adversaries, often turning their backs, and making as though they were all flying away, on which the barbarians would rush after them with much noise and shouting, when the Spartans at their approach would wheel round and face their pursuers, in this way destroying vast numbers of the enemy. Some Spartans likewise fell in these encounters, but only a very few. At last the Persians, finding that all their efforts to gain the pass availed nothing, and that whether they attacked by divisions or in any other way, it was to no purpose, withdrew to their own quarters.

212. During these assaults, it is said that Xerxes, who was watching the battle, thrice leaped from the throne on which he sat, in terror for his army.

Next day the combat was renewed, but with no better success on the part of the barbarians. The Greeks were so few that the barbarians hoped to find them disabled, by reason of their wounds, from offering any further resistance; and so they once more attacked them. But the Greeks were drawn up in detachments according to their cities, and bore the brunt of the battle in turns, all except the Phocians, who had been stationed on the mountain to guard the pathway. So when the Persians found no difference between that day and the preceding, they again retired to their quarters.

213. Now, as the king was at a loss, and knew not how he should deal with the emergency, Ephialtes, the son of Eurydemus, a man of Malis, came to him and was admitted to a conference. Stirred by the hope of receiving a rich reward at the king's hands, he had come to tell him of the pathway which led across the mountain to Thermopylae; by which disclosure he brought destruction on the band of Greeks who had there withstood the barbarians. This Ephialtes afterwards, from fear of the Lacedaemonians, fled into Thessaly; and during his exile, in an assembly of the Amphictyons held at Pylae, a price was set upon his head by the Pylagorae. When some time had gone by, he returned from exile, and went to Anticyra, where he was slain by Athenades, a native of Trachis. Athenades did not slay him for his treachery, but for another reason, which I shall mention in a later part of my history: yet still the Lacedaemonians honoured him none the less. Thus then did Ephialtes perish a long time afterwards.

214. Besides this there is another story told, which I do not at all believe, that Onetas the son of Phanagoras, a native of Carystus, and Corydallus, a man of Anticyra, were the persons who spoke on this matter to the king, and took the Persians across the mountain. One may guess which story is true, from the fact that the deputies of the Greeks, the Pylagorae, who must have had the best means of ascertaining the truth, did not offer the reward for the heads of Onetas and Corydallus, but for that of Ephialtes of Trachis; and again from the flight of Ephialtes, which we know to have been on this account. Onetas, I allow, although he was not a Malian, might have been acquainted with the path, if he had lived much in that part of the country; but as Ephialtes was the person who actually led the Persians round the mountain by the pathway, I leave his name on record as that of the man who did the deed.

215. Great was the joy of Xerxes on this occasion; and as he approved highly of the enterprise which Ephialtes undertook to accomplish, he forthwith sent upon the errand Hydarnes, and the

Persians under him. The troops left the camp about the time of the lighting of the lamps. The pathway along which they went was first discovered by the Malians of these parts, who soon afterwards led the Thessalians by it to attack the Phocians, at the time when the Phocians fortified the pass with a wall, and so put themselves under covert from danger. And ever since, the path has always been put to an ill use by the Malians.

216. The course which it takes is the following: Beginning at the Asopus, where that stream flows through the cleft in the hills, it runs along the ridge of the mountain (which is called, like the pathway over it, Anopaea), and ends at the city of Alpenus—the first Locrian town as you come from Malis—by the stone called Black-buttock and the seats of the Cercopians. Here it is as narrow as at any other point.

217. The Persians took this path, and crossing the Asopus, continued their march through the whole of the night, having the mountains of Oeta on their right hand, and on their left those of Trachis. At dawn of day they found themselves close to the summit. Now the hill was guarded, as I have already said, by 1,000 Phocian men-at-arms, who were placed there to defend the pathway, and at the same time to secure their own country. They had been given the guard of the mountain path, while the other Greeks defended the pass below, because they had volunteered for the service, and had pledged themselves to Leonidas to maintain the post.

218. The ascent of the Persians became known to the Phocians in the following manner: During all the time that they were making their way up, the Greeks remained unconscious of it, inasmuch as the whole mountain was covered with groves of oak; but it happened that the air was very still, and the leaves which the Persians stirred with their feet made, as it was likely they would, a loud rustling, whereupon the Phocians jumped up and flew to seize their arms. In a moment the barbarians came in sight, and perceiving men arming themselves, were greatly amazed; for they had fallen in with an enemy when they expected no opposition. Hydarnes, alarmed at the sight, and fearing lest the Phocians might be Lacedaemonians, inquired of Ephialtes to what nation these troops

belonged. Ephialtes told him the exact truth, whereupon he arrayed his Persians for battle. The Phocians, galled by the showers of arrows to which they were exposed, and imagining themselves the special object of the Persian attack, fled hastily to the crest of the mountain, and there made ready to meet death; but while their mistake continued, the Persians, with Ephialtes and Hydarnes, not thinking it worth their while to delay on account of Phocians, passed on and descended the mountain with all possible speed.

219. The Greeks at Thermopylae received the first warning of the destruction which the dawn would bring on them from the seer Megistias, who read their fate in the victims as he was sacrificing. After this deserters came in, and brought the news that the Persians were marching round by the hills: it was still night when these men arrived. Last of all, the scouts came running down from the heights, and brought in the same accounts, when the day was just beginning to break. Then the Greeks held a council to consider what they should do, and here opinions were divided: some were strong against quitting their post, while others contended to the contrary. So when the council had broken up, part of the troops departed and went their ways homeward to their several states; part however resolved to remain, and to stand by Leonidas to the last.

220. It is said that Leonidas himself sent away the troops who departed, because he tendered their safety, but thought it unseemly that either he or his Spartans should quit the post which they had been especially sent to guard. For my own part, I incline to think that Leonidas gave the order, because he perceived the allies to be out of heart and unwilling to encounter the danger to which his own mind was made up.* He therefore commanded them to retreat, but said that he himself could not draw back with honour; knowing that, if he stayed, glory awaited him, and that Sparta in

---

* Herodotus, by accident or design, has practically ignored the Greek plan of campaign in the relation between operations on land and sea. Leonidas was perhaps surprised that the Persians came around by the short route of the Anopaea but his main task, so far as he knew, was to hold the land route until the Greek fleet could force a decisive action. This could be done if the allies met the Persians near Mount Callidromus, the longer route to the rear of Thermopylae. Leonidas believed that he could hold the pass with his remaining force—tr.

that case would not lose her prosperity. For when the Spartans, at the very beginning of the war, sent to consult the oracle concerning it, the answer which they received from the priestess was that either Sparta must be overthrown by the barbarians, or one of her kings must perish. The prophecy was delivered in hexameter verse, and ran thus:

> Oh! ye men who dwell in the streets of broad Lacedaemon,
> Either your glorious town shall be sacked by the children of Perseus,
> Or, in exchange, must all through the whole Laconian country
> Mourn for the loss of a king, descendant of great Heracles.
> He cannot be withstood by the courage of bulls or of lions,
> Strive as they may; he is mighty as Zeus; there is nought that shall stay him,
> Till he have got for his prey your king, or your glorious city.

The remembrance of this answer, I think, and the wish to secure the whole glory for the Spartans, caused Leonidas to send the allies away. This is more likely than that they quarrelled with him, and took their departure in such unruly fashion.

221. To me it seems no small argument in favour of this view, that the seer also who accompanied the army, Megistias, the Acarnanian, said to have been of the blood of Melampus, and the same who was led by the appearance of the victims to warn the Greeks of the danger which threatened them, received orders to retire (as it is certain he did) from Leonidas, that he might escape the coming destruction. Megistias, however, though bidden to depart, refused, and stayed with the army; but he had an only son present with the expedition, whom he now sent away.

222. So the allies, when Leonidas ordered them to retire, obeyed him and forthwith departed. Only the Thespians and the Thebans remained with the Spartans; and of these the Thebans were kept back by Leonidas as hostages, very much against their will. The Thespians, on the contrary, stayed entirely of their own accord, refusing to retreat, and declaring that they would not forsake Leonidas and his followers. So they abode with the Spartans, and

died with them. Their leader was Demophilus, the son of Diadromes.

223. At sunrise Xerxes made libations, after which he waited until the time when the market-place is wont to fill, and then began his advance. Ephialtes had instructed him thus, as the descent of the mountain is much quicker, and the distance much shorter, than the way round the hills, and the ascent. So the barbarians under Xerxes began to draw nigh; and the Greeks under Leonidas, as they now went forth determined to die, advanced much further than on previous days, until they reached the more open portion of the pass. Hitherto they had held their station within the wall, and from this had gone forth to fight at the point where the pass was the narrowest. Now they joined battle beyond the defile, and carried slaughter among the barbarians, who fell in heaps. Behind them the captains of the squadrons, armed with whips, urged their men forward with continual blows. Many were thrust into the sea, and there perished; a still greater number were trampled to death by their own soldiers; no one heeded the dying. For the Greeks, reckless of their own safety and desperate, since they knew that, as the mountain had been crossed, their destruction was nigh at hand, exerted themselves with the most furious valour against the barbarians.

224. By this time the spears of the greater number were all shivered, and with their swords they hewed down the ranks of the Persians; and here, as they strove, Leonidas fell fighting bravely, together with many other famous Spartans, whose names I have taken care to learn on account of their great worthiness, as indeed I have those of all the 300.* There fell too at the same time very many famous Persians: among them, two sons of Darius, Abrocomes and Hyperanthes, his children by Phratagune, the daughter of Artanes. Artanes was brother of King Darius, being a son of Hystaspes, the son of Arsames; and when he gave his daughter to the king, he made him heir likewise of all his substance; for she was his only child.

225. Thus two brothers of Xerxes here fought and fell. And now there arose a fierce struggle between the Persians and the La-

---

* These names were all inscribed on a pillar at Sparta, which remained standing in the time of Pausanias—tr.

cedaemonians over the body of Leonidas, in which the Greeks four times drove back the enemy, and at last by their great bravery succeeded in bearing off the body. This combat was scarcely ended when the Persians with Ephialtes approached; and the Greeks, informed that they drew nigh, made a change in the manner of their fighting. Drawing back into the narrowest part of the pass, and retreating even behind the cross wall, they posted themselves upon a hillock, where they stood all drawn up together in one close body, except only the Thebans. The hillock whereof I speak is at the entrance of the straits, where the stone lion stands which was set up in honour of Leonidas. Here they defended themselves to the last, such as still had swords using them, and the others resisting with their hands and teeth; till the barbarians, who in part had pulled down the wall and attacked them in front, in part had gone round and now encircled them upon every side, overwhelmed and buried the remnant left beneath showers of missile weapons.

226. Thus nobly did the whole body of Lacedaemonians and Thespians behave, but nevertheless one man is said to have distinguished himself above all the rest, to wit, Dieneces the Spartan. A speech which he made before the Greeks engaged the Medes, remains on record. One of the Trachinians told him, "Such was the number of the barbarians, that when they shot forth their arrows the sun would be darkened by their multitude." Dieneces, not at all frightened at these words, but making light of the Median numbers, answered, "Our Trachinian friend brings us excellent tidings. If the Medes darken the sun, we shall have our fight in the shade." Other sayings too of a like nature are said to have been left on record by this same person.

227. Next to him two brothers, Lacedaemonians, are reputed to have made themselves conspicuous: they were named Alpheus and Maro, and were the sons of Orsiphantus. There was also a Thespian who gained greater glory than any of his countrymen: he was a man called Dithyrambus, the son of Harmatidas.

228. The slain were buried where they fell; and in their honour, nor less in honour of those who died before Leonidas sent the allies away, an inscription was set up, which said:

> Here did four thousand men from Pelops' land
> Against three hundred myriads bravely stand.

This was in honour of all. Another was for the Spartans alone:

> Go, stranger, and to Lacedaemon tell
> That here, obeying her behests, we fell.

This was for the Lacedaemonians. The seer had the following:

> The great Megistias' tomb you here may view,
>   Whom slew the Medes, fresh from Spercheius' fords.
> Well the wise seer the coming death foreknew,
>   Yet scorned he to forsake his Spartan lords.

These inscriptions, and the pillars likewise, were all set up by the Amphictyons, except that in honour of Megistias, which was inscribed to him (on account of their sworn friendship) by Simonides, the son of Leoprepes.

229. Two of the 300, it is said, Aristodemus and Eurytus, having been attacked by a disease of the eyes, had received orders from Leonidas to quit the camp, and both lay at Alpeni in the worst stage of the malady. These two men might, had they been so minded, have agreed together to return alive to Sparta; or if they did not like to return, they might have gone both to the field and fallen with their countrymen. But at this time, when either way was open to them, unhappily they could not agree, but took contrary courses. Eurytus no sooner heard that the Persians had come round the mountain than straightway he called for his armour, and having buckled it on, bade his Helot* lead him to the place where his friends were fighting. The Helot did so, and then turned and fled; but Eurytus plunged into the thick of the battle, and so perished. Aristodemus, on the other hand, was faint of heart, and remained at Alpeni. It is my belief that if Aristodemus only had been sick and returned, or if both had come back together, the Spartans would have been content and felt no anger; but when there were two men with the very same excuse, and one of them

---

* By the expression his Helot, we are to understand the special servant whose business it was to attend constantly upon the Spartan warrior—tr.

was chary of his life, while the other freely gave it, they could not but be very wroth with the former.

230. This is the account which some give of the escape of Aristodemus. Others say, that he, with another, had been sent on a message from the army, and, having it in his power to return in time for the battle, purposely loitered on the road, and so survived his comrades; while his fellow-messenger came back in time, and fell in the battle.

231. When Aristodemus returned to Lacedaemon, reproach and disgrace awaited him; disgrace, inasmuch as no Spartan would give him a light to kindle his fire, or so much as address a word to him; and reproach, since all spoke of him as the craven. However he wiped away all his shame afterwards at the battle of Plataea.

232. Another of the 300 is likewise said to have survived the battle, a man named Pantites, whom Leonidas had sent on an embassy into Thessaly. He, they say, on his return to Sparta, found himself in such disgrace that he hanged himself.

233. The Thebans under the command of Leontiades remained with the Greeks, and fought against the barbarians, only so long as necessity compelled them. No sooner did they see victory inclining to the Persians, and the Greeks under Leonidas hurrying with all speed towards the hillock, than they moved away from their companions, and with hands upraised advanced towards the barbarians, exclaiming, as was indeed most true, "They for their part wished well to the Medes, and had been among the first to give earth and water to the king; force alone had brought them to Thermopylae, and so they must not be blamed for the slaughter which had befallen the king's army." These words, the truth of which was attested by the Thessalians, sufficed to obtain the Thebans the grant of their lives. However, their good fortune was not without some drawback; for several of them were slain by the barbarians on their first approach; and the rest, who were the greater number, had the royal mark branded upon their bodies by the command of Xerxes, Leontiades, their captain, being the first to suffer. (This man's son, Eurymachus, was afterwards slain by the Plataeans, when he came with a band of 400 Thebans, and seized their city.)

234. Thus fought the Greeks at Thermopylae. And Xerxes, after the fight was over, called for Demaratus to question him; and began as follows, "Demaratus, you are a worthy man; your true-speaking proves it. All has happened as you forewarned me. Now, then, tell me, how many Lacedaemonians are there left, and of those left how many are such brave warriors as these? Or are they all alike?"

"O King," replied the other, "the whole number of the Lacedaemonians is very great, and many are the cities which they inhabit. But I will tell you what you really wish to learn. There is a town of Lacedaemon called Sparta, which contains within it about 8,000 full-grown men. They are, one and all, equal to those who have fought here. The other Lacedaemonians are brave men, but not such warriors as these."

"Tell me now, Demaratus," rejoined Xerxes, "how we may with least trouble subdue these men. You must know all the paths of their counsels, as you were once their king."

235. Then Demaratus answered, "O king, since you ask my advice so earnestly, it is fitting that I should inform you what I consider to be the best course. Detach 300 vessels from the body of your fleet, and send them to attack the shores of Laconia. There is an island called Cythera in those parts, not far from the coast, concerning which Chilon, one of our wisest men, made the remark, that Sparta would gain if it were sunk to the bottom of the sea—so constantly did he expect that it would give occasion to some project like that which I now recommend to you. I mean not to say that he had a foreknowledge of your attack upon Greece; but in truth he feared all armaments. Send your ships then to this island, and thence frighten the Spartans. If once they have a war of their own close to their doors, fear not their giving any help to the rest of the Greeks while your land-force is engaged in conquering them. In this way may all Greece be subdued; and then Sparta, left to herself, will be powerless. But if you will not take this advice, I will tell you what you may expect. When you come to the Peloponnese, you will find a narrow neck of land, where all the Peloponnesians who are leagued against you will be gathered together; and there you

will have to fight bloodier battles than any which you have yet witnessed. If, however, you follow my plan, the isthmus and the cities of Peloponnese will yield to you without a battle."

236. Achaemenes, who was present at their conversation, now spoke—he was brother to Xerxes, and having the command of the fleet, feared lest Xerxes might be prevailed upon to do as Demaratus advised. "I perceive, O king," he said, "that you are listening to the words of a man who is envious of your good-fortune, and seeks to betray your cause. This is indeed the common temper of the Grecian people—they envy good-fortune, and hate power greater than their own. If in this state of our affairs, after we have lost 400 vessels by shipwreck, 300 more be sent away to make a voyage round the Peloponnese, our enemies will become a match for us. But let us keep our whole fleet in one body, and it will be dangerous for them to venture on an attack, as they will certainly be no match for us then. Besides, while our sea and land forces advance together, the fleet and army can each help the other; but if they be parted, no aid will come either from you to the fleet, or from the fleet to you. Only order your own matters well, and trouble not to inquire concerning the enemy, where they will fight, or what they will do, or how many they are. Surely they can manage their own concerns without us, as we can ours without them. If the Lacedaemonians come out against the Persians to battle, they will scarce repair the disaster which has befallen them now."

237. Xerxes replied, "Achaemenes, your counsel pleases me well, and I will do as you say. But Demaratus advised what he thought best—only his judgment was not so good as yours. Never will I believe that he does not wish well to my cause; for that is disproved both by his former counsels, and also by the circumstances of the case. A citizen does indeed envy any fellow-citizen who is more lucky than himself, and often hates him secretly; if such a man be called on for counsel, he will not give his best thoughts, unless indeed he be a man of very exalted virtue; and such are but rarely found. But a friend of another country delights in the good fortune of his foreign bond-friend, and will give him,

when asked, the best advice in his power. Therefore I warn all men to abstain henceforth from speaking ill of Demaratus, who is my bond-friend."

238. When Xerxes had thus spoken, he proceeded to pass through the slain; and finding the body of Leonidas, whom he knew to have been the Lacedaemonian king and captain, he ordered that the head should be struck off, and the trunk fastened to a cross. This proves to me most clearly, what is plain also in many other ways,—namely, that King Xerxes was more angry with Leonidas, while he was still in life, than with any other mortal. Otherwise he would not have used his body so shamefully. For the Persians usually honour those who show themselves valiant in fight more highly than any nation that I know. They, however, to whom the orders were given, obeyed the commands of the king.

239. I return now to a point in my history, which at the time I left incomplete. The Lacedaemonians were the first of the Greeks to hear of the king's design against their country; and it was at this time that they sent to consult the Delphic oracle, and received the answer of which I spoke a while ago. The discovery was made to them in a very strange way. Demaratus, the son of Ariston, after he took refuge with the Medes, was not, in my judgment, which is supported by probability, a well-wisher to the Lacedaemonians. It may be questioned, therefore, whether he did what I am about to mention from good-will or from insolent triumph. It happened that he was at Susa at the time when Xerxes determined to lead his army into Greece; and in this way becoming acquainted with his design, he resolved to send tidings of it to Sparta. So as there was no other way of effecting his purpose, since the danger of being discovered was great, Demaratus framed the following contrivance. He took a pair of tablets, and clearing the wax away from them, wrote what the king was purposing to do upon the wood whereof the tablets were made; having done this, he spread the wax once more over the writing, and so sent it. By these means, the guards placed to watch the roads, observed nothing but a blank tablet, were sure to give no trouble to the bearer. When the tablet reached Lacedaemon, there was no one, I understand, who could find out the secret, till Gorgo, the daughter of Cleomenes and wife of

Leonidas, discovered it, and told the others. "If they would scrape the wax off the tablet," she said, "they would be sure to find the writing upon the wood." The Lacedaemonians took her advice, found the writing, and read it; after which they sent it round to the other Greeks. Such then is the account which is given of this matter.

Map of Greece according to Thucydides

THUCYDIDES · THE HISTORY*

Thucydides' evaluation of historical events of the past and his declaration of his own methods of historical inquiry. Book I: 1–23

1. THUCYDIDES, an Athenian, wrote the history of the war in which the Peloponnesians and the Athenians fought against one another. He began to write when they first took up arms, believing that it would be great and memorable above any previous war. For he argued that both states were then at the full height of their military power, and he saw the rest of the Hellenes either siding or intending to side with one or other of them. No movement ever stirred Hellas more deeply than this; it was shared by many of the Barbarians, and might be said even to affect the world at large. The character of the events which preceded, whether immediately or in more remote antiquity, owing to the lapse of time cannot be made out with certainty. But, judging from the evidence which I am able to trust after most careful enquiry, I should imagine that former ages were not great either in their wars or in anything else.

2. The country which is now called Hellas was not regularly settled in ancient times. The people were migratory, and readily left their homes whenever they were overpowered by numbers. There was no commerce, and they could not safely hold intercourse with one another either by land or sea. The several tribes cultivated their own soil just enough to obtain a maintenance from it. But they had no accumulations of wealth, and did not plant the ground; for, being without walls, they were never sure that an invader might not come and despoil them. Living in this manner and know-

* Selections from the translation by Benjamin Jowett, *Thucydides,* 2nd ed. rev. (Oxford: Clarendon Press, 1900), 2 vols.

ing that they could anywhere obtain a bare subsistence, they were always ready to migrate; so that they had neither great cities nor any considerable resources. The richest districts were most constantly changing their inhabitants; for example, the countries which are now called Thessaly and Boeotia, the greater part of the Peloponnesus with the exception of Arcadia, and all the best parts of Hellas. For the productiveness of the land increased the power of individuals; this in turn was a source of quarrels by which communities were ruined, while at the same time they were more exposed to attacks from without. Certainly Attica, of which the soil was poor and thin, enjoyed a long freedom from civil strife, and therefore retained its original inhabitants. And a striking confirmation of my argument is afforded by the fact that Attica through immigration increased in population more than any other region. For the leading men of Hellas, when driven out of their own country by war or revolution, sought an asylum at Athens; and from the very earliest times, being admitted to rights of citizenship, so greatly increased the number of inhabitants that Attica became incapable of containing them, and was at last obliged to send out colonies to Ionia.

3. The feebleness of antiquity is further proved to me by the circumstance that there appears to have been no common action in Hellas before the Trojan War. And I am inclined to think that the very name was not as yet given to the whole country, and in fact did not exist at all before the time of Hellen, the son of Deucalion; the different tribes, of which the Pelasgian was the most widely spread, gave their own names to different districts. But when Hellen and his sons became powerful in Phthiotis, their aid was invoked by other cities, and those who associated with them gradually began to be called Hellenes, though a long time elapsed before the name prevailed over the whole country. Of this Homer affords the best evidence; for he, although he lived long after the Trojan War, nowhere uses this name collectively, but confines it to the followers of Achilles from Phthiotis, who were the original Hellenes; when speaking of the entire host he calls them Danaäns, or Argives, or Achaeans. Neither is there any mention of Barbarians in his poems,

clearly because there were as yet no Hellenes opposed to them by a common distinctive name. Thus the several Hellenic tribes (and I mean by the term Hellenes those who, while forming separate communities, had a common language, and were afterwards called by a common name), owing to their weakness and isolation, were never united in any great enterprise before the Trojan War. And they only made the expedition against Troy after they had gained considerable experience of the sea.

4. Minos is the first to whom tradition ascribes the possession of a navy. He made himself master of a great part of what is now termed the Hellenic sea; he conquered the Cyclades, and was the first coloniser of most of them, expelling the Carians and appointing his own sons to govern in them. Lastly, it was he who, from a natural desire to protect his growing revenues, sought, as far as he was able, to clear the sea of pirates.

5. For in ancient times both the Hellenes, and those Barbarians, whose homes were on the coast of the mainland or in islands, when they began to find their way to one another by sea had recourse to piracy. They were commanded by powerful chiefs, who took this means of increasing their wealth and providing for their poorer followers. They would fall upon the unwalled and straggling towns, or rather villages, which they plundered, and maintained themselves chiefly by the plunder of them; for, as yet, such an occupation was held to be honourable and not disgraceful. This is proved by the practice of certain tribes on the mainland who, to the present day, glory in piratical exploits, and by the witness of the ancient poets, in whose verses the question is invariably asked of newly-arrived voyagers, whether they are pirates; which implies that neither those who are questioned disclaim, nor those who are interested in knowing censure the occupation. On land also neighbouring communities plundered each other; and there are many parts of Hellas in which the old practices still continue, as for example, among the Ozolian Locrians, Aetolians, Acarnanians, and the adjacent regions of the continent. The fashion of wearing arms among these continental tribes is a relic of their old predatory habits. For in ancient times all Hellenes carried weapons because their

homes were undefended and intercourse was unsafe; like the Barbarians they went armed in their every-day life. And the continuance of the custom in certain parts of the country indicates that it once prevailed everywhere.

6. The Athenians were the first who laid aside arms and adopted an easier and more luxurious way of life. Quite recently the old-fashioned refinement of dress still lingered among the elder men of their richer class, who wore under-garments of linen, and bound back their hair in a knot with golden clasps in the form of grasshoppers; and the same customs long survived among the elders of Ionia, having been derived from their Athenian ancestors. On the other hand, the simple dress which is now common was first worn at Sparta; and there, more than anywhere else, the life of the rich was assimilated to that of the people. The Lacedaemonians too were the first who in their athletic exercises stripped naked and rubbed themselves over with oil. But this was not the ancient custom; athletes formerly, even when they were contending at Olympia, wore girdles about their loins, a practice which lasted until quite lately, and still prevails among Barbarians, especially those of Asia, where the combatants in boxing and wrestling matches wear girdles. And many other customs which are now confined to the Barbarians might be shown to have existed formerly in Hellas.

7. In later times, when navigation had become general and wealth was beginning to accumulate, cities were built upon the seashore and fortified; peninsulas too were occupied and walled-off with a view to commerce and defence against the neighbouring tribes. But the older towns both in the islands and on the continent, in order to protect themselves against the piracy which so long prevailed, were built inland; and there they remain to this day. For the piratical tribes plundered, not only one another, but all those who, without being seamen, lived on the sea-coast.

8. The islanders were even more addicted to piracy than the inhabitants of the mainland. They were mostly Carian or Phoenician settlers. This is proved by the fact that when the Athenians purified Delos during the Peloponnesian War and the tombs of the dead were opened, more than half of them were found to be

Carians. They were known by the fashion of their arms which were buried with them, and by their mode of burial, the same which is still practised among them.

After Minos had established his navy, communication by sea became more general. For, he having expelled the marauders when he colonised the greater part of the islands, the dwellers on the seacoast began to grow richer and to live in a more settled manner; and some of them, finding their wealth increased beyond their expectations, surrounded their towns with walls. The love of gain made the weaker willing to serve the stronger, and the command of wealth enabled the more powerful to subjugate the lesser cities. This was the state of society which was beginning to prevail at the time of the Trojan War.

9. I am inclined to think that Agamemnon succeeded in collecting the expedition, not because the suitors of Helen had bound themselevs by oath to Tyndareus, but because he was the most powerful king of his time. Those Peloponnesians who possess the most accurate traditions say that* originally Pelops gained his power by the great wealth which he brought with him from Asia into a poor country, whereby he was enabled, although a stranger, to give his name to the Peloponnesus; and that still greater fortune attended his descendants after the death of Eurystheus, king of Mycenae, who was slain in Attica by the Heraclidae. For Atreus the son of Pelops was the maternal uncle of Eurystheus, who, when he went on the expedition, naturally committed to his charge the kingdom of Mycenae. Now Atreus had been banished by his father on account of the murder of Chrysippus. But Eurystheus never returned; and the Mycenaeans, dreading the Heraclidae were ready to welcome Atreus, who was considered a powerful man and had ingratiated himself with the multitude. So he succeeded to the throne of Mycenae and the other dominions of Eurystheus. Thus the house of Pelops prevailed over that of Perseus.

And it was, as I believe, because Agamemnon inherited this power and also because he was the greatest naval potentate of his time that he was able to assemble the expedition; and the other

---

* Or, 'Those who possess the most accurate traditions respecting the history of Peloponnesus say that' etc.—tr.

princes followed him, not from good-will, but from fear. Of the chiefs who came to Troy, he, if the witness of Homer be accepted, brought the greatest number of ships himself, besides supplying the Arcadians with them. In the 'Handing down of the Sceptre' he is described as 'The king of many islands, and of all Argos.' But, living on the mainland, he could not have ruled over any except the adjacent islands (which would not be 'many') unless he had possessed a considerable navy. From this expedition we must form our conjectures about the character of still earlier times.

10. When it is said that Mycenae was but a small place, or that any other city which existed in those days is inconsiderable in our own, this argument will hardly prove that the expedition was not as great as the poets relate and as is commonly imagined. Suppose the city of Sparta to be deserted, and nothing left but the temples and the ground-plan, distant ages would be very unwilling to believe that the power of the Lacedaemonians was at all equal to their fame. And yet they own two-fifths of the Peloponnesus, and the acknowledged leaders of the whole, as well as of numerous allies in the rest of Hellas. But their city is not built continuously, and has no splendid temples or other edifices; it rather resembles a group of villages like the ancient towns of Hellas, and would therefore make a poor show. Whereas, if the same fate befell the Athenians, the ruins of Athens would strike the eye, and we should infer their power to have been twice as great as it really is. We ought not then to be unduly sceptical. The greatness of cities should be estimated by their real power and not by appearances. And we may fairly suppose the Trojan expedition to have been greater than any which preceded it, although according to Homer, if we may once more appeal to his testimony, not equal to those of our own day. He was a poet, and may therefore be expected to exaggerate; yet, even upon his showing, the expedition was comparatively small. For it numbered, as he tells us, twelve hundred ships, those of the Boeotians carrying one hundred and twenty men each, those of Philoctetes fifty; and by these numbers he may be presumed to indicate the largest and the smallest ships; else why in the catalogue is nothing said about the size of any others? That the crews were all fighting men as well as rowers he clearly implies when speaking of the ships

of Philoctetes; for he tells us that all the oarsmen were likewise archers. And it is not to be supposed that many who were not sailors would accompany the expedition, except the kings and principal officers; for the troops had to cross the sea, bringing with them the materials of war, in vessels without decks, build after the old piratical fashion. Now if we take a mean between the crews, the invading forces will appear not to have been very numerous when we remember that they were drawn from the whole of Hellas.

11. The cause of the inferiority was not so much the want of men as the want of money; the invading army was limited, by the difficulty of obtaining supplies, to such a number as might be expected to live on the country in which they were to fight. After their arrival at Troy, when they had won a battle (as they clearly did, for otherwise they could not have fortified their camp), even then they appear not to have used the whole of their force, but to have been driven by want of provisions to the cultivation of the Chersonese and to pillage. And in consequence of this dispersion of their forces, the Trojans were enabled to hold out against them during the whole ten years, being always a match for those who remained on the spot. Whereas if the besieging army had brought abundant supplies, and, instead of betaking themselves to agriculture or pillage, had carried on the war persistently with all their forces, they would easily have been masters of the field and have taken the city; since, even divided as they were, and with only a part of their army available at any one time, they held their ground. Or, again, they might have regularly invested Troy, and the place would have been captured in less time and with less trouble. Poverty was the real reason why the achievements of former ages were insignificant, and why the Trojan War, the most celebrated of them all, when brought to the test of facts, falls short of its fame and of the prevailing traditions to which the poets have given authority.

12. Even in the age which followed the Trojan War, Hellas was still in process of ferment and settlement, and had no time for peaceful growth. The return of the Hellenes from Troy after their long absence led to many changes: quarrels too arose in nearly every city, and those who were expelled by them went and

founded other cities. Thus in the sixtieth year after the fall of Troy, the Boeotian people, having been expelled from Arnè by the Thessalians, settled in the country formerly called Cadmeis, but now Boeotia: a portion of the tribe already dwelt there, and some of these had joined in the Trojan expedition. In the eightieth year after the war, the Dorians led by the Heraclidae conquered the Peloponnesus. A considerable time elapsed before Hellas became finally settled; after a while, however, she recovered tranquillity and began to send out colonies. The Athenians colonised Ionia and most of the islands; the Peloponnesians the greater part of Italy and Sicily, and various places in Hellas. These colonies were all founded after the Trojan War.

13. As Hellas grew more powerful and the acquisition of wealth became more and more rapid, the revenues of her cities increased, and in most of them tyrannies were established; they had hitherto been ruled by hereditary kings, have fixed prerogatives. The Hellenes likewise began to build navies and to make the sea their element. The Corinthians are said to have first adopted something like the modern style of marine, and the oldest Hellenic triremes to have been constructed at Corinth. A Corinthian ship-builder, Ameinocles, appears to have built four ships for the Samians; he went to Samos about three hundred years before the end of the Peloponnesian War. And the earliest naval engagement on record is that between the Corinthians and Corcyraeans which occurred about forty years later. Corinth, being seated on an isthmus, was naturally from the first a centre of commerce; for the Hellenes within and without the Peloponnese in the old days, when they communicated chiefly by land, had to pass through her territory in order to reach one another. Her wealth too was a source of power, as the ancient poets testify, who speak of 'Corinth the rich.' When navigation grew more common, the Corinthians, having already acquired a fleet, were able to put down piracy; they offered a market both by sea and land, and with the increase of riches the power of their city increased yet more. Later, in the time of Cyrus [559–529 B.C.] the first Persian king, and of Cambyses his son, the Ionians had a large navy; they fought with Cyrus, and were for a time masters of the sea around their own coasts [529–522 B.C.].

Polycrates, too, who was a tyrant of Samos in the reign of Cambyses had a powerful navy and subdued several of the islands, among them Rhenea, which he dedicated to the Delian Apollo. And the Phocaeans, when they were colonising Massalia, defeated the Carthaginians on the sea.

14. These were the most powerful navies, and even these, which came into existence many generations after the Trojan War, appear to have consisted chiefly of fifty-oared vessels and galleys of war, as in the days of Troy; as yet triremes were not common. But a little before the Persian War and the death of Darius [485 B.C.], who succeeded Cambyses, the Sicilian tyrants and the Corcyraeans had them in considerable numbers. No other maritime powers of any consequence arose in Hellas before the expedition of Xerxes. The Aeginetans, Athenians, and a few more had small fleets, and these mostly consisted of fifty-oared vessels. Even the ships which the Athenians built quite recently at the instigation of Themistocles, when they were at war with the Aeginetans and in expectation of the Barbarian, even these ships with which they fought at Salamis were not completely decked.

15. So inconsiderable were the Hellenic navies in recent as well as in more ancient times. And yet those who applied their energies to the sea obtained a great accession of strength by the increase of their revenues and the extension of their dominion. For they attacked and subjugated the islands, especially when the pressure of population was felt by them. Whereas by land, no conflict of any kind which brought increase of power ever occurred; what wars they had were mere border feuds. Foreign and distant expeditions of conquest the Hellenes never undertook; for they were not as yet ranged under the command of the great states, nor did they form voluntary leagues or make expeditions on an equal footing. Their wars were only the wars of the several neighbouring tribes with one another. The conflict in which the rest of Hellas was most divided, allying itself with one side or the other, was the ancient war between the Chalcidians and Eretrians.

16. There were different impediments to the progress of the different states. The Ionians had attained great prosperity when Cyrus and the Persians, having overthrown Croesus and subdued

the countries between the river Halys and the sea, made war against them and enslaved the cities on the mainland. Some time afterwards, Darius, strong in the possession of the Phoenician fleet, conquered the islands also.

17. Nor again did the tyrants of the Hellenic cities extend their thoughts beyond their own interest, that is, the security of their persons, and the aggrandisement of themselves and their families. They were extremely cautious in the administration of their government, and nothing considerable was ever effected by them; except in wars with their neighbours, as in Sicily, where their power attained its greatest height. Thus for a long time everything conspired to prevent Hellas from uniting in any great action and to paralyse enterprise in the individual states.

18. At length the tyrants both at Athens and in the rest of Hellas (which had been under their dominion long before Athens), at least the greater number of them, and with the exception of the Sicilian the last who ever ruled, were put down by the Lacedaemonians. For although Lacedaemon, after the conquest of the country by the Dorians who now inhabit it, remained long unsettled, and indeed longer than any country which we know, nevertheless she obtained good laws at an earlier period than any other, and has never been subject to tyrants; she has preserved the same form of government for rather more than four hundred years, reckoning to the end of the Peloponnesian War. It was the excellence of her constitution which gave her power, and thus enabled her to regulate the affairs of other states. Not long after the overthrow of the tyrants by the Lacedaemonians, the battle of Marathon was fought between the Athenians and the Persians; ten years later, the Barbarian returned with the vast armament which was to enslave Hellas. In the greatness of the impending danger, the Lacedaemonians, who were the most powerful state in Hellas, assumed the lead of the confederates, while the Athenians, as the Persian host advanced, resolved to forsake their city, broke up their homes, and, taking to their ships, became seamen. The Barbarian was repelled by a common effort; but soon the Hellenes, as well those who had revolted from the King as those who formed the

original confederacy, took different sides and became the allies either of the Athenians or of the Lacedaemonians; for these were now the two leading powers, the one strong by land and the other by sea. The league between them was of short duration; they speedily quarrelled and, with their respective allies, went to war. Any of the other Hellenes who had differences of their own now resorted to one or other of them. So that from the Persian to the Peloponnesian War, the Lacedaemonians and the Athenians were perpetually fighting or making peace, either with one another or with their own revolted allies; thus they attained military efficiency, and learned experience in the school of danger.

19. The Lacedaemonians did not make tributaries of those who acknowledged their leadership, but took care that they should be governed by oligarchies in the exclusive interest of Sparta. The Athenians, on the other hand, after a time deprived the subject cities of their ships and made all of them pay a fixed tribute, except Chios and Lesbos. And the single power of Athens at the beginning of this war was greater than that of Athens and Sparta together at their greatest, while the confederacy remained intact.

20. Such are the results of my enquiries, though the early history of Hellas is of a kind which forbids implicit reliance on every particular of the evidence. Men do not discriminate, and are too ready to receive ancient traditions about their own as well as about other countries. Athenians think that Hipparchus was actually tyrant when he was slain by Harmodius and Aristogeiton; they are not aware that Hippias was the eldest of the sons of Peisistratus, and succeeded him, and that Hipparchus and Thessalus were only his brothers. At the last moment, Harmodius and Aristogeiton suddenly suspected that Hippias had been forewarned by some of their accomplices. They therefore abstained from attacking him, but, wishing to do something before they were seized, and not to risk their lives in vain, they slew Hipparchus, with whom they fell in near the temple called Leocorium as he was marshalling the Panathenaic procession. There are many other matters, not obscured by time, but contemporary, about which the other Hellenes are equally mistaken. For example, they imagine that the kings of

Lacedaemon in their council have not one but two votes each, and that in the army of the Lacedaemonians there is a division called the Pitanate division; whereas they never had anything of the sort. So little trouble do men take in the search after truth; so readily do they accept whatever comes first to hand.

21. Yet any one who upon the grounds which I have given arrives at some such conclusion as my own about those ancient times, would not be far wrong. He must not be misled by the exaggerated fancies of the poets, or by the tales of chroniclers who seek to please the ear rather than to speak the truth. Their accounts cannot be tested by him; and most of the facts in the lapse of ages have passed into the region of romance. At such a distance of time he must make up his mind to be satisfied with conclusions resting upon the clearest evidence which can be had. And, though men will always judge any war in which they are actually fighting to be the greatest at the time, but, after it is over, revert to their admiration of some other which has preceded, still the Peloponnesian, if estimated by the actual facts, will certainly prove to have been the greatest ever known.

22. As to the speeches which were made either before or during the war, it was hard for me, and for others who reported them to me, to recollect the exact words. I have therefore put into the mouth of each speaker the sentiments proper to the occasion, expressed as I thought he would be likely to express them, while at the same time I endeavoured, as nearly as I could, to give the general purport of what was actually said. Of the events of the war I have not ventured to speak from any chance information, nor according to any notion of my own; I have described nothing but what I either saw myself, or learned from others of whom I made the most careful and particular enquiry. The task was a laborious one, because eye-witnesses of the same occurrences gave different accounts of them, as they remembered or were interested in the actions of one side or the other. And very likely the strictly historical character of my narrative may be disappointing to the ear. But if he who desires to have before his eyes a true picture of the events which have happened, and of the like events which may be expected to happen hereafter in the order of human things, shall

pronounce what I have written to be useful, then I shall be satisfied. My history is an everlasting possession, not a prize composition which is heard and forgotten.

23. The greatest achievement of former times was the Persian War; yet even this was speedily decided in two battles by sea and two by land. But the Peloponnesian War was a protracted struggle, and attended by calamities such as Hellas had never known within a like period of time. Never were so many cities captured and depopulated—some by Barbarians, others by Hellenes themselves fighting against one another; and several of them after their capture were repeopled by strangers. Never were exile and slaughter more frequent, whether in the war or brought about by civil strife. And traditions which had often been current before, but rarely verified by fact, were now no longer doubted. For there were earthquakes unparalleled in their extent and fury, and eclipses of the sun more numerous than are recorded to have happened in any former age; there were also in some places great droughts causing famines, and lastly the plague which did immense harm and destroyed numbers of the people. All these calamities fell upon Hellas simultaneously with the war, which began when the Athenians and Peloponnesians violated the thirty years' truce concluded by them after the recapture of Euboea. Why they broke it and what were the grounds of quarrel I will first set forth, that in time to come no man may be at a loss to know what was the origin of this great war. The real though unavowed cause I believe to have been the growth of the Athenian power, which terrified the Lacedaemonians and forced them into war; but the reasons publicly alleged on either side were as follows.

Pericles' speech delivered at the funeral ceremonies at the end of the first year of the Peloponnesian War
Book II:34–37

34. DURING THE same winter, in accordance with an old national custom, the funeral of those who first fell in this war was celebrated by the Athenians at the public charge. The ceremony is as follows: Three days before the celebration they erect a tent in

which the bones of the dead are laid out, and every one brings to his own dead any offering which he pleases. At the time of the funeral the bones are placed in chests of cypress wood, which are conveyed on hearses; there is one chest for each tribe. They also carry a single empty litter decked with a pall for all whose bodies are missing, and cannot be recovered after the battle. The procession is accompanied by any one who chooses, whether citizen or stranger, and the female relatives of the deceased are present at the place of interment and make lamentation. The public sepulchre is situated in the most beautiful spot outside the walls; there they always bury those who fall in war; only after the battle of Marathon the dead, in recognition of their pre-eminent valour, were interred on the field. When the remains have been laid in the earth, some man of know ability and high reputation, chosen by the city, delivers a suitable oration over them; after which the people depart. Such is the manner of interment; and the ceremony was repeated from time to time throughout the war. Over those who were the first buried Pericles was chosen to speak. At the fitting moment he advanced from the sepulchre to a lofty stage, which had been erected in order that he might be heard as far as possible by the multitude, and spoke as follows:—

(FUNERAL SPEECH.)

35. 'Most of those who have spoken here before me have commended the lawgiver who added this oration to our other funeral customs; it seemed to them a worthy thing that such an honour should be given at their burial to the dead who have fallen on the field of battle. But I should have preferred that, when men's deeds have been brave, they should be honoured in deed only, and with such an honour as this public funeral, which you are now witnessing. Then the reputation of many would not have been imperilled on the eloquence or want of eloquence of one, and their virtues believed or not as he spoke well or ill. For it is difficult to say neither too little nor too much; and even moderation is apt not to give the impression of truthfulness. The friend of the dead who knows the facts is likely to think that the words of the speaker fall short of his

knowledge and of his wishes; another who is not so well informed, when he hears of anything which surpasses his own powers, will be envious and will suspect exaggeration. Mankind are tolerant of the praises of others so long as each hearer thinks that he can do as well or nearly as well himself, but, when the speaker rises above him, jealousy is aroused and he begins to be incredulous. However, since our ancestors have set the seal of their approval upon the practice, I must obey, and to the utmost of my power shall endeavour to satisfy the wishes and beliefs of all who hear me.

36. 'I will speak first of our ancestors, for it is right and seemly that now, when we are lamenting the dead, a tribute should be paid to their memory. There has never been a time when they did not inhabit this land, which by their valour they have handed down from generation to generation, and we have received from them a free state. But if they were worthy of praise, still more were our fathers, who added to their inheritance, and after many a struggle transmitted to us their sons this great empire. And we ourselves assembled here to-day, who are still most of us in the vigour of life, have carried the work of improvement further, and have richly endowed our city with all things, so that she is sufficient for herself both in peace and war. Of the military exploits by which our various possessions were acquired, or of the energy with which we or our fathers drove back the tide of war, Hellenic or Barbarian, I will not speak; for the tale would be long and is familiar to you. But before I praise the dead, I should like to point out by what principles of action we rose to power, and under what institutions and through what manner of life our empire became great. For I conceive that such thoughts are not unsuited to the occasion, and that this numerous assembly of citizens and strangers may profitably listen to them.

37. 'Our form of government does not enter into rivalry with the institutions of others. We do not copy our neighbours, but are an example to them. It is true that we are called a democracy, for the administration is in the hands of the many and not of the few. But while the law secures equal justice to all alike in their private disputes, the claim of excellence is also recognised; and when a citizen is in any way distinguished, he is preferred to the public

service, not as a matter of privilege, but as the reward of merit. Neither is poverty a bar, but a man may benefit his country whatever be the obscurity of his condition. There is no exclusiveness in our public life, and in our private intercourse we are not suspicious of one another, nor angry with our neighbour if he does what he likes; we do not put on sour looks at him which, though harmless, are not pleasant. While we are thus unconstrained in our private intercourse, a spirit of reverence pervades our public acts; we are prevented from doing wrong by respect for the authorities and for the laws, having an especial regard to those which are ordained for the protection of the injured as well as to those unwritten laws which bring upon the transgressor of them the reprobation of the general sentiment.

38. 'And we have not forgotten to provide for our weary spirits many relaxations from toil; we have regular games and sacrifices throughout the year; our homes are beautiful and elegant; and the delight which we daily feel in all these things helps to banish melancholy. Because of the greatness of our city the fruits of the whole earth flow in upon us; so that we enjoy the goods of other countries as freely as of our own.

39. 'Then, again, our military training is in many respects superior to that of our adversaries. Our city is thrown open to the world, and we never expel a foreigner or prevent him from seeing or learning anything of which the secret if revealed to an enemy might profit him. We rely not upon management or trickery, but upon our own hearts and hands. And in the matter of education, whereas they from early youth are always undergoing laborious exercises which are to make them brave, we live at ease, and yet are equally ready to face the perils which they face. And here is the proof. The Lacedaemonians come into Attica not by themselves, but with their whole confederacy following; we go alone into a neighbour's country; and although our opponents are fighting for their homes and we on a foreign soil, we have seldom any difficulty in overcoming them. Our enemies have never felt our united strength; the care of a navy divides our attention, and on land we are obliged to send our own citizens everywhere. But they, if they meet and defeat a part of our army, are as proud as if they had

routed us all, and when defeated they pretend to have been vanquished by us all.

40. 'If then we prefer to meet danger with a light heart but without laborious training, and with a courage which is gained by habit and not enforced by law, are we not greatly the gainers? Since we do not anticipate the pain, although, when the hour comes, we can be as brave as those who never allow themselves to rest; and thus too our city is equally admirable in peace and in war. For we are lovers of the beautiful, yet simple in our tastes, and we cultivate the mind without loss of manliness. Wealth we employ, not for talk and ostentation, but when there is a real use for it. To avow poverty with us is no disgrace; the true disgrace is in doing nothing to avoid it. An Athenian citizen does not neglect the state because he takes care of his own household; and even those of us who are engaged in business have a very fair idea of politics. We alone regard a man who takes no interest in public affairs, not as a harmless, but as a useless character; and if few of us are originators, we are all sound judges of a policy. The great impediment to action is, in our opinion, not discussion, but the want of that knowledge which is gained by discussion preparatory to action. For we have a peculiar power of thinking before we act and of acting too, whereas other men are courageous from ignorance but hesitate upon reflection. And they are surely to be esteemed the bravest spirits who, having the clearest sense both of the pains and pleasures of life, do not on that account shrink from danger. In doing good, again, we are unlike others; we make our friends by conferring, not by receiving favours. Now he who confers a favour is the firmer friend, because he would fain by kindness keep alive the memory of an obligation; but the recipient is colder in his feelings, because he knows that in requiting another's generosity he will not be winning gratitude but only paying a debt. We alone do good to our neighbours not upon a calculation of interest, but in the confidence of freedom and in a frank and fearless spirit.

41. 'To sum up: I say that Athens is the school of Hellas, and that the individual Athenian in his own person seems to have the power of adapting himself to the most varied forms of action with the utmost versatility and grace. This is no passing and idle word,

but truth and fact; and the assertion is verified by the position to which these qualities have raised the state. For in the hour of trial Athens alone among her contemporaries is superior to the report of her. No enemy who comes against her is indignant at the reverses which he sustains at the hands of such a city; no subject complains that his masters are unworthy of him. And we shall assuredly not be without witnesses; there are mighty monuments of our power which will make us the wonder of this and of succeeding ages; we shall not need the praises of Homer or of any other panegyrist whose poetry may please for the moment, although his representation of the facts will not bear the light of day. For we have compelled every land and every sea to open a path for our valour, and have everywhere planted eternal memorials of our friendship and of our enmity. Such is the city for whose sake these men nobly fought and died; they could not bear the thought that she might be taken from them; and every one of us who survive should gladly toil on her behalf.

42. 'I have dwelt upon the greatness of Athens because I want to show you that we are contending for a higher prize than those who enjoy none of these privileges, and to establish by manifest proof the merit of these men whom I am now commemorating. Their loftiest praise has been already spoken. For in magnifying the city I have magnified them, and men like them whose virtues made her glorious. And of how few Hellenes can it be said as of them, that their deeds when weighed in the balance, have been found equal to their fame! Methinks that a death such as theirs has been gives the true measure of a man's worth; it may be the first revelation of his virtues, but is at any rate their final seal. For even those who come short in other ways may justly plead the valour with which they have fought for their country; they have blotted out the evil with the good, and have benefited the state more by their public services than they have injured her by their private actions. None of these men were enervated by wealth or hesitated to resign the pleasures of life; none of them put off the evil day in the hope, natural to poverty, that a man, though poor, may one day become rich. But, deeming that the punishment of their enemies was sweeter than

any of these things, and that they could fall in no nobler cause, they determined at the hazard of their lives to be honourably avenged, and to leave the rest. They resigned to hope their unknown chance of happiness; but in the face of death they resolved to rely upon themselves alone. And when the moment came they were minded to resist and suffer, rather than to fly and save their lives; they ran away from the word of dishonour, but on the battle-field their feet stood fast, and in an instant, at the height of their fortune, they passed away from the scene, not of their fear, but of their glory.

43. 'Such was the end of these men; they were worthy of Athens, and the living need not desire to have a more heroic spirit, although they may pray for a less fatal issue. The value of such a spirit is not to be expressed in words. Any one can discourse to you for ever about the advantages of a brave defence, which you know already. But instead of listening to him I would have you day by day fix your eyes upon the greatness of Athens, until you become filled with the love of her; and when you are impressed by the spectacle of her glory, reflect that this empire has been acquired by men who knew their duty and had the courage to do it, who in the hour of conflict had the fear of dishonour always present to them, and who, if ever they failed in an enterprise, would not allow their virtues to be lost to their country, but freely gave their lives to her as the fairest offering which they could present at her feast. The sacrifice which they collectively made was individually repaid to them; for they received again each one for himself a praise which grows not old, and the noblest of all sepulchres—I speak not of that in which their remains are laid, but of that in which their glory survives, and is proclaimed always and on every fitting occasion both in word and deed. For the whole earth is the sepulchre of famous men; not only are they commemorated by columns and inscriptions in their own country, but in foreign lands there dwells also an unwritten memorial of them, graven not on stone but in the hearts of men. Make them your examples, and, esteeming courage to be freedom and freedom to be happiness, do not weigh too nicely the perils of war. The unfortunate who has no hope of a change for

the better has less reason to throw away his life than the prosperous who, if he survive, is always liable to a change for the worse, and to whom any accident fall makes the most serious difference. To a man of spirit, cowardice and disaster coming together are far more bitter than death striking him unperceived at a time when he is full of courage and animated by the general hope.

44. 'Wherefore I do not now commiserate the parents of the dead who stand here; I would rather comfort them. You know that your life has been passed amid manifold vicissitudes; and that they may be deemed fortunate who have gained most honour, whether an honourable death like theirs, or an honourable sorrow like yours, and whose days have been so ordered that the term of their happiness is likewise the term of their life. I know how hard it is to make you feel this, when the good fortune of others will too often remind you of the gladness which once lightened your hearts. And sorrow is felt at the want of those blessings, not which a man never knew, but which were a part of his life before they were taken from him. Some of you are of an age at which they may hope to have other children, and they ought to bear their sorrow better; not only will the children who may hereafter be born make them forget their own lost ones, but the city will be doubly a gainer. She will not be left desolate, and she will be safer. For a man's counsel cannot have equal weight or worth, when he alone has no children to risk in the general danger. To those of you who have passed their prime, I say: "Congratulate yourselves that you have been happy during the greater part of your days; remember that your life of sorrow will not last long, and be comforted by the glory of those who are gone. For the love of honour alone is ever young, and not riches, as some say, but honour is the delight of men when they are old and useless."

45. 'To you who are the sons and brothers of the departed, I see that the struggle to emulate them will be an arduous one. For all men praise the dead, and, however preeminent your virtue may be, hardly will you be thought, I do not say to equal, but even to approach them. The living have their rivals and detractors, but when a man is out of the way, the honour and good-will which he receives is unalloyed. And, if I am to speak of womanly virtues to

those of you who will henceforth be widows, let me sum them up in one short admonition: To a woman not to show more weakness than is natural to her sex is a great glory, and not to be talked about for good or for evil among men.

46. 'I have paid the required tribute, in obedience to the law, making use of such fitting words as I had. The tribute of deeds has been paid in part; for the dead have been honourably interred, and it remains only that their children should be maintained at the public charge until they are grown up: this is the solid prize with which, as with a garland, Athens crowns her sons living and dead, after a struggle like theirs. For where the rewards of virtue are greatest, there the noblest citizens are enlisted in the service of the state. And now, when you have duly lamented, every one his own dead, you may depart.'

47. Such was the order of the funeral celebrated in this winter, with the end of which ended the first year of the Peloponnesian War.

Thucydides' description of the Plague at Athens.
Book II: 48–54

48. THE DISEASE is said to have begun south of Egypt in Aethiopia; thence it descended into Egypt and Libya, and after spreading over the greater part of the Persian empire, suddenly fell upon Athens. It first attacked the inhabitants of the Piraeus, and it was supposed that the Peloponnesians had poisoned the cisterns, no conduits having as yet been made there. It afterwards reached the upper city, and then the mortality became far greater. As to its probable origin or the causes which might or could have produced such a disturbance of nature, every man, whether a physician or not, will give his own opinion. But I shall describe its actual course, and the symptoms by which any one who knows them beforehand may recognise the disorder should it ever reappear. For I was myself attacked, and witnessed the sufferings of others.

49. The season was admitted to have been remarkably free from ordinary sickness; and if anybody was already ill of any other

disease, it was absorbed in this. Many who were in perfect health, all in a moment, and without any apparent reason, were seized with violent heats in the head and with redness and inflammation of the eyes. Internally the throat and the tongue were quickly suffused with blood, and the breath became unnatural and fetid. There followed sneezing and hoarseness; in a short time the disorder, accompanied by a violent cough, reached the chest; then fastening lower down, it would move the stomach and bring on all the vomits of bile to which physicians have ever given names; and they were very distressing. An ineffectual retching producing violent convulsions attacked most of the sufferers; some as soon as the previous symptoms had abated, others not until long afterwards. The body externally was not so very hot to the touch, nor yet pale; it was of a livid colour inclining to red, and breaking out in pustules and ulcers. But the internal fever was intense; the sufferers could not bear to have on them even the finest linen garment; they insisted on being naked, and there was nothing which they longed for more eagerly than to throw themselves into cold water. And many of those who had no one to look after them actually plunged into the cisterns, for they were tormented by unceasing thirst, which was not in the least assuaged whether they drank little or much. They could not sleep; a restlessness which was intolerable never left them. While the disease was at its height the body, instead of wasting away, held out amid these sufferings in a marvellous manner, and either they died on the seventh or ninth day, not of weakness, for their strength was not exhausted, but of internal fever, which was the end of most; or, if they survived, then the disease descended into the bowels and there produced violent ulceration; severe diarrhoea at the same time set in, and at a later stage caused exhaustion, which finally with few exceptions carried them off. For the disorder which had originally settled in the head passed gradually through the whole body, and, if a person got over the worst, would often seize the extremities and leave its mark, attacking the privy parts and the fingers and the toes; and some escaped with the loss of these, some with the loss of their eyes. Some again had no sooner recovered than they were seized with a forgetfulness of all things and knew neither themselves nor their friends.

50. The general character of the malady no words can describe, and the fury with which it fastened upon each sufferer was too much for human nature to endure. There was one circumstance in particular which distinguished it from ordinary diseases. The birds and animals which feed on human flesh, although so many bodies were lying unburied, either never came near them, or died if they touched them. This was proved by a remarkable disappearance of the birds of prey, which were not to be seen either about the bodies or anywhere else; while in the case of the dogs the result was even more obvious, because they live with man.

51. Such was the general nature of the disease: I omit many strange peculiarities which characterised individual cases. None of the ordinary sicknesses attacked any one while it lasted, or, if they did, they ended in the plague. Some of the sufferers died from want of care, others equally who were receiving the greatest attention. No single remedy could be deemed a specific; for that which did good to one did harm to another. No constitution was of itself strong enough to resist or weak enough to escape the attacks; the disease carried off all alike and defied every mode of treatment. Most appalling was the despondency which seized upon any one who felt himself sickening; for he instantly abandoned his mind to despair and, instead of holding out, absolutely threw away his chance of life. Appalling too was the rapidity with which men caught the infection; dying like sheep if they attended on one another; and this was the principal cause of mortality. When they were afraid to visit one another, the sufferers died in their solitude, so that many houses were empty because there had been no one left to take care of the sick; or if they ventured they perished, especially those who aspired to heroism. For they went to see their friends without thought of themselves and were ashamed to leave them, at a time when the very relations of the dying were at last growing weary and ceased even to make lamentations, overwhelmed by the vastness of the calamity. But whatever instances there may have been of such devotion, more often the sick and the dying were tended by the pitying care of those who had recovered, because they knew the course of the disease and were themselves free from apprehension. For no one was ever attacked a second time, or not

with a fatal result. All men congratulated them, and they themselves, in the excess of their joy at the moment, had an innocent fancy that they could not die of any other sickness.

52. The crowding of the people out of the country into the city aggravated the misery; and the newly-arrived suffered most. For, having no houses of their own, but inhabiting in the height of summer stifling huts, the mortality among them was dreadful, and they perished in wild disorder. The dead lay as they had died, one upon another, while others hardly alive wallowed in the streets and crawled about every fountain craving for water. The temples in which they lodged were full of the corpses of those who died in them; for the violence of the calamity was such that men, not knowing where to turn, grew reckless of all law, human and divine. The customs which had hitherto been observed at funerals were universally violated, and they buried their dead each one as best he could. Many, having no proper appliances, because the deaths in their household had been so numerous already, lost all shame in the burial of the dead. When one man had raised a funeral pile, others would come, and throwing on their dead first, set fire to it; or when some other corpse was already burning, before they could be stopped would throw their own dead upon it and depart.

53. There were other and worse forms of lawlessness which the plague introduced at Athens. Men who had hitherto concealed what they took pleasure in, now grew bolder. For, seeing the sudden change,—how the rich died in a moment, and those who had nothing immediately inherited their property,—they reflected that life and riches were alike transitory, and they resolved to enjoy themselves while they could, and to think only of pleasure. Who would be willing to sacrifice himself to the law of honour when he knew not whether he would ever live to be held in honour? The pleasure of the moment and any sort of thing which conduced to it took the place both of honour and of expediency. No fear of Gods or law of man deterred a criminal. Those who saw all perishing alike, thought that the worship or neglect of the Gods made no difference. For offences against human law no punishment was to be feared; no one would live long enough to be called to account. Already a far heavier sentence had been passed and was hanging

over a man's head; before that fell, why should he not take a little pleasure?

54. Such was the grievous calamity which now afflicted the Athenians; within the walls their people were dying, and without, their country was being ravaged.

Thucydides' description of the demoralizing effect of the civil strife (stasis) at Corcyraea.
Book III: 82–85

82. FOR NOT LONG afterwards nearly the whole Hellenic world was in commotion; in every city the chiefs of the democracy and of the oligarchy were struggling, the one to bring in the Athenians, the other the Lacedaemonians. Now in time of peace, men would have had no excuse for introducing either, and no desire to do so; but, when they were at war, the introduction of a foreign alliance on one side or the other to the hurt of their enemies and the advantage of themselves was easily effected by the dissatisfied party. And revolution brought upon the cities of Hellas many terrible calamities, such as have been and always will be while human nature remains the same, but which are more or less aggravated and differ in character with every new combination of circumstances. In peace and prosperity both states and individuals are actuated by higher motives, because they do not fall under the dominion of imperious necessities; but war, which takes away the comfortable provision of daily life, is a hard master and tends to assimilate men's characters to their conditions.

When troubles had once begun in the cities, those who followed carried the revolutionary spirit further and further, and determined to outdo the report of all who had preceded them by the ingenuity of their enterprises and the atrocity of their revenges. The meaning of words had no longer the same relation to things, but was changed by them as they thought proper. Reckless daring was held to be loyal courage; prudent delay was the excuse of a coward; moderation was the disguise of unmanly weakness; to know everything was to do nothing. Frantic energy was the true quality of a man. A conspirator who wanted to be safe was a recreant in disguise. The lover of violence was always trusted, and his opponent suspected. He who succeeeeded in a plot was deemed knowing, but a still greater master in craft was he who detected one. On the other hand, he who plotted from the first to have nothing to do with plots was a breaker up of parties and a poltroon who was afraid of the enemy. In a word, he who could outstrip another in a bad action was applauded, and so was he who encouraged to evil one who had no idea of it. The tie of party was stronger than the tie of blood, because a partisan was more ready to dare without asking why. (For party associations are not based upon any established law, nor do they seek the public good; they are formed in defiance of the laws and from self-interest.) The seal of good faith was not divine law, but fellowship in crime. If an enemy when he was in the ascendant offered fair words, the opposite party received them not in a generous spirit, but by a jealous watchfulness of his actions. Revenge was dearer than self-preservation. Any agreements sworn to by either party, when they could do nothing else, were binding as long as both were powerless. But he who on a favourable opportunity first took courage, and struck at his enemy when he saw him off his guard, had greater pleasure in a perfidious than he would have had in an open act of revenge; he congratulated himself that he had taken the safer course, and also that he had overreached his enemy and gained the prize of superior ability. In general the dishonest more easily gain credit for cleverness than the simple for goodness; men take a pride in the one, but are ashamed of the other.

The cause of all these evils was the love of power, originating in avarice and ambition, and the party-spirit which is engendered by them when men are fairly embarked in a contest. For the leaders on either side used specious names, the one party professing to uphold the constitutional equality of the many, the other the wisdom of an aristocracy, while they made the public interests, to which in name they were devoted, in reality their prize. Striving in every way to overcome each other, they committed the most monstrous crimes; yet even these were surpassed by the magnitude of their revenges which they pursued to the very utmost, neither party observing any definite limits either of justice or public expediency, but both alike making the caprice of the moment their law. Either by the help of an unrighteous sentence, or grasping power with the strong hand, they were eager to satiate the impatience of party-spirit. Neither faction cared for religion; but any fair pretence which succeeded in effecting some odious purpose was greatly lauded. And the citizens who were of neither party fell a prey to both; either they were disliked because they held aloof, or men were jealous of their surviving.

83. Thus revolution gave birth to every form of wickedness in Hellas. The simplicity which is so large an element in a noble nature was laughed to scorn and disappeared. An attitude of perfidious antagonism everywhere prevailed; for there was no word binding enough, nor oath terrible enough to reconcile enemies. Each man was strong only in the conviction that nothing was secure; he must look to his own safety, and could not afford to trust others. Inferior intellects generally succeeded best. For, aware of their own deficiencies, and fearing the capacity of their opponents, for whom they were no match in powers of speech, and whose subtle wits were likely to anticipate them in contriving evil, they struck boldly and at once. But the cleverer sort, presuming in their arrogance that they would be aware in time, and disdaining to act when they could think, were taken off their guard and easily destroyed.

84. Now in Corcyra most of these deeds were perpetrated, and for the first time. There was every crime which men could commit in revenge who had been governed not wisely, but tyrannically, and now had the oppressor at their mercy. There were the dishonest designs of others who were longing to be relieved from their habitual poverty, and were naturally animated by a passionate desire for their neighbour's goods; and there were crimes of another class which men commit, not from covetousness, but, from the enmity which equals foster towards one another until they are carried away by their blind rage into the extremes of pitiless cruelty. At such a time the life of the city was all in disorder, and human nature, which is always ready to transgress the laws, having now trampled them under foot, delighted to show that her passions were ungovernable, that she was stronger than justice, and the enemy of

everything above her. If malignity had not exercised a fatal power, how could any one have preferred revenge to piety, and gain to innocence? But, when men are retaliating upon others, they are reckless of the future, and do not hesitate to annul those common laws of humanity to which every individual trusts for his own hope of deliverance should he ever be overtaken by calamity; they forget that in their own hour of need they will look for them in vain.

85. Such were the passions which the citizens of Corcyra first of all Hellenes displayed towards one another. . . .

> *Description of the incident at Pylos during the Peloponnesian War. Though only a relatively few men were involved in the battle, it marked a significant moment in the War, a moment which, as Thucydides points out, the Athenians let slip through their own obstinacy.*
> Book IV: 1–42

1. IN THE following summer, about the time when the corn comes into ear, ten Syracusan and ten Locrian ships took possession of Messenè in Sicily, whither they had gone by the invitation of the inhabitants. And so Messenè revolted from the Athenians. The Syracusans took part in this affair chiefly because they saw that Messenè was the key to Sicily. They were afraid that the Athenians would one day establish themselves there and come and attack them with a larger force. The Locrians took part because the Rhegians were their enemies, and they wanted to crush them by sea as well as by land. They had already invaded the territory of Rhegium with their whole army, in order to hinder the Rhegians from assisting the Messenians; they were also partly instigated by certain Rhegian exiles who had taken refuge with them. For the Rhegians had been for a long time torn by revolution, and in their present condition could not resist the Locrians, who for this very reason were the more disposed to attack them. After wasting the country, the Locrians withdrew their land forces; but the ships remained to protect Messenè. Another fleet which the allies were manning was intended to lie in the harbour of Messenè, and to carry on the war from thence.

2. During the spring and about the same time, before the corn was in full ear, the Peloponnesians and their allies invaded Attica, under the command of Agis the son of Archidamus, the Lacedaemonian king. They encamped and ravaged the country.

The Athenians sent to Sicily the forty ships, which were now ready, under the command of Eurymedon and Sophocles, the third general, Pythodorus, having gone thither beforehand. Orders were given to them, as they passed Corcyra, to assist the Corcyraeans in the city, who were harassed by the exiles in the mountain. The Peloponnesians had already sent sixty ships to the assistance of the exiles, expecting to make themselves masters of the situation with little difficulty; for there was a great famine in the city. Demosthenes, since his return from Acarnania, had been in no command, but now at his own request the Athenians allowed him to make use of the fleet about the Peloponnese according to his judgment.

3. When they arrived off the coast of Laconia and heard that the Peloponnesian ships were already at Corcyra, Eurymedon and Sophocles wanted to hasten thither, but Demosthenes desired them first to put in at Pylos and not to proceed on their voyage until they had done what he wanted. They objected, but it so happened that a storm came on and drove them into Pylos. Instantly Demosthenes urged them to fortify the place; this being the project which he had in view when he accompanied the fleet. He pointed out to them that there was abundance of timber and stone ready to their hand, and that the position was naturally strong, while both the place itself and the country for a long way round was uninhabited. Pylos is distant about forty-six miles from Sparta, and is situated in the territory which once belonged to the Messenians; by the Lacedaemonians it is called Coryphasium. The other generals argued that there were plenty of desolate promontories on the coast of Peloponnesus which he might occupy if he wanted to waste the public money. But Demosthenes thought that this particular spot had exceptional advantages. There was a harbour ready at hand; the Messenians, who were the ancient inhabitants of the country and spoke the same language with the Lacedaemonians, would make descents from the fort and do the greatest mischief; and they would be a trusty garrison.

4. As neither generals nor soldiers would listen to him, he at last communicated his idea to the officers of divisions; who would not listen to him either. The weather was still unfit for sailing; he was therefore compelled to remain doing nothing; until at length the soldiers, who had nothing to do, were themselves seized with a desire to come round and fortify the place forthwith. So they put their hands to the work; and, being unprovided with iron tools, brought stones which they picked out and put them together as they happened to fit; if they required to use mortar, having no hods, they carried it on their backs, which they bent so as to form a resting-place for it, clasping their hands behind them that it might not fall off. By every means in their power they hurried on the weaker points, wanting to finish them before the Lacedaemonians arrived. The position was in most places so strongly fortified by nature as to have no need of a wall.

5. The Lacedaemonians, who were just then celebrating a festival, made light of the news, being under the impression that they could easily storm the fort whenever they chose to attack it, even if the Athenians did not run away of themselves at their approach. They were also delayed by the absence of their army in Attica. In six days the Athenians finished the wall on the land side, and in places towards the sea where it was most required; they then left Demosthenes with five ships to defend it, and with the rest hastened on their way to Corcyra and Sicily.

6. The Peloponnesian army in Attica, when they heard that Pylos had been occupied, quickly returned home, Agis and the Lacedaemonians thinking that this matter touched them very nearly. The invasion had been made quite early in the year while the corn was yet green, and they were in want of food for their soldiers; moreover the wet and unseasonable weather had distressed them, so that on many grounds they were inclined to return sooner than they had intended. This was the shortest of all the Peloponnesian invasions; they only remained fifteen days in Attica. . . .

8. On the return of the Peloponnesians from Attica, the Spartans and the Perioeci in the neighbourhood of the city went at once to attack Pylos, but the other Lacedaemonians, having only just returned from an expedition, were slower in arriving. A message

was sent round the Peloponnesus bidding the allies come without a moment's delay and meet at Pylos; another message summoned the sixty Peloponnesian ships from Corcyra. These were carried over the Leucadian isthmus, and, undiscovered by the Athenian ships, which were by this time at Zacynthus, reached Pylos, where their land forces had already assembled. While the Peloponnesian fleet was still on its way, Demosthenes succeeded in despatching unobserved two vessels to let Eurymedon and the Athenian fleet know of his danger, and to bid them come at once.

While the Athenian ships were hastening to the assistance of Demosthenes in accordance with his request, the Lacedaemonians prepared to attack the fort both by sea and by land; they thought that there would be little difficulty in taking a work hastily constructed and defended by a handful of men. But as they expected the speedy arrival of the Athenian fleet they meant to close the entrances to the harbour, and prevent the Athenians from anchoring there should they fail in taking the fort before their arrival.

The island which is called Sphacteria stretches along the land and is quite close to it, making the harbour safe and the entrances narrow; there is only a passage for two ships at the one end, which was opposite Pylos and the Athenian fort, while at the other the strait between the island and the mainland is wide enough to admit eight or nine. The length of the island is about a mile and three-quarters; it was wooded, and being uninhabited had no roads. The Lacedaemonians were intending to block up the mouths of the harbour by ships placed close together with their prows outwards; meanwhile, fearing lest the Athenians should use the island for military operations, they conveyed thither some hoplites, and posted others along the shore of the mainland. Thus both the island and the mainland would be hostile to the Athenians; and nowhere on the mainland would there be a possibility of landing. For on the shore of Pylos itself, outside the entrance of the strait, and where the land faced the open sea, there were no harbours, and the Athenians would find no position from which they could assist their countrymen. Meanwhile the Lacedaemonians, avoiding the risk of an engagement at sea, might take the fort, which had been occupied in a hurry and was not provisioned. Acting on this impression they conveyed their hoplites over to the island, selecting them by lot out of each division of the army. One detachment relieved another; those who went over last and were taken in the island were four hundred and twenty men, besides the Helots who attended them; they were under the command of Epitadas the son of Molobrus.

9. Demosthenes, seeing that the Lacedaemonians were about to attack him both by sea and by land, made his own preparations. He drew up on shore under the fort the three triremes remaining to him out of the five which had not gone on to Corcyra, and protected them by a stockade; their crews he armed with shields, but of a poor sort, most of them made of wicker-work. In an uninhabited country there was no possibility of procuring arms, and these were only obtained from a thirty-oared privateer and a light boat belonging to some Messenians who had just arrived. Of these Messenians about forty were hoplites, whom Demosthenes used with the others. He placed the greater part of his forces, armed and unarmed, upon the side of the place which looks towards the mainland and was stronger and better fortified; these he ordered, if they should be attacked, to repel the land forces, while he himself selected out of the whole body of his troops sixty hoplites and a few archers, and marched out of the fort to the sea-shore at the point where the Lacedaemonians seemed most likely to attempt a landing. The spot which he chose lay towards the open sea, and was rocky and dangerous; but he thought that the enemy would be attracted thither and would be sure to make a dash at that point because the fortifications were weaker. For the Athenians, not expecting to be defeated at sea, had left the wall just there less strong, while if the enemy could once force a landing, the place would easily be taken. Accordingly, marching down to the very edge of the sea, he there posted his hoplites; he was determined to keep the enemy off if he could, and in this spirit he addressed his men: —

10. 'My companions in danger, let none of you now on the eve of battle desire to display his wits by reckoning up the sum of the perils which surround us; let him rather resolve to meet the enemy without much thought, but with a lively hope that he will survive them all. In cases like these, when there is no choice, reflection is

useless, and the sooner danger comes the better. I am sure that our chances are more than equal if we will only stand firm, and, having so many advantages, do not take fright at the numbers of the enemy and throw them all away. The inaccessibility of the place is one of them; this, however, will only aid us if we maintain our position; when we have once retreated, the ground, though difficult in itself, will be easy enough to the enemy, for there will be no one to oppose him. And if we turn and press upon him he will be more obstinate than ever; for his retreat will be next to impossible. On ship-board the Peloponnesians are easily repelled, but once landed they are as good as we are. Of their numbers again we need not be so much afraid; for, numerous as they are, few only can fight at a time, owing to the difficulty of bringing their ships to shore. We are contending against an army superior indeed in numbers, but they are not our equals in other respects; for they are not on land but on water, and ships require many favourable accidents before they can act with advantage. So that I consider their embarrassments to counterbalance our want of numbers. You are Athenians, who know by experience the difficulty of disembarking in the presence of an enemy, and that if a man is not frightened out of his wits at the splashing of oars and the threatening look of a ship bearing down upon him, but is determined to hold his ground, no force can move him. It is now your turn to be attacked, and I call on you to stand fast and not to let the enemy touch the beach at all. Thus you will save yourselves and the place.'

11. The Athenians, inspirited by the words of Demosthenes, went down to the shore and formed a line along the water's edge. The Lacedaemonians now began to move, and assaulted the fort with their army by land, and with their fleet, consisting of forty-three ships, by sea. The admiral in command was Thrasymelidas, son of Cratesicles, a Spartan; he made his attack just where Demosthenes expected. The Athenians defended themselves both by sea and land. The Peloponnesians had divided their fleet into relays of a few ships—the space would not allow of more—and so resting and fighting by turns they made their attack with great spirit, loudly exhorting one another to force back the enemy and take the fort. Brasidas distinguished himself above all other men in

the engagement; he was captain of a ship, and seeing his fellow-captains and the pilots, even if they could touch anywhere, hesitating and afraid of running their ships on the rocks, he called out to them: 'Not to be sparing of timber when the enemy had built a fort in their country; let them wreck their ships to force a landing': this he said to his own countrymen, and to the allies that 'they should not hesitate at such a moment to make a present of their ships to the Lacedaemonians, who had done so much for them; they must run aground, and somehow or other get to land and take the fort and the men in it.'

12. While thus upbraiding the others he compelled his own pilot to run his ship aground, and made for the gangway. But in attempting to disembark he was struck by the Athenians, and, after receiving many wounds, he swooned away and fell into the fore part of the ship; his shield slipped off his arm into the sea, and, being washed ashore, was taken up by the Athenians and used for the trophy which they raised in commemoration of this attack. The Peloponnesians in the other ships made great efforts to disembark, but were unable on account of the roughness of the ground and the tenacity with which the Athenians held their position. It was a singular turn of fortune which drove the Athenians to repel the Lacedaemonians, who were attacking them by sea, from the Lacedaemonian coast, and the Lacedaemonians to fight for a landing on their own soil, now hostile to them, in the face of the Athenians. For in those days it was the great glory of the Lacedaemonians to be a land power distinguished for their military prowess, and of the Athenians to be a nation of sailors and the first sea power in Hellas.

13. The Peloponnesians, having continued their efforts during this day and a part of the next, at length desisted; on the third day they sent some of their ships to Asinè for timber with which to make engines, hoping by their help to take the part of the fort looking towards the harbour where the landing was easier, although it was built higher. Meanwhile the Athenian ships arrived from Zacynthus; they had been increased in number to fifty by the arrival of some guardships from Naupactus and of four Chian vessels. Their commanders saw that both the mainland and the island were full of hoplites, and that the ships were in the harbour and were

not coming out: so, not knowing where to find anchorage, they sailed away for the present to the island of Protè, which is close at hand and uninhabited, and there passed the night. Next day, having made ready for action, they put off to sea, intending, if, as they hoped, the Peloponnesians were willing to come out against them, to give battle in the open; if not, to sail into the harbour. The Peloponnesians did not come out, and had somehow neglected to close the mouths as they had intended. They showed no sign of moving, but were on shore, manning their ships and preparing to fight, if any one entered the harbour, which was of considerable size.

14. The Athenians, seeing how matters stood, rushed in upon them at both mouths of the harbour. Most of the enemies' ships had by this time got into deep water and were facing them. These they put to flight and pursued them as well as they could in such a narrow space, damaging many and taking five, one of them with the crew. They charged the remaining vessels even after they had reached the land, and there were some which they disabled while the crews were getting into them and before they put out at all. Others they succeeded in tying to their own ships and began to drag them away empty, the sailors having taken flight. At this sight the Lacedaemonians were in an agony, for their friends were being cut off in the island; they hurried to the rescue, and dashing armed as they were into the sea, took hold of the ships and pulled them back; that was a time when every one thought that the action was at a stand where he himself was not engaged. The confusion was tremendous; the two combatants in this battle for the ships interchanging their usual manner of fighting; for the Lacedaemonians in their excitement and desperation did, as one may say, carry on a sea-fight from the land, and the Athenians, who were victorious and eager to push their good fortune to the utmost, waged a land-fight from their ships. At length, after giving each other much trouble and inflicting great damage, they parted. The Lacedaemonians saved their empty ships, with the exception of those which were first taken. Both sides retired to their encampments; the Athenians then raised a trophy, gave up the dead, and took possession of the wrecks. They lost no time in sailing round the island

and establishing a guard over the men who were cut off there. The Peloponnesians on the mainland, who had now been joined by all their contingents, remained in their position before Pylos.

15. At Sparta, when the news arrived, there was great consternation; it was resolved that the magistrates should go down to the camp and see for themselves; they could then take on the spot any measures which they thought necessary. Finding on their arrival that nothing could be done for their soldiers in the island, and not liking to run the risk of their being starved to death or overcome by force of numbers, they decided that with the consent of the Athenian generals they would suspend hostilities at Pylos, and sending ambassadors to ask for peace at Athens, would endeavour to recover their men as soon as possible.

16. The Athenian commanders accepted their proposals, and a truce was made on the following conditions:—

'The Lacedaemonians shall deliver into the hands of the Athenians at Pylos the ships in which they fought, and shall also bring thither and deliver over any other ships of war which are in Laconia; and they shall make no assault upon the fort either by sea or land. The Athenians shall permit the Lacedaemonians on the mainland to send to those on the island a fixed quantity of kneaded flour, viz. two Attic quarts of barley-meal for each man, and a pint of wine, and also a piece of meat; for an attendant, half these quantities; they shall send them into the island under the inspection of the Athenians, and no vessel shall sail in by stealth. The Athenians shall guard the island as before, but not land, and shall not attack the Peloponnesian forces by land or by sea. If either party violate this agreement in any particular, however slight, the truce is to be at an end. The agreement is to last until the Lacedaemonian ambassadors return from Athens, and the Athenians are to convey them thither and bring them back in a trireme. When they return the truce is to be at an end, and the Athenians are to restore the ships in the same condition in which they received them.' Such were the terms of the truce. The ships, which were about sixty in number, were given up to the Athenians. The ambassadors went on their way, and arriving at Athens spoke as follows:—

17. 'Men of Athens, the Lacedaemonians have sent us to nego-

tiate for the recovery of our countrymen in the island, in the hope that you may be induced to grant us terms such as will be at once advantageous to you and not inglorious to us in our present misfortune. If we speak at length, this will be no departure from the custom of our country. On the contrary, it is our manner not to say much where few words will suffice, but to be more liberal of speech when something important has to be said and words are the ministers of action. Do not receive what we say in a hostile spirit, or imagine that we deem you ignorant and are instructing you, but regard us simply as putting you in mind of what you already know to be good policy. For you may turn your present advantage to excellent account, not only keeping what you have won, but gaining honour and glory as well. You will then escape the reverse which is apt to be experienced by men who attain any unusual good fortune; for, having already succeeded beyond all expectation, they see no reason why they should set any limit to their hopes and desires. Whereas they who have oftenest known the extremes of either kind of fortune ought to be most suspicious of prosperity; and this may naturally be expected to be the lesson which experience has taught both us and you.

18. 'Look only at the calamity which has just overtaken us, who formerly enjoyed the greatest prestige of any Hellenic state, but are now come hither to ask of you the boon which at one time we should have thought ourselves better able to confer. You cannot attribute our mishap to any want of power; nor to the pride which an incerase of power fosters. We were neither stronger nor weaker than before, but we erred in judgment, and to such errors all men are liable. Therefore you should not suppose that, because your city and your empire are powerful at this moment, you will always have fortune on your side. The wise ensure their own safety by not making too sure of their gains, and when disasters come they can meet them more intelligently; they know that war will go on its way whithersoever chance may lead, and will not restrict itself to the limits which he who begins to meddle with it would fain prescribe. They of all men will be least likely to meet with reverses, because they are not puffed up with military success, and they will be most inclined to end the struggle in the hour of victory. It will be for

your honour, Athenians, to act thus towards us. And then the victories which you have gained already cannot be attributed to mere luck; as they certainly will be if, rejecting our prayer, you should hereafter encounter disasters, a thing which is not unlikely to happen. Whereas you may if you will leave to posterity a reputation for power and wisdom which no danger can affect.

19. 'The Lacedaemonians invite you to make terms with them and to finish the war. They offer peace and alliance and a general friendly and happy relation, and they ask in return their countrymen who are cut off in the island. They think it better that neither city should run any further risk, you of the escape of the besieged, who may find some means of forcing their way out, we of their being compelled to surrender and passing absolutely into your hands. We think that great enmities are most effectually reconciled, not when one party seeks revenge and, getting a decided superiority, binds his adversary by enforced oaths and makes a treaty with him on unequal terms, but when, having it in his power to do all this, he from a generous and equitable feeling overcomes his resentment, and by the moderation of his terms surprises his adversary, who, having suffered no violence at his hands, is bound to recompense his generosity not with evil but with good, and who therefore, from a sense of honour, is more likely to keep his word. And mankind are more ready to make such a concession to their greater enemies than to those with whom they have only a slight difference. Again, they joyfully give way to those who first give way themselves, although against overbearing power they will risk a conflict even contrary to their own better judgment.

20. 'Now, if ever, is the time of reconciliation for us both, before either has suffered any irremediable calamity, which must cause, besides the ordinary antagonism of contending states, a personal and inveterate hatred, and will deprive you of the advantages which we now offer. While the contest is still undecided, while you may acquire reputation and our friendship, and while our disaster can be repaired on tolerable terms, and disgrace averted, let us be reconciled, and choosing peace instead of war ourselves, let us give relief and rest to all the Hellenes. The chief credit of the peace will be yours. Whether we or you drove them into war is uncertain; but

to give them peace lies with you, and to you they will be grateful. If you decide for peace, you may assure to yourselves the lasting friendship of the Lacedaemonians freely offered by them, you on your part employing no force but kindness only. Consider the great advantages which such a friendship will yield. If you and we are at one, you may be certain that the rest of Hellas, which is less powerful than we, will pay to both of us the greatest deference.'

21. Thus spoke the Lacedaemonians, thinking that the Athenians, who had formerly been desirous of making terms with them, and had only been prevented by their refusal, would now, when peace was offered to them, joyfully agree and would restore their men. But the Athenians reflected that, since they had the Lacedaemonians shut up in the island, it was at any time in their power to make peace, and they wanted more. These feelings were chiefly encouraged by Cleon the son of Cleaenetus, a popular leader of the day who had the greatest influence over the multitude. He persuaded them to reply that the men in the island must first of all give up themselves and their arms and be sent to Athens; the Lacedaemonians were then to restore Nisaea, Pegae, Troezen, and Achaia—places which had not been taken in war, but had been surrendered under a former treaty in a time of reverse, when the Athenians were more anxious to obtain peace than they now were. On these conditions they might recover the men and make a treaty of such duration as both parties should approve.

22. To this reply the Lacedaemonians said nothing, but only requested that the Athenians would appoint commissioners to discuss with them the details of the agreement and quietly arrive at an understanding about them if they could. This proposal was assailed by Cleon in unmeasured language: he had always known, he said, that they meant no good, and now their designs were unveiled; for they were unwilling to speak a word before the people, but wanted to be closeted with a select few; if they had any honesty in them, let them say what they wanted to the whole city. But the Lacedaemonians knew that, although they might be willing to make concessions under the pressure of their calamities, they could not speak openly before the assembly (for if they spoke and did not succeed, the terms which they offered might injure them in the opinion of

their allies); they saw too that the Athenians would not grant what was asked of them on any tolerable conditions. So, after a fruitless negotiation, they returned home.

23. Upon their return the truce at Pylos instantly came to an end, and the Lacedaemonians demanded back their ships according to the agreement. But the Athenians accused them of making an assault upon the fort, and of some other petty infractions of the treaty which seemed hardly worth mentioning. Accordingly they refused to restore them, insisting upon the clause which said that if 'in any particular, however slight,' the agreement were violated, the treaty was to be at an end. The Lacedaemonians remonstrated, and went away protesting against the injustice of detaining their ships. Both parties then renewed the war at Pylos with the utmost vigour. The Athenians had two triremes sailing round Sphacteria in opposite directions throughout the day, and at night their whole fleet was moored about the island, except on the side towards the sea when the wind was high. Twenty additional ships had come from Athens to assist in the blockade, so that the entire number was seventy. The Peloponnesians lay encamped on the mainland and made assaults upon the fort, watching for any opportunity which might present itself of rescuing their men.

26. At Pylos the Athenians continued to blockade the Lacedaemonians in the island, and the Peloponnesian forces on the mainland remained in their old position. The watch was harassing to the Athenians, for they were in want both of food and water; there was only one small well, which was in the acropolis, and the soldiers were commonly in the habit of scraping away the shingle on the seashore, and drinking such water as they could get. The Athenian garrison was crowded into a narrow space, and, their ships having no regular anchorage, the crews took their meals on land by turns; one half of the army eating while the other lay at anchor in the open sea. The unexpected length of the siege was a great discouragement to them; they had hoped to starve their enemies out in a few days, for they were on a desert island, and had only brackish water to drink. The secret of this protracted resistance was a proclamation issued by the Lacedaemonians offering large fixed prices, and freedom if he were a Helot, to any one who would convey into

the island meal, wine, cheese or any other provision suitable for a besieged place. Many braved the danger, especially the Helots; they started from all points of Peloponnesus, and before daybreak bore down upon the shore of the island looking towards the open sea. They took especial care to have a strong wind in their favour, since they were less likely to be discovered by the triremes when it blew hard from the sea. The blockade was then impracticable, and the crews of the boats were perfectly reckless in running them aground; for a value had been set upon them, and Lacedaemonian hoplites were waiting to receive them about the landing-places of the island. All however who ventured when the sea was calm were captured. Some too dived and swam by way of the harbour, drawing after them by a cord skins containing pounded linseed and poppy-seeds mixed with honey. At first they were not found out, but afterwards watches were posted. The two parties had all sorts of devices, the one determined to send in food, the other to detect them.

27. When the Athenians heard that their own army was suffering and that supplies were introduced into the island, they began to be anxious and were apprehensive that the blockade might extend into the winter. They reflected that the conveyance of necessaries round the Peloponnese would then be impracticable. Their troops were in a desert place, to which, even in summer, they were not able to send a sufficient supply. The coast was without harbours; and therefore it would be impossible to maintain the blockade. Either the watch would be relaxed and the men would escape; or, taking advantage of a storm, they might sail away in the ships which brought them food. Above all they feared that the Lacedaemonians, who no longer made overtures to them, must now be reassured of the strength of their own position, and they regretted having rejected their advances. Cleon, knowing that he was an object of general mistrust because he had stood in the way of peace, challenged the reports of the messengers from Pylos; who rejoined that, if their words were not believed, the Athenians should send commissioners of their own. And so Theogenes and Cleon himself were chosen commissioners. As he knew that he could only confirm the report of the messengers whom he was calumniating, or would

be convicted of falsehood if he contradicted them, observing too that the Athenians were now more disposed to take active measures, he advised them not to send commissioners, which would only be a loss of valuable time, but, if they were themselves satisfied with the report, to send a fleet against the island. Pointedly alluding to Nicias the son of Niceratus, who was one of the generals and an enemy of his, he declared sarcastically that, if the generals were men, they might easily sail with an expedition to the island and take the garrison, and that this was what he would certainly have done, had he been general.

28. Nicias perceived that the multitude were murmuring at Cleon, and asking 'why he did not sail in any case—now was his time if he thought the capture of Sphacteria to be such an easy matter'; and hearing him find fault, he told him that, as far as they, the generals, were concerned, he might take any force which he required and try. Cleon at first imagined that the offer of Nicias was only a pretence, and was willing to go; but finding that he was in earnest, he tried to back out, and said that not he but Nicias was general. He was now alarmed, for he never imagined that Nicias would go so far as to give up his place to him. Again Nicias bade him take the command of the expedition against Pylos, which he formally gave up to him in the presence of the assembly. And the more Cleon declined the proffered command and tried to retract what he had said, so much the more the multitude, as their manner is, urged Nicias to resign and shouted to Cleon that he should sail. At length, not knowing how to escape from his own words, he undertook the expedition, and, coming forward, said that he was not afraid of the Lacedaemonians, and that he would sail without taking a single man from the city if he were allowed to have the Lemnian and Imbrian forces now at Athens, the auxiliaries from Aenus, who were targeteers, and four hundred archers from other places. With these and with the troops already at Pylos he gave his word that within twenty days he would either bring the Lacedaemonians alive or kill them on the spot. His vain words moved the Athenians to laughter; nevertheless the wiser sort of men were pleased when they reflected that of two good things they could not fail to obtain one—either there would be no more trouble with

Cleon, which they would have greatly preferred, or, if they were disappointed, he would put the Lacedaemonians into their hands.

29. When he had concluded the affair in the assembly, and the Athenians had passed the necessary vote for his expedition, he made choice of Demosthenes, one of the generals at Pylos, to be his colleague, and proceeded to sail with all speed. He selected Demosthenes because he heard that he was already intending to make an attack upon the island; for the soldiers, who were suffering much from the discomfort of the place, in which they were rather besieged than besiegers, were eager to strike a decisive blow. He had been much encouraged by a fire which had taken place in the island. It had previously been nearly covered with wood and was pathless, having never been inhabited; and he had feared that the nature of the country would give the enemy an advantage. For, however large the force with which he landed, the Lacedaemonians might attack him from some place of ambush and do him much injury. Their mistakes and the character of their forces would be concealed by the wood; whereas all the errors made by his own army would be palpable, and so the enemy, with whom the power of attack would rest, might come upon them suddenly wherever they liked. And if they were compelled to go into the wood and there engage, a smaller force which knew the ground would be more than a match for the larger number who were unacquainted with it. Their own army, however numerous, would be destroyed without knowing it, for they would not be able to see where they needed one another's assistance.

30. Demosthenes was led to make these reflections from his experience in Aetolia, where his defeat had been in a great measure owing to the forest. However, while the Athenian soldiers were taking their midday meal, with a guard posted in advance, at the extremity of the island, compelled as they were by want of room to land on the edge of the shore at meal-times, some one unintentionally set fire to a portion of the wood; a wind came on; and from this accident, before they knew what was happening, the greater part of it was burnt. Demosthenes, who had previously suspected that the Lacedaemonians when they sent in provisions to the besieged had exaggerated their number, saw that the men were more numerous

than he had imagined. He saw too the increased zeal of the Athenians, who were now convinced that the attempt was worth making; and the island seemed to him more accessible. So he prepared for the descent, despatching messengers to the allies in the neighbourhood for additional forces and putting all in readiness. Cleon sent and announced to Demosthenes his approach, and soon afterwards, bringing with him the army which he had requested, himself arrived at Pylos. On the meeting of the two generals they first of all sent a herald to the Lacedaemonian force on the mainland, proposing that they should avoid any further risk by ordering the men in the island to surrender with their arms; they were to be placed under surveillance but well treated until a general peace was concluded.

31. Finding that their proposal was rejected, the Athenians waited for a day, and on the night of the day following put off, taking with them all their heavy-armed troops, whom they had embarked in a few ships. A little before dawn they landed on both sides of the island, towards the sea and towards the harbour, a force amounting in all to about eight hundred men. They then ran as fast as they could to the first station on the island. Now the disposition of the enemy was as follows: This first station was garrisoned by about thirty hoplites, while the main body under the command of Epitadas was posted near the spring in the centre of the island, where the ground was most level. A small force guarded the furthest extremity of the island opposite Pylos, which was precipitous towards the sea, and on the land side the strongest point of all, being protected to some extent by an ancient wall made of rough stones, which the Spartans thought would be of use to them if they were overpowered and compelled to retreat. Such was the disposition of the Lacedaemonian troops.

32. The Athenians rushed upon the first garrison and cut them down, half asleep as they were and just snatching up their arms. Their landing had been unobserved, the enemy supposing that the ships were only gone to keep the customary watch for the night. When the dawn appeared, the rest of the army began to disembark. They were the crews of rather more than seventy ships, including all but the lowest rank of rowers, variously equipped. There were

also archers to the number of eight hundred, and as many targeteers, besides the Messenian auxiliaries and all who were on duty about Pylos, except the guards who could not be spared from the walls of the fortress. Demosthenes divided them into parties of two hundred more or less, who seized the highest points of the island in order that the enemy, being completely surrounded and distracted by the number of their opponents, might not know whom they should face first, but might be exposed to missiles on every side. For if they attacked those who were in front, they would be assailed by those behind; and if those on one flank, by those posted on the other; and whichever way they moved, the light-armed troops of the enemy were sure to be in their rear. These were their most embarrassing opponents, because they were armed with bows and javelins and slings and stones, which could be used with effect at a distance. Even to approach them was impossible, for they conquered in their very flight, and when an enemy retreated, pressed close at his heels. Such was the plan of the descent which Demosthenes had in his mind, and which he now carried into execution.

33. The main body of the Lacedaemonians on the island under Epitadas, when they saw the first garrison cut to pieces and an army approaching them, drew up in battle array. The Athenian hoplites were right in front, and the Lacedaemonians advanced against them, wanting to come to close quarters; but having light-armed adversaries both on their flank and rear, they could not get at them or profit by their own military skill, for they were impeded by a shower of missiles from both sides. Meanwhile the Athenians instead of going to meet them remained in position, while the light-armed again and again ran up and attacked the Lacedaemonians, who drove them back where they pressed closest. But though compelled to retreat they still continued fighting, being lightly equipped and easily getting the start of their enemies. The ground was difficult and rough, the island having been uninhabited; and the Lacedaemonians, who were incumbered by their arms, could not pursue them in such a place.

34. For some little time these skirmishes continued. But soon the Lacedaemonians became too weary to rush out upon their assailants, who began to be sensible that their resistance grew feebler.

The sight of their own number, which was many times that of the enemy, encouraged them more than anything; they soon found that their losses were trifling compared with what they had expected; and familiarity made them think their opponents much less formidable than when they first landed cowed by the fear of facing Lacedaemonians. They now despised them and with a loud cry rushed upon them in a body, hurling at them stones, arrows, javelins, whichever came first to hand. The shout with which they accompanied the attack dismayed the Lacedaemonians, who were unaccustomed to this kind of warfare. Clouds of dust arose from the newly-burnt wood, and there was no possibility of a man's seeing what was before him, owing to the showers of arrows and stones hurled by their assailants which were flying amid the dust. And now the Lacedaemonians began to be sorely distressed, for their felt cuirasses did not protect them against the arrows, and the points of the javelins broke off where they struck them. They were at their wits' end, not being able to see out of their eyes or to hear the word of command, which was drowned by the cries of the enemy. Destruction was staring them in the face, and they had no means or hope of deliverance.

35. At length, finding that so long as they fought in the same narrow spot more and more of their men were wounded, they closed their ranks and fell back on the last fortification of the island, which was not far off, and where their other garrison was stationed. Instantly the light-armed troops of the Athenians pressed upon them with fresh confidence, redoubling their cries. Those of the Lacedaemonians who were caught by them on the way were killed, but the greater number escaped to the fort and ranged themselves with the garrison, resolved to defend the heights wherever they were assailable. The Athenians followed, but the strength of the position made it impossible to surround and cut them off, and so they attacked them in face and tried to force them back. For a long time, and indeed during the greater part of the day, both armies, although suffering from the battle and thirst and the heat of the sun, held their own; the one endeavouring to thrust their opponents from the high ground, the other determined not to give

way. But the Lacedaemonians now defended themselves with greater ease, because they were not liable to be taken in flank.

36. There was no sign of the end. At length the general of the Messenian contingent came to Cleon and Demosthenes and told them that the army was throwing away its pains, but if they would give him some archers and light-armed troops and let him find a path by which he might get round in the rear of the Lacedaemonians, he thought that he could force the approach. Having obtained his request he started from a point out of sight of the enemy, and making his way wherever the broken ground afforded a footing and where the cliff was so steep that no guards had been set, he and his men with great difficulty got round unseen and suddenly appeared on the summit in their rear, striking panic into the astonished enemy and redoubling the courage of his own friends who were watching for his reappearance. The Lacedaemonians were now assailed on both sides, and to compare a smaller thing to a greater, were in the same case with their own countrymen at Thermopylae. For as they perished when the Persians found a way round by the path, so now the besieged garrison were attacked on both sides, and no longer resisted. The disparity of numbers, and the failure of bodily strength arising from want of food, compelled them to fall back, and the Athenians were at length masters of the approaches.

37. Cleon and Demosthenes saw that if the Lacedaemonians gave way one step more they would be destroyed by the Athenians; so they stopped the engagement and held back their own army, for they wanted, if possible, to bring them alive to Athens. They were in hopes that when they heard the offer of terms their courage might be broken, and that they might be induced by their desperate situation to yield up their arms. Accordingly they proclaimed to them that they might, if they would, surrender at discretion to the Athenians themselves and their arms.

38. Upon hearing the proclamation most of them lowered their shields and waved their hands in token of their willingness to yield. A truce was made, and then Cleon and Demosthenes on the part of the Athenians, and Styphon the son of Pharax on the part of the Lacedaemonians, held a parley. Epitadas, who was the first in command, had been already slain; Hippagretas, who was next in

succession, lay among the slain for dead; and Styphon had taken the place of the two others, having been appointed, as the law prescribed, in case anything should happen to them. He and his companions expressed their wish to communicate with the Lacedaemonians on the mainland as to the course which they should pursue. The Athenians allowed none of them to stir, but themselves invited heralds from the shore; and after two or three communications, the herald who came over last from the body of the army brought back word, 'The Lacedaemonians bid you act as you think best, but you are not to dishonour yourselves.' Whereupon they consulted together, and then gave up themselves and their arms. During that day and the following night the Athenians kept guard over them; on the next day they set up a trophy on the island and made preparations to sail, distributing the prisoners among the trierarchs. The Lacedaemonians sent a herald and conveyed away their own dead. The number of the dead and the prisoners was as follows:—Four hundred and twenty hoplites in all passed over into the island; of these, two hundred and ninety-two were brought to Athens alive, the remainder had perished. Of the survivors the Spartans numbered about a hundred and twenty. But few Athenians fell, for there was no regular engagement.

39. Reckoned from the sea-fight to the final battle in the island, the time during which the blockade lasted was ten weeks and two days. For about three weeks the Lacedaemonians were supplied with food while the Spartan ambassadors were gone to solicit peace, but during the rest of this time they lived on what was brought in by stealth. A store of corn and other provisions was found in the island at the time of the capture; for the commander Epitadas had not served out full rations. The Athenians and Peloponnesians now withdrew their armies from Pylos and returned home. And the mad promise of Cleon was fulfilled; for he did bring back the prisoners within twenty days, as he has said.

40. Nothing which happened during the war caused greater amazement in Hellas; for it was universally imagined that the Lacedaemonians would never give up their arms, either under the pressure of famine or in any other extremity, but would fight to the last and die sword in hand. No one would believe that those who

surrendered were men of the same quality with those who perished. There is a story of a reply made by a captive taken in the island to one of the Athenian allies who had sneeringly asked 'Where were their brave men—all killed?' He answered that 'The spindle' (meaning the arrow) 'would be indeed a valuable weapon if it picked out the brave.' He meant to say that the destruction caused by the arrows and stones was indiscriminate.

41. On the arrival of the captives the Athenians resolved to put them in chains until peace was concluded, but if in the meantime the Lacedaemonians invaded Attica, to bring them out and put them to death. They placed a garrison in Pylos; and the Messenians of Naupactus, regarding the place as their native land (for Pylos is situated in the territory which was once Messenia), sent thither some of themselves, being such troops as were best suited for the service, who ravaged Laconia and did great harm, because they spoke the same language with the inhabitants. The Lacedaemonians had never before experienced this irregular and predatory warfare; and finding the Helots desert, and dreading some serious domestic calamity, they were in great trouble. Although reluctant to expose their condition before the Athenians, they sent envoys to them and endeavoured to recover Pylos and the prisoners. But the Athenians only raised their terms, and at last, after they had made many fruitless journeys, dismissed them. Thus ended the affair of Pylos.

> *The Melian Debate. It has stood as a classic debate between a large imperialist power and a small independent state on the nature and responsibilities of power. It is, furthermore, perhaps the most damning indictment of Athens in the whole of Thucydides' History, for, as he has the Athenians themselves say, the Athenians now consider their enemies to be not only the Spartans but any state which refuses to align itself with Athens. Athens recognizes now only two groups: subjects and enemies. The Melians paid heavily for their attempt at neutrality. Athens put the island under seige; when the island finally capitulated the Athenian as-*

sembly had all the male citizens slaughtered and women and children sold into slavery.

Book V:84–114

84. IN THE ensuing summer, Alcibiades sailed to Argos with twenty ships, and seized any of the Argives who were still suspected to be of the Lacedaemonian faction, to the number of three hundred; and the Athenians deposited them in the subject islands near at hand. The Athenians next made an expedition against the island of Melos with thirty ships of their own, six Chian, and two Lesbian, twelve hundred hoplites and three hundred archers besides twenty mounted archers of their own, and about fifteen hundred hoplites furnished by their allies in the islands. The Melians are colonists of the Lacedaemonians who would not submit to Athens like the other islanders. At first they were neutral and took no part. But when the Athenians tried to coerce them by ravaging their lands, they were driven into open hostilities. The generals, Cleomedes the son of Lycomedes and Tisias the son of Tisimachus, encamped with the Athenian forces on the island. But before they did the country any harm they sent envoys to negotiate with the Melians. Instead of bringing these envoys before the people, the Melians desired them to explain their errand to the magistrates and to the dominant class. They spoke as follows:—

85. 'Since we are not allowed to speak to the people, lest, . . . a multitude should be deceived by seductive and unanswerable arguments which they would hear set forth in a single uninterrupted oration (for we are perfectly aware that this is what you mean in bringing us before a select few), you who are sitting here may as well make assurance yet surer. Let us have no set speeches at all, but do you reply to each several statement of which you disapprove, and criticise it at once. Say first of all how you like this mode of proceeding.'

86. The Melian representatives answered:—'The quiet interchange of explanations is a reasonable thing, and we do not object to that. But your warlike movements, which are present not only to our fears but to our eyes, seem to belie your words. We see that,

although you may reason with us, you mean to be our judges; and that at the end of the discussion, if the justice of our cause prevail and we therefore refuse to yield, we may expect war; if we are convinced by you, slavery.'

87. *Ath.* 'Nay, but if you are only going to argue from fancies about the future, or if you meet us with any other purpose than that of looking your circumstances in the face and saving your city, we have done; but if this is your intention we will proceed.'

88. *Mel.* 'It is an excusable and natural thing that men in our position should neglect no argument and no view which may avail. But we admit that this conference has met to consider the question of our preservation; and therefore let the argument proceed in the manner which you propose.'

89. *Ath.* 'Well, then, we Athenians will use no fine words; we will not go out of our way to prove at length that we have a right to rule, because we overthrew the Persians; or that we attack you now because we are suffering any injury at your hands. We should not convince you if we did; nor must you expect to convince us by arguing that, although a colony of the Lacedaemonians, you have taken no part in their expeditions, or that you have never done us any wrong. But you and we should say what we really think, and aim only at what is possible, for we both alike know that into the discussion of human affairs the question of justice only enters where there is equal power to enforce it, and that the powerful exact what they can, and the weak grant what they must.'

90. *Mel.* 'Well, then, since you set aside justice and invite us to speak of expediency, in our judgment it is certainly expedient that you should respect a principle which is for the common good; that to every man when in peril a reasonable claim should be accounted a claim of right, and that any plea which he is disposed to urge, even if failing of the point a little, should help his cause. Your interest in this principle is quite as great as ours, inasmuch as you, if you fall, will incur the heaviest vengeance, and will be the most terrible example to mankind.'

91. *Ath.* 'The fall of our empire, if it should fall, is not an event to which we look forward with dismay; for ruling states such as Lacedaemon are not cruel to their vanquished enemies. With the

Lacedaemonians, however, we are not now contending; the real danger is from our many subject states, who may of their own motion rise up and overcome their masters. But this is a danger which you may leave to us. And we will now endeavour to show that we have come in the interests of our empire, and that in what we are about to say we are only seeking the preservation of your city. For we want to make you ours with the least trouble to ourselves, and it is for the interests of us both that you should not be destroyed.'

92. *Mel.* 'It may be your interest to be our masters, but how can it be ours to be your slaves?'

93. *Ath.* 'To you the gain will be that by submission you will avert the worst; and we shall be all the richer for your preservation.'

94. *Mel.* "But must we be your enemies? Will you not receive us as friends if we are neutral and remain at peace with you?'

95. *Ath.* 'No, your enmity is not half so mischievous to us as your friendship; for the one is in the eyes of our subjects an argument of our power, the other of our weakness.'

96. *Mel.* 'But are your subjects really unable to distinguish between states in which you have no concern, and those which are chiefly your own colonies, and in some cases have revolted and been subdued by you?'

97. *Ath.* 'Why, they do not doubt that both of them have a good deal to say for themselves on the score of justice, but they think that states like yours are left free because they are able to defend themselves, and that we do not attack them because we dare not. So that your subjection will give us an increase of security, as well as an extension of empire. For we are masters of the sea, and you who are islanders, and insignificant islanders too, must not be allowed to escape us.'

98. *Mel.* 'But do you not recognise another danger? For, once more, since you drive us from the plea of justice and press upon us your doctrine of expediency, we must show you what is for our interest, and, if it be for yours also, may hope to convince you:— Will you not be making enemies of all who are now neutrals? When they see how you are treating us they will expect you some day to turn against them; and if so, are you not strengthening the

enemies whom you already have, and bringing upon you others who, if they could help, would never dream of being your enemies at all?'

99. *Ath.* 'We do not consider our really dangerous enemies to be any of the peoples inhabiting the mainland who, secure in their freedom, may defer indefinitely any measures of precaution which they take against us, but islanders who, like you, happen to be under no control, and all who may be already irritated by the necessity of submission to our empire—these are our real enemies, for they are the most reckless and most likely to bring themselves as well as us into a danger which they cannot but foresee.'

100. *Mel.* 'Surely then, if you and your subjects will brave all this risk, you to preserve your empire and they to be quit of it, how base and cowardly would it be in us, who retain our freedom, not to do and suffer anything rather than be your slaves.'

101. *Ath.* 'Not so, if you calmly reflect: for you are not fighting against equals to whom you cannot yield without disgrace, but you are taking counsel whether or no you shall resist an overwhelming force. The question is not one of honour but of prudence.'

102. *Mel.* 'But we know that the fortune of war is sometimes impartial, and not always on the side of numbers. If we yield now, all is over; but if we fight, there is yet a hope that we may stand upright.'

103. *Ath.* 'Hope is a good comforter in the hour of danger, and when men have something else to depend upon, although hurtful, she is not ruinous. But when her spend-thrift nature has induced them to stake their all, they see her as she is in the moment of their fall, and not till then. While the knowledge of her might enable them to be ware of her, she never fails. You are weak and a single turn of the scale might be your ruin. Do not . . . be thus deluded; avoid the error of which so many are guilty, who, although they might still be saved if they would take the natural means, when visible grounds of confidence forsake them, have recourse to the invisible, to prophecies and oracles and the like, which ruin men by the hopes which they inspire in them.'

104. *Mel.* 'We know only too well how hard the struggle must be against your power, and against fortune, if she does not mean to

be impartial. Nevertheless we do not despair of fortune; for we hope to stand as high as you in the favour of heaven, because we are righteous and you against whom we contend are unrighteous; and we are satisfied that our deficiency in power will be compensated by the aid of our allies the Lacedaemonians; they cannot refuse to help us, if only because we are their kinsmen, and for the sake of their own honour. And therefore our confidence is not so utterly blind as you suppose.'

105. *Ath.* 'As for the Gods, we expect to have quite as much of their favour as you: for we are not doing or claiming anything which goes beyond common opinion about divine or men's desires about human things. For of the Gods we believe, and of men we know, that by a law of their nature wherever they can rule they will. This law was not made by us, and we are not the first who have acted upon it; we did but inherit it, and shall bequeath it to all time, and we know that you and all mankind, if you were as strong as we are, would do as we do. So much for the Gods; we have told you why we expect to stand as high in their good opinion as you. And then as to the Lacedaemonians—when you imagine that out of very shame they will assist you, we admire the innocence of your idea, but we do not envy you the folly of it. The Lacedaemonians are exceedingly virtuous among themselves, and according to their national standard of morality. But, in respect of their dealings with others, although many things might be said, they can be described in few words—of all men whom we know they are the most notorious for identifying what is pleasant with what is honourable, and what is expedient with what is just. But how inconsistent is such a character with your present blind hope of deliverance!'

106. *Mel.* 'That is the very reason why we trust them; they will look to their interest, and therefore will not be willing to betray the Melians, who are their own colonists, lest they should be distrusted by their friends in Hellas and play into the hands of their enemies.'

107. *Ath.* 'But do you not see that the path of expediency is safe, whereas justice and honour involve danger in practice, and such dangers the Lacedaemonians seldom care to face?'

108. *Mel.* 'On the other hand, we think that whatever perils there may be, they will be ready to face them for our sakes, and will

consider danger less dangerous where we are concerned. For if they need our aid we are close at hand, and they can better trust our loyal feeling because we are their kinsmen.'

109. *Ath.* 'Yes, but what encourages men who are invited to join in a conflict is clearly not the good-will of those who summon them to their side, but a decided superiority in real power. To this no men look more keenly than the Lacedaemonians; so little confidence have they in their own resources, that they only attack their neighbours when they have numerous allies, and therefore they are not likely to find their way by themselves to an island, when we are masters of the sea.'

110. *Mel.* 'But they may send their allies: the Cretan sea is a large place; and the masters of the sea will have more difficulty in overtaking vessels which want to escape than the pursued in escaping. If the attempt should fail they may invade Attica itself, and find their way to allies of yours whom Brasidas did not reach: and then you will have to fight, not for the conquest of a land in which you have no concern, but nearer home, for the preservation of your confederacy and of your own territory.'

111. *Ath.* 'Help may come from Lacedaemon to you as it has come to others, and should you ever have actual experience of it, then you will know that never once have the Athenians retired from a siege through fear of a foe elsewhere. You told us that the safety of your city would be your first care, but we remark that, in this long discussion, not a word has been uttered by you which would give a reasonable man expectation of deliverance. Your strongest grounds are hopes deferred, and what power you have is not to be compared with that which is already arrayed against you. Unless after we have withdrawn you mean to come, as even now you may, to a wiser conclusion, you are showing a great want of sense. For surely you cannot dream of flying to that false sense of honour which has been the ruin of so many when danger and dishonour were staring them in the face. Many men with their eyes still open to the consequences have found the word "honour" too much for them, and have suffered a mere name to lure them on, until it has drawn down upon them real and irretrievable calamities; through their own folly they have incurred a worse dishonour

than fortune would have inflicted upon them. If you are wise you will not run this risk; you ought to see that there can be no disgrace in yielding to a great city which invites you to become her ally on reasonable terms, keeping your own land, and merely paying tribute; and that you will certainly gain no honour if, having to choose between two alternatives, safety and war, you obstinately prefer the worse. To maintain our rights against equals, to be politic with superiors, and to be moderate towards inferiors is the path of safety. Reflect once more when we have withdrawn, and say to yourselves over and over again that you are deliberating about your one and only country, which may be saved or may be destroyed by a single decision.'

112. The Athenians left the conference: the Melians, after consulting among themselves, resolved to persevere in their refusal, and made answer as follows:—'Men of Athens, our resolution is unchanged; and we will not in a moment surrender that liberty which our city, founded seven hundred years ago, still enjoys; we will trust to the good fortune which, by the favour of the Gods, has hitherto preserved us, and for human help to the Lacedaemonians, and endeavour to save ourselves. We are ready however to be your friends, and the enemies neither of you nor of the Lacedaemonians, and we ask you to leave our country when you have made such a peace as may appear to be in the interest of both parties.'

113. Such was the answer of the Melians; the Athenians, as they quitted the conference, spoke as follows:—'Well, we must say, judging from the decision at which you have arrived, that you are the only men who deem the future to be more certain than the present, and regard things unseen as already realised in your fond anticipation, and that the more you cast yourselves upon the Lacedaemonians and fortune and hope, and trust them, the more complete will be your ruin.'

114. The Athenian envoys returned to the army; and the generals, when they found that the Melians would not yield, immediately commenced hostilities. They surrounded the town of Melos with a wall, dividing the work among the several contingents. They then left troops of their own and of their allies to keep guard both by land and by sea, and retired with the greater part of their army; the remainder carried on the blockade.

Roman patrician with ancestral masks

POLYBIUS · HISTORIES*

―――――――――――――――――――――――――――――――――――

Book I: 1–5, 14

1. HAD THE PRAISE of History been passed over by former Chroniclers it would perhaps have been incumbent upon me to urge the choice and special study of records of this sort, as the readiest means men can have of correcting their knowledge of the past. But my predecessors have not been sparing in this respect. They have all begun and ended, so to speak, by enlarging on this theme: asserting again and again that the study of History is in the truest sense an education, and a training for political life; and that the most instructive, or rather the only, method of learning to bear with dignity the vicissitudes of fortune is to recall the catastrophes of others. It is evident, therefore, that no one need think it his duty to repeat what has been said by many, and said well. Least of all myself: for the surprising nature of the events which I have undertaken to relate is in itself sufficient to challenge and stimulate the attention of every one, old or young, to the study of my work. Can any one be so indifferent or idle as not to care to know by what means, and under what kind of polity, almost the whole inhabited world was conquered and brought under the dominion of the single city of Rome, and that too within a period of not quite fifty-three years? [219–167 B.C.] Or who again can be so completely absorbed in other subjects of contemplation or study, as to think any

―――――

* The selections made from Polybius have been chosen for their aptness in demonstrating Polybius' historiographic standards, his interest in political analysis, his pragmatic view of history, and his narrative skill. The translation is by Evelyn S. Shuckburgh, originally published in 1889, issued in a new edition *The Histories of Polybius,* introduction by F. W. Walbank (Bloomington: Indiana University Press, 1962), 2 vols.

of them superior in importance to the accurate understanding of an event for which the past affords no precedent.

2. We shall best show how marvellous and vast our subject is by comparing the most famous Empires which preceded, and which have been the favourite themes of historians, and measuring them with the superior greatness of Rome. There are but three that deserve even to be so compared and measured: and they are these. The Persians for a certain length of time were possessed of a great empire and dominion. But every time they ventured beyond the limits of Asia, they found not only their empire, but their own existence also in danger. The Lacedaemonians, after contending for supremacy in Greece for many generations, when they did get it, held it without dispute for barely twelve years. [Sparta. 405–394 B.C.] The Macedonians obtained dominion in Europe from the lands bordering on the Adriatic to the Danube,—which after all is but a small fraction of this continent,—and, by the destruction of the Persian Empire, they afterwards added to that the dominion of Asia. And yet, though they had the credit of having made themselves masters of a larger number of countries and states than any people had ever done, they still left the greater half of the inhabited world in the hands of others. They never so much as thought of attempting Sicily, Sardinia, or Libya: and as to Europe, to speak the plain truth, they never even knew of the most warlike tribes of the West. The Roman conquest, on the other hand, was not partial. Nearly the whole inhabited world was reduced by them to obedience: and they left behind them an empire not to be paralleled in the past or rivalled in the future. Students will gain from my narrative a clearer view of the whole story, and of the numerous and important advantages which such exact record of events offers.

3. My History begins in the 140th Olympiad [220–217 B.C.]. The events from which it starts are these. In Greece, what is called the Social war: the first waged by Philip, son of Demetrius and father of Perseus, in league with the Achaeans against the Aetolians. In Asia, the war for the possession of Coele-Syria which Antiochus and Ptolemy Philopator carried on against each other. In Italy, Libya, and their neighbourhood, the conflict between Rome

and Carthage, generally called the Hannibalian war. My work thus begins where that of Aratus of Sicyon leaves off. Now up to this time the world's history had been, so to speak, a series of disconnected transactions, as widely separated in their origin and results as in their localities. But from this time forth History becomes a connected whole: the affairs of Italy and Libya are involved with those of Asia and Greece, and the tendency of all is to unity. This is why I have fixed upon this era as the starting-point of my work. For it was their victory over the Carthaginians in this war, and their conviction that thereby the most difficult and most essential step towards universal empire had been taken, which encouraged the Romans for the first time to stretch out their hands upon the rest, and to cross with an army into Greece and Asia.

Now, had the states that were rivals for universal empire been familiarly known to us, no reference perhaps to their previous history would have been necessary, to show the purpose and the forces with which they approached an undertaking of this nature and magnitude. But the fact is that the majority of the Greeks have no knowledge of the previous constitution, power, or achievements either of Rome or Carthage. I therefore concluded that it was necessary to prefix this and the next book to my History. I was anxious that no one, when fairly embarked upon my actual narrative, should feel at a loss, and have to ask what were the designs entertained by the Romans, or the forces and means at their disposal, that they entered upon those undertakings, which did in fact lead to their becoming masters of land and sea everywhere in our part of the world. I wished, on the contrary, that these books of mine, and the prefatory sketch which they contained, might make it clear that the resources they started with justified their original idea, and sufficiently explained their final success in grasping universal empire and dominion.

4. There is this analogy between the plan of my History and the marvellous spirit of the age with which I have to deal. Just as Fortune made almost all the affairs of the world incline in one direction, and forced them to converge upon one and the same point; so it is my task as an historian to put before my readers a

compendious view of the part played by Fortune in bringing about the general catastrophe.* It was this peculiarity which originally challenged my attention, and determined me on undertaking this work. And combined with this was the fact that no writer of our time has undertaken a general history. Had any one done so my ambition in this direction would have been much diminished. But, in point of fact, I notice that by far the greater number of historians concern themselves with isolated wars and the incidents that accompany them: while as to a general and comprehensive scheme of events, their date, origin, and catastrophe, no one as far as I know has undertaken to examine it. I thought it, therefore, distinctly my duty neither to pass by myself, nor allow any one else to pass by, without full study, a characteristic specimen of the dealings of Fortune at once brilliant and instructive in the highest degree. For fruitful as Fortune is in change, and constantly as she is producing dramas in the life of men, yet never assuredly before this did she work such a marvel, or act such a drama, as that which we have witnessed. And of this we cannot obtain a comprehensive view from writers of mere episodes. It would be as absurd to expect to do so as for a man to imagine that he has learnt the shape of the whole world, its entire arrangement and order, because he has visited one after the other the most famous cities in it; or perhaps merely examined them in separate pictures. That would be indeed absurd: and it has always seemed to me that men, who are persuaded that they get a competent view of universal from episodical history, are very like persons who should see the limbs of some body, which had once been living and beautiful, scattered and remote; and should imagine that to be quite as good as actually beholding the activity and beauty of the living creature itself. But if some one could there and then reconstruct the animal once more, in the perfection of its beauty and the charm of its vitality, and could display it to the same people, they would beyond doubt confess that they had been far from conceiving the truth, and had been little better than dreamers. For indeed some idea of a whole may be got from a part, but an accurate knowledge and clear comprehension cannot. Wherefore we must conclude that episodical history con-

* "The general catastrophe" should read "her general purpose"—tr.

tributes exceedingly little to the familiar knowledge and secure grasp of universal history. While it is only by the combination and comparison of the separate parts of the whole,—by observing their likeness and their difference,—that a man can attain his object: can obtain a view at once clear and complete; and thus secure both the profit and the delight of History.

5. I shall adopt as the starting-point of this book the first occasion on which the Romans crossed the sea from Italy [264–261 B.C.]. This is just where the History of Timaeus left off; and it falls in the 129th Olympiad. I shall accordingly have to describe what the state of their affairs in Italy was, how long that settlement had lasted, and on what resources they reckoned, when they resolved to invade Sicily. For this was the first place outside Italy in which they set foot. The precise cause of their thus crossing I must state without comment; for if I let one cause lead me back to another, my point of departure will always elude my grasp, and I shall never arrive at the view of my subject which I wish to present. As to dates, then, I must fix on some era agreed upon and recognised by all: and as to events, one that admits of distinctly separate treatment; even though I may be obliged to go back some short way in point of time, and take a summary review of the intermediate transactions. For if the facts with which one starts are unknown, or even open to controversy, all that comes after will fail of approval and belief. But opinion being once formed on that point, and a general assent obtained, all the succeeding narrative becomes intelligible.

14. But it was not these considerations only which induced me to undertake the history of this war. I was influenced quite as much by the fact that Philinus and Fabius, who have the reputation of writing with the most complete knowledge about it, have given us an inadequate representation of the truth. Now, judging from their lives and principles, I do not suppose that these writers have intentionally stated what was false; but I think that they are much in the same state of mind as men in love. Partisanship and complete prepossession made Philinus think that all the actions of the Carthaginians were characterised by wisdom, honour, and courage: those of the Romans by the reverse. Fabius thought the exact oppo-

site. Now in other relations of life one would hesitate to exclude such warmth of sentiment: for a good man ought to be loyal to his friends and patriotic to his country; ought to be at one with his friends in their hatreds and likings. But directly a man assumes the moral attitude of an historian he ought to forget all considerations of that kind. There will be many occasions on which he will be bound to speak well of his enemies, and even to praise them in the highest terms if the facts demand it: and on the other hand many occasions on which it will be his duty to criticise and denounce his own side, however dear to him, if their errors of conduct suggest that course. For as a living creature is rendered wholly useless if deprived of its eyes, so if you take truth from History what is left is but an idle unprofitable tale. Therefore, one must not shrink either from blaming one's friends or praising one's enemies; nor be afraid of finding fault with and commending the same persons at different times. For it is impossible that men engaged in public affairs should always be right, and unlikely that they should always be wrong. Holding ourselves, therefore, entirely aloof from the actors, we must as historians make statements and pronounce judgment in accordance with the actions themselves.

Polybius' survey and analysis of the Greek and Roman constitutions
Book VI: 1–18

1. I AM aware that some will be at a loss to account for my interrupting the course of my narrative for the sake of entering upon the following disquisition on the Roman constitution. But I think that I have already in many passages made it fully evident that this particular branch of my work was one of the necessities imposed on me by the nature of my original design; and I pointed this out with special clearness in the preface which explained the scope of my history. I there stated that the feature of my work which was at once the best in itself, and the most instructive to the students of it, was that it would enable them to know and fully realise in what manner, and under what kind of constitution, it came about that nearly the whole world fell under the power of Rome in somewhat

less than fifty-three years,—an event certainly without precedent. This being my settled purpose, I could see no more fitting period than the present for making a pause, and examining the truth of the remarks about to be made on this constitution. In private life if you wish to satisfy yourself as to the badness or goodness of particular persons, you would not, if you wish to get a genuine test, examine their conduct at a time of uneventful repose, but in the hour of brilliant success or conspicuous reverse. For the true test of a perfect man is the power of bearing with spirit and dignity violent changes of fortune. An examination of a constitution should be conducted in the same way: and therefore being unable to find in our day a more rapid or more signal change than that which has happened to Rome, I reserved my disquisition on its constitution for this place. . . .

What is really educational and beneficial to students of history is the clear view of the causes of events, and the consequent power of choosing the better policy in a particular case. Now in every practical undertaking by a state we must regard as the most powerful agent for success or failure the form of its constitution; for from this as from a fountain-head all conceptions and plans of action not only proceed, but attain their consummation. . . .

3. Of the Greek republics, which have again and again risen to greatness and fallen into insignificance, it is not difficult to speak, whether we recount their past history or venture an opinion on their future. For to report what is already known is an easy task, nor is it hard to guess what is to come from our knowledge of what has been. But in regard to the Romans it is neither an easy matter to describe their present state, owing to the complexity of their constitution; nor to speak with confidence of their future, from our inadequate acquaintance with their peculiar institutions in the past whether affecting their public or their private life. It will require then no ordinary attention and study to get a clear and comprehensive conception of the distinctive features of this constitution.

Now, it is undoubtedly the case that most of those who profess to give us authoritative instruction on this subject distinguish three kinds of constitutions, which they designate *kingship, aristocracy, democracy*. But in my opinion the question might fairly be put to them, whether they name these as being the *only* ones, or as the *best*. In either case I think they are wrong. For it is plain that we must regard as the *best* constitution that which partakes of all these three elements. And this is no mere assertion, but has been proved by the example of Lycurgus, who was the first to construct a constitution—that of Sparta—on this principle. Nor can we admit that these are the *only* forms: for we have had before now examples of absolute and tyrannical forms of government, which, while differing as widely as possible from kingship, yet appear to have some points of resemblance to it; on which account all absolute rulers falsely assume and use, as far as they can, the title of king. Again there have been many instances of oligarchical governments having in appearance some analogy to aristocracies, which are, if I may say so, as different from them as it is possible to be. The same also holds good about democracy.

4. I will illustrate the truth of what I say. We cannot hold every absolute government to be a kingship, but only that which is accepted voluntarily, and is directed by an appeal to reason rather than to fear and force. Nor again is every oligarchy to be regarded as an aristocracy; the latter exists only where the power is wielded by the justest and wisest men selected on their merits. Similarly, it is not enough to constitute a democracy that the whole crowd of citizens should have the right to do whatever they wish or propose. But where reverence to the gods, succour of parents, respect to elders, obedience to laws, are traditional and habitual, in such communities, if the will of the majority prevail, we may speak of the form of government as a democracy. So then we enumerate six forms of government,—the three commonly spoken of which I have just mentioned, and three more allied forms, I mean *despotism, oligarchy* and *mob-rule*. The first of these arises without artificial aid and in the natural order of events. Next to this, and produced from it by the aid of art and adjustment, comes *kingship;* which degenerating into the evil form allied to it, by which I mean *tyranny*, both are once more destroyed and *aristocracy* produced. Again the latter being in the course of nature perverted to *oligarchy*, and the people passionately avenging the unjust acts of their rulers, *democracy* comes into existence; which again by its

violence and contempt of law becomes sheer *mob-rule*. No clearer proof of the truth of what I say could be obtained than by a careful observation of the natural origin, genesis, and decadence of these several forms of government. For it is only by seeing distinctly how each of them is produced that a distinct view can also be obtained of its growth, zenith, and decadence, and the time, circumstance, and place in which each of these may be expected to recur. This method I have assumed to be especially applicable to the Roman constitution, because its origin and growth have from the first followed natural causes.

5. Now the natural laws which regulate the merging of one form of government into another are perhaps discussed with greater accuracy by Plato and some other philosophers. But their treatment, from its intricacy and exhaustiveness, is only within the capacity of a few. I will therefore endeavour to give a summary of the subject, just so far as I suppose it to fall within the scope of a practical history and the intelligence of ordinary people. For if my exposition appear in any way inadequate, owing to the general terms in which it is expressed, the details contained in what is immediately to follow will amply atone for what is left for the present unsolved.

What is the origin then of a constitution, and whence is it produced? Suppose that from floods, pestilences, failure of crops, or some such causes the race of man is reduced almost to extinction. Such things we are told have happened, and it is reasonable to think will happen again. Suppose accordingly all knowledge of social habits and arts to have been lost. Suppose that from the survivors, as from seeds, the race of man to have again multiplied. In that case I presume they would, like the animals, herd together; for it is but reasonable to suppose that bodily weakness would induce them to seek those of their own kind to herd with. And in that case too, as with the animals, he who was superior to the rest in strength of body or courage of soul would lead and rule them. For what we see happen in the case of animals that are without the faculty of reason, such as bulls, goats, and cocks,—among whom there can be no dispute that the strongest take the lead,—that we must regard as in the truest sense the teaching of nature. Originally then it is probably that the condition of life among men was this,—herding together like animals and following the strongest and bravest as leaders. The limit of this authority would be physical strength, and the name we should give it would be despotism. But as soon as the idea of family ties and social relation has arisen amongst such agglomerations of men, then is born also the idea of kingship, and then for the first time mankind conceives the notion of goodness and justice and their reverse.

6. The way in which such conceptions originate and come into existence is this. The intercourse of the sexes is an instinct of nature, and the result is the birth of children. Now, if any one of these children who have been brought up, when arrived at maturity, is ungrateful and makes no return to those by whom he was nurtured, but on the contrary presumes to injure them by word and deed, it is plain that he will probably offend and annoy such as are present, and have seen the care and trouble bestowed by the parents on the nurture and bringing up of their children. For seeing that men differ from the other animals in being the only creatures possessed of reasoning powers, it is clear that such a difference of conduct is not likely to escape their observation; but that they will remark it when it occurs, and express their displeasure on the spot: because they will have an eye to the future, and will reason on the likelihood of the same occurring to each of themselves. Again, if a man has been rescued or helped in an hour of danger, and, instead of showing gratitude to his preserver, seeks to do him harm, it is clearly probable that the rest will be displeased and offended with him, when they know it: sympathising with their neighbour and imagining themselves in his case. Hence arises a notion in every breast of the meaning and theory of duty, which is in fact the beginning and end of justice. Similarly, again, when any one man stands out as the champion of all in a time of danger, and braves with firm courage the onslaught of the most powerful wild beasts, it is probable that such a man would meet with marks of favour and pre-eminence from the common people; while he who acted in a contrary way would fall under their contempt and dislike. From this, once more, it is reasonable to suppose that there would arise in the minds of the multitude a theory of the disgraceful and the

honourable, and of the difference between them; and that one should be sought and imitated for its advantages, the other shunned. When, therefore, the leading and most powerful man among his people ever encourages such persons in accordance with the popular sentiment, and thereby assumes in the eyes of his subject the appearance of being the distributor to each man according to his deserts, they no longer obey him and support his rule from fear of violence, but rather from conviction of its utility, however old he may be, rallying round him with one heart and soul, and fighting against all who form designs against his government. In this way he becomes a *king* instead of a *despot* by imperceptible degrees, reason having ousted brute courage and bodily strength from this supremacy.

7. This then is the natural process of formation among mankind of the notion of goodness and justice, and their opposites; and this is the origin and genesis of genuine kingship: for people do not only keep up the government of such men personally, but for their descendants also for many generations; from the conviction that those who are born from and educated by men of this kind will have principles also like theirs. But if they subsequently become displeased with their descendants, they do not any longer decide their choice of rulers and kings by their physical strength or brute courage; but by the differences of their intellectual and reasoning faculties, from practical experience of the decisive importance of such a distinction. In old times, then, those who were once thus selected, and obtained this office, grew old in their royal functions, making magnificent strongholds and surrounding them with walls and extending their frontiers, partly for the security of their subjects, and partly to provide them with abundance of the necessaries of life; and while engaged in these works they were exempt from all vituperation or jealousy; because they did not make their distinctive dress, food, or drink, at all conspicuous, but lived very much like the rest, and joined in the everyday employments of the common people. But when their royal power became hereditary in their family, and they found every necessary for security ready to their hands, as well as more than was necessary for their personal support, then they gave the rein to their appetites; imagined that rulers

must needs wear different clothes from those of subjects; have different and elaborate luxuries of the table; and must even seek sensual indulgence, however unlawful the source, without fear of denial. These things having given rise in the one case to jealousy and offence, in the other to outburst of hatred and passionate resentment, the kingship became a tyranny: the first step in disintegration was taken; and plots began to be formed against the government, which did not now proceed from the worst men but from the noblest, most high-minded, and most courageous, because these are the men who can least submit to the tyrannical acts of their rulers.

8. But as soon as the people got leaders, they cooperated with them against the dynasty for the reasons I have mentioned; and then *kingship* and *despotism* were alike entirely abolished, and *aristocracy* once more began to revive and start afresh. For in their immediate gratitude to those who had deposed the despots, the people employed them as leaders, and entrusted their interests to them; who, looking upon this charge at first as a great privilege, made the public advantage their chief concern, and conducted all kinds of business, public or private, with diligence and caution. But when the sons of these men received the same position of authority from their fathers,—having had no experience of misfortunes, and none at all of civil equality and freedom of speech, but having been bred up from the first under the shadow of their fathers' authority and lofty position,—some of them gave themselves up with passion to avarice and unscrupulous love of money, others to drinking and the boundless debaucheries which accompanies it, and others to the violation of women or the forcible appropriation of boys; and so they turned an *aristocracy* into an *oligarchy*. But it was not long before they roused in the minds of the people the same feelings as before; and their fall therefore was very like the disaster which befel the tyrants.

9. For no sooner had the knowledge of the jealousy and hatred existing in the citizens against them emboldened some one to oppose the government by word or deed, than he was sure to find the whole people ready and prepared to take his side. Having then got rid of these rulers by assassination or exile, they do not venture to

set up a king again, being still in terror of the injustice to which this led before; nor dare they intrust the common interests again to more than one, considering the recent example of their misconduct: and therefore, as the only sound hope left them is that which depends upon themselves, they are driven to take refuge in that; and so changed the constitution from an oligarchy to a *democracy,* and took upon themselves the superintendence and charge of the state. And as long as any survive who have had experience of oligarchical supremacy and domination, they regard their present constitution as a blessing, and hold equality and freedom as of the utmost value. But as soon as a new generation has arisen, and the democracy has descended to their children's children, long association weakens their value for equality and freedom, and some seek to become more powerful than the ordinary citizen; and the most liable to this temptation are the rich. So when they begin to be fond of office, and find themselves unable to obtain it by their own unassisted efforts and their own merits, they ruin their estates, while enticing and corrupting the common people in every possible way. By which means when, in their senseless mania for reputation, they have made the populace ready and greedy to receive bribes, the virtue of democracy is destroyed, and it is transformed into a government of violence and the strong hand. For the mob, habituated to feed at the expense of others, and to have its hopes of a livelihood in the property of its neighbours, as soon as it has got a leader sufficiently ambitious and daring, being excluded by poverty from the sweets of civil honours, produces a reign of mere violence. Then come tumultuous assemblies, massacres, banishments, redivisions of land; until, after losing all trace of civilisation, it has once more found a master and a despot.

This is the regular cycle of constitutional revolutions, and the natural order in which constitutions change, are transformed, and return again to their original stage. If a man have a clear grasp of these principles he may perhaps make a mistake as to the dates at which this or that will happen to a particular constitution; but he will rarely be entirely mistaken as to the stage of growth or decay at which it has arrived, or as to the point at which it will undergo some revolutionary change. However, it is in the case of the Roman constitution that this method of inquiry will most fully teach us its formation, its growth, and zenith, as well as the changes awaiting it in the future; for this, if any constitution ever did, owed, as I said just now, its original foundation and growth to natural causes, and to natural causes will owe its decay. My subsequent narrative will be the best illustration of what I say.

10. For the present I will make a brief reference to the legislation of Lycurgus: for such a discussion is not at all alien to my subject. That statesman was fully aware that all those changes which I have enumerated come about by an undeviating law of nature; and reflected that every form of government that was unmixed, and rested on one species of power, was unstable; because it was swiftly perverted into that particular form of evil peculiar to it and inherent in its nature. For just as rust is the natural dissolvent of iron, wood-worms and grubs to timber, by which they are destroyed without any external injury, but by that which is engendered in themselves; so in each constitution there is naturally engendered a particular vice inseparable from it: in kingship it is absolutism; in aristocracy it is oligarchy; in democracy lawless ferocity and violence; and to these vicious states all these forms of government are, as I have lately shown, inevitably transformed. Lycurgus, I say, saw all this, and accordingly combined together all the excellences and distinctive features of the best constitutions, that no part should become unduly predominant, and be perverted into its kindred vice; and that, each power being checked by the others, no one part should turn the scale or decisively out-balance the others; but that, by being accurately adjusted and in exact equilibrium, the whole might remain long steady like a ship sailing close to the wind. The royal power was prevented from growing insolent by fear of the people, which had also assigned to it an adequate share in the constitution. The people in their turn were restrained from a bold contempt of the kings by fear of the Gerusia: the members of which, being selected on grounds of merit, were certain to throw their influence on the side of justice in every question that arose; and thus the party placed at a disadvantage by its conservative tendency was always strengthened and supported

by the weight and influence of the Gerusia. The result of this combination has been that the Lacedaemonians retained their freedom for the longest period of any people with which we are acquainted.

Lycurgus however established his constitution without the discipline of adversity, because he was able to foresee by the light of reason the course which events naturally take and the source from which they come. But though the Romans have arrived at the same result in framing their commonwealth, they have not done so by means of abstract reasoning, but through many struggles and difficulties, and by continually adopting reforms from knowledge gained in disaster. The result has been a constitution like that of Lycurgus, and the best of any existing in my time. . . .

11. I have given an account of the constitution of Lycurgus, I will now endeavour to describe that of Rome at the period of their disastrous defeat at Cannae.

I am fully conscious that to those who actually live under this constitution I shall appear to give an inadequate account of it by the omission of certain details. Knowing accurately every portion of it from personal experience, and from having been bred up in its customs and laws from childhood, they will not be struck so much by the accuracy of the description, as annoyed by its omissions; nor will they believe that the historian has purposely omitted unimportant distinctions, but will attribute his silence upon the origin of existing institutions or other important facts to ignorance. What is told they depreciate as insignificant or beside the purpose; what is omitted they desiderate as vital to the question: their object being to appear to know more than the writers. But a good critic should not judge a writer by what he leaves unsaid, but from what he says: if he detects mis-statement in the latter, he may then feel certain that ignorance accounts of the former; but if what he says is accurate, his omissions ought to be attributed to deliberate judgment and not to ignorance. So much for those whose criticisms are prompted by personal ambition rather than by justice. . . .

Another requisite for obtaining a judicious approval for an historical disquisition, is that it should be germane to the matter in hand; if this is not observed, though its style may be excellent and its matter irreproachable, it will seem out of place and disgust rather than please. . . .

As for the Roman constitution, it had three elements, each of them possessing sovereign powers; and their respective share of power in the whole state had been regulated with such a scrupulous regard to equality and equilibrium, that no one could say for certain, not even a native, whether the constitution as a whole were an aristocracy or democracy or despotism. And no wonder: for if we confine our observation to the power of the Consuls we should be inclined to regard it as despotic; if on that of the Senate, as aristocratic; and if finally one looks at the power possessed by the people it would seem a clear case of a democracy. What the exact powers of these several parts were, and still, with slight modifications, are, I will now state.

12. The Consuls, before leading out the legions, remain in Rome and are supreme masters of the administration. All other magistrates, except the Tribunes, are under them and take their orders. They introduce foreign ambassadors to the Senate; bring matters requiring deliberation before it; and see to the execution of its decrees. If, again, there are any matters of state which require the authorisation of the people, it is their business to see to them, to summon the popular meetings, to bring the proposals before them, and to carry out the decrees of the majority. In the preparations for war also, and in a word in the entire administration of a campaign, they have all but absolute power. It is competent to them to impose on the allies such levies as they think good, to appoint the Military Tribunes, to make up the roll for soldiers and select those that are suitable. Besides they have absolute power of inflicting punishment on all who are under their command while on active service: and they have authority to expend as much of the public money as they choose, being accompanied by a quaestor who is entirely at their orders. A survey of these powers would in fact justify our describing the constitution as despotic,—a clear case of royal government. Nor will it affect the truth of my description, if any of the institutions I have described are changed in our time, or in that of our posterity: and the same remarks apply to what follows.

13. The Senate has first of all the control of the treasury, and regulates the receipts and disbursements alike. For the Quaestors cannot issue any public money for the various departments of the state without a decree of the Senate, except for the service of the Consuls. The Senate controls also what is by far the largest and most important expenditure, that, namely, which is made by the censors every *lustrum* for the repair or construction of public buildings; this money cannot be obtained by the censors except by the grant of the Senate. Similarly all crimes committed in Italy requiring a public investigation, such as treason, conspiracy, poisoning, or wilful murder, are in the hands of the Senate. Besides, if any individual or state among the Italian allies requires a controversy to be settled, a penalty to be assessed, help or protection to be afforded,—all this is the province of the Senate. Or again, outside Italy, if it is necessary to send an embassy to reconcile warring communities, or to remind them of their duty, or sometimes to impose requisitions upon them, or to receive their submission, or finally to proclaim war against them,—this too is the business of the Senate. In like manner the reception to be given to foreign ambassadors in Rome, and the answers to be returned to them, are decided by the Senate. With such business the people have nothing to do. Consequently, if one were staying at Rome when the consuls were not in town, one would imagine the constitution to be a complete aristocracy: and this has been the idea entertained by many Greeks, and by many kings as well, from the fact that nearly all the business they had with Rome was settled by the Senate.

14. After this one would naturally be inclined to ask what part is left for the people in the constitution, when the Senate has these various functions, especially the control of the receipts and expenditure of the exchequer; and when the Consuls, again, have absolute power over the details of military preparation, and an absolute authority in the field? There is, however, a part left the people, and it is a most important one. For the people is the sole fountain of honour and of punishment; and it is by these two things and these alone that dynasties and constitutions and, in a word, human society are held together: for where the distinction between them is not sharply drawn both in theory and practice,

there no undertaking can be properly administered,—as indeed we might expect when good and bad are held in exactly the same honour. The people then are the only court to decide matters of life and death; and even in cases where the penalty is money, if the sum to be assessed is sufficiently serious, and especially when the accused have held the higher magistracies. And in regard to this arrangement there is one point deserving especial commendation and record. Men who are on trial for their lives at Rome, while sentence is in process of being voted,—if even only one of the tribes whose votes are needed to ratify the sentence has not voted,—have the privilege at Rome of openly departing and condemning themselves to a voluntary exile. Such men are safe at Naples or Praeneste or at Tibur, and at other towns with which this arrangement has been duly ratified on oath.

Again, it is the people who bestow offices on the deserving, which are the most honourable rewards of virtue. It has also the absolute power of passing or repealing laws; and, most important of all, it is the people who deliberate on the question of peace or war. And when provisional terms are made for alliance, suspension of hostilities, or treaties, it is the people who ratify them or the reverse.

These considerations again would lead one to say that the chief power in the state was the people's and that the constitution was a democracy.

15. Such, then, is the distribution of power between the several parts of the state. I must now show how each of these several parts can, when they choose, oppose or support each other.

The Consul, then, when he has started on an expedition with the powers I have described, is to all appearance absolute in the administration of the business in hand; still he has need of the support both of people and Senate, and, without them, is quite unable to bring the matter to a successful conclusion. For it is plain that he must have supplies sent to his legions from time to time; but without a decree of the Senate they can be supplied neither with corn, nor clothes, nor pay, so that all the plans of a commander must be futile, if the Senate is resolved either to shrink from danger or hamper his plans. And again, whether a Consul shall bring any undertaking to a conclusion or no depends entirely upon the Senate: for it has absolute authority at the end of a year to send another Consul to supersede him, or to continue the existing one in his command. Again, even to the successes of the generals the Senate has the power to add distinction and glory, and on the other hand to obscure their merits and lower their credit. For these high achievements are brought in tangible form before the eyes of the citizens by what are called "triumphs." But these triumphs the commanders cannot celebrate with proper pomp, or in some cases celebrate at all, unless the Senate concurs and grants the necessary money. As for the people, the Consuls are pre-eminently obliged to court their favour, however distant from home may be the field of their operations; for it is the people, as I have said before, that ratifies, or refuses to ratify, terms of peace and treaties; but most of all because when laying down their office they have to give an account of their administration before it. Therefore in no case is it safe for the Consuls to neglect either the Senate or the goodwill of the people.

16. As for the Senate, which possesses the immense power I have described, in the first place it is obliged in public affairs to take the multitude into account, and respect the wishes of the people; and it cannot put into execution the penalty for offences against the republic, which are punishable with death, unless the people first ratify its decrees. Similarly even in matters which directly affect the senators,—for instance, in the case of a law diminishing the Senate's traditional authority, or depriving senators of certain dignities and offices, or even actually cutting down their property,—even in such cases the people have the sole power of passing or rejecting the law. But most important of all is the fact that, if the Tribunes interpose their veto, the Senate not only are unable to pass a decree, but cannot even hold a meeting at all, whether formal or informal. Now, the Tribunes are always bound to carry out the decree of the people, and above all things to have regard to their wishes: therefore, for all these reasons the Senate stands in awe of the multitude, and cannot neglect the feelings of the people.

17. In like manner the people on its part is far from being

independent of the Senate, and is bound to take its wishes into account both collectively and individually. For contracts, too numerous to count, are given out by the censors in all parts of Italy for the repairs or construction of public buildings; there is also the collection of revenue from any rivers, harbours, gardens, mines, and land—everything, in a word, that comes under the control of the Roman government: and in all these the people at large are engaged; so that there is scarcely a man, so to speak, who is not interested either as a contractor or as being employed in the works. For some purchase the contracts from the censors for themselves; and others go partners with them; while others again go security for these contractors, or actually pledge their property to the treasury for them. Now over all these transactions the Senate has absolute control. It can grant an extension of time; and in case of unforeseen accident can relieve the contractors from a portion of their obligation, or release them from it altogether, if they are absolutely unable to fulfil it. And there are many details in which the Senate can inflict great hardships, or, on the other hand, grant great indulgences to the contractors: for in every case the appeal is to it. But the most important point of all is that the judges are taken from its members in the majority of trials, whether public or private, in which the charges are heavy. Consequently, all citizens are much at its mercy; and being alarmed at the uncertainty as to when they may need its aid, are cautious about resisting or actively opposing its will. And for a similar reason men do not rashly resist the wishes of the Consuls, because one and all may become subject to their absolute authority on a campaign.

18. The result of this power of the several estates for mutual help or harm is a union sufficiently firm for all emergencies, and a constitution than which it is impossible to find a better. For whenever any danger from without compels them to unite and work together, the strength which is developed by the State is so extraordinary, that everything required is unfailingly carried out by the eager rivalry shown by all classes to devote their whole minds to the need of the hour, and to secure that any determination come to should not fail for want of promptitude; while each individual works, privately and publicly alike, for the accomplishment of the

business in hand. Accordingly, the peculiar constitution of the State makes it irresistible, and certain of obtaining whatever it determines to attempt. Nay, even when these external alarms are past, and the people are enjoying their good fortune and the fruits of their victories, and, as usually happens, growing corrupted by flattery and idleness, show a tendency to violence and arrogance,— it is in these circumstances, more than ever, that the constitution is seen to possess within itself the power of correcting abuses. For when any one of the three classes becomes puffed up, and manifests an inclination to be contentious and unduly encroaching, the mutual interdependency of all the three, and the possibility of the pretensions of any one being checked and thwarted by the others, must plainly check this tendency: and so the proper equilibrium is maintained by the impulsiveness of the one part being checked by its fear of the other. . . .

Polybius' Criticism of Earlier Historians, particularly Timaeus
Book XII: 25, 28

WHAT EPITHET ought one to apply to Timaeus, and what word will properly characterise him? A man of his kind appears to me to deserve the very bitterest of the terms which he has applied to others. It has already been sufficiently proved that he is a carping, false and impudent writer; and from what remains to be said he will be shown to be unphilosophical, and, in short, utterly uninstructed. For towards the end of his twenty-first book, in the course of his "harangue of Timoleon," he remarks that "the whole sublunary world being divided into three parts—Asia, Libya, and Europe. . . ." One could scarcely believe such a remark to have come, I don't say from Timaeus, but even from the proverbial Margites. . . .

25. (*a*) The proverb tells us that one drop from the largest vessel is sufficient to show the whole contents. This is applicable to the present case. When one or two false statements have been discovered in a history, and they have been shown to be wilful, it is clear that nothing which such an historian may say can be regarded

as certain or trustworthy. But in order to convince the more careful student, I must speak on his method and practice in regard to public speeches, military harangues, ambassador's orations, and all compositions of that class; which are, as it were, a compendium of events and an epitome of all history. Now that he has given these in his writings with entire disregard of truth, and that of set purpose, can any reader of Timaeus fail to be aware? He has not written down the words actually used, nor the real drift of these speeches; but imagining how they ought to have been expressed, he enumerates all the arguments used, and makes the words tally with the circumstances, like a school-boy declaiming on a set theme: as though his object were to display his own ability, not to give a report of what was in reality said. . . .

(b) The special province of history is, first, to ascertain what the actual words used were; and secondly, to learn why it was that a particular policy or argument failed or succeeded. For a bare statement of an occurrence is interesting indeed, but not instructive: but when this is supplemented by a statement of cause, the study of history becomes fruitful. For it is by applying analogies to our own circumstances that we get the means and basis for calculating the future; and for learning from the past when to act with caution, and when with greater boldness, in the present. The historian therefore who omits the words actually used, as well as all statement of the determining circumstances, and gives us instead conjectures and mere fancy compositions, destroys the special use of history. In this respect Timaeus is an eminent offender, for we all know that his books are full of such writing.

(c) But perhaps some one may raise the queston as to how it comes about that, being the sort of writer that I am showing him to be, he has obtained acceptance and credit among certain people. The reason is that his work abounds with hostile criticism and invective against others: and he has been judged, not by the positive merits of his own composition and his independent narrative, but by his skill in refuting his fellow historians; to which department he appears to me to have brought great diligence and an extraordinary natural aptitude. The case of the physicist Strato is almost precisely similar. As long as this man is endeavouring to descredit and refute the opinions of others, he is admirable: directly he brings forward anything of his own, or expounds any of his own doctrines, he at once seems to men of science to lose his faculties and become stupid and unintelligent. And for my part, I look upon this difference in writers as strictly analogous to the facts of everyday life. In this too it is easy to criticise our neighbours, but to be faultless ourselves is hard. One might almost say that those who are most ready at finding fault with others are most prone to errors in their own life.

(*d*) Besides these I may mention another error of Timaeus. Having stayed quietly at Athens for about fifty years, during which he devoted himself to the study of written history, he imagined that he was in possession of the most important means of writing it. To my mind this was a great mistake. History and the science of medicine are alike in this respect, that both may be divided broadly into three departments; and therefore those who study either must approach them in three ways. For instance the three departments of medicine are the rhetorical, the dietetic, and the surgical and pharmaceutical. . . . The first, which takes its rise from the school of Herophilus and Callimachus of Alexandria, does indeed rightly claim a certain position in medical science; but by its speciousness and liberal promises acquires so much reputation that those who are occupied with other branches of the art are supposed to be completely ignorant. But just bring one of these professors to an actual invalid: you will find that they are as completely wanting in the necessary skill as men who have never read a medical treatise. Nay, it has happened before now that certain persons, who had really nothing serious the matter with them, have been persuaded by their powerful arguments to commit themselves to their treatment, and have thereby endangered their lives: for they are like men trying to steer a ship out of a book. Still such men go from city to city with great *éclât*, and get the common people together to listen to them. But if, when this is done, they induce certain people to submit as a specimen to their practical treatment; they only succeed in reducing them to state of extreme discomfort, and making them a laughing stock to the audience. So completely does a persuasive address frequently get the advantage over practical experience. The third branch of the medical science, though it involves genuine skill in the treatment of the several cases, is not only rare in itself, but is also frequently cast into the shade, thanks to the folly of popular judgment, by volubility and impudence.

25. (e) In the same way the science of genuine history is threefold: first, the dealing with written documents and the arrangement of the material thus obtained; second, topography, the appearance of cities and localities, the description of rivers and harbours, and, speaking generally, the peculiar features of seas and countries and their relative distances; thirdly, political affairs. Now, as in the case of medicine, it is the last branch that many attach themselves to, owing to their preconceived opinions on the subject. And the majority of writers bring to the undertaking no spirit of fairness at all: nothing but dishonesty, impudence and unscrupulousness. Like vendors of drugs, their aim is to catch popular credit and favour, and to seize every opportunity of enriching themselves. About such writers it is not worth while to say more.

(f) But some of those who have the reputation of approaching history in a reasonable spirit are like the theoretical physicians. They spend all their time in libraries, and acquire generally all the learning which can be got from books, and then persuade themselves that they are adequately equipped for their task. . . . Yet in my opinion they are only partially qualified for the production of genuine history. To inspect ancient records indeed, with the view of ascertaining the notions entertained by the ancients of certain places, nations, politics and events, and of understanding the several circumstances and contingencies experienced in former times, is useful; for the history of the past directs our attention in a proper spirit to the future, if a writer can be found to give a statement of facts as they really occurred. But to persuade one's self, as Timaeus does, that such ability in research is sufficient to enable a man to describe subsequent transactions with success is quite foolish. It is as though a man were to imagine that an inspection of the works of the old masters would enable him to become a painter and a master of the art himself.

This will be rendered still more evident from what I have now to say, particularly from certain passages in the history of Ephorus.

This writer in his history of war seems to me to have had some idea of naval tactics, but to be quite unacquainted with fighting on shore. Accordingly, if one turns one's attention to the naval battles at Cyprus and Cnidus, in which the generals of the king were engaged against Evagoras of Salamis* and then against the Lacedaemonians, one will be struck with admiration of the historian, and will learn many useful lessons as to what to do in similar circumstances. But when he tells the story of the battle of Leuctra between the Thebans and Lacedaemonians, or again that of Mantinea between the same combatants, in which Epaminondas lost his life, if in these one examines attentively and in detail the arrangements and evolutions in the line of battle, the historian will appear quite ridiculous, and betray his entire ignorance and want of personal experience of such matters. The battle of Leuctra indeed was simple, and confined to one division of the forces engaged, and therefore does not make the writer's lack of knowledge so very glaring: but that of Mantinea was complicated and technical, and is accordingly unintelligible, and indeed completely inconceivable, to the historian. This will be rendered clear by first laying down a correct plan of the ground, and then measuring the extent of the movements as described by him. The same is the case with Theopompus, and above all with Timaeus, the subject of this book. These latter writers also can conceal their ignorance, so long as they deal with generalities; but directly they attempt minute and detailed description, they show that they are no better than Ephorus. . . .

25. (g) It is in fact as impossible to write well on the operations in a war, if a man has had no experience of actual service, as it is to write well on politics without having been engaged in political transactions and vicissitudes. And when history is written by the book-learned, without technical knowledge, and without clearness of detail, the work loses all its value. For if you take from history its element of practical instruction, what is left of it has nothing to attract and nothing to teach. Again, in the topography of cities and localities, when such men attempt to go into details, being entirely without personal knowledge, they must in a similar manner necessarily pass over many points of importance; while they waste words

* Tyrant of Salamis in Cyprus, B.C. 404–374.—tr.

on many that are not worth the trouble. And this is what his failure to make personal inspection brings upon Timaeus. . . .

(*h*) In his thirty-fourth book Timaeus says that "he spent fifty continuous years at Athens as an alien, and never took part in any military service, or went to inspect the localities." Accordingly, when he comes upon any such matters in the course of his history, he shows much ignorance and makes many misstatements; and if he ever does come near the truth, he is like one of those animal-painters who draw from models of stuffed skins. Such artists sometimes preserve the correct outline, but the vivid look and life-like portraiture of the real animal, the chief charm of the painter's art, are quite wanting. This is just the case with Timaeus, and in fact with all who start with mere book-learning; there is nothing vivid in their presentment of events, for that can only come from the personal experience of the writers. And hence it is, that those who have gone through no such course of actual experience produce no genuine enthusiasm in the minds of their readers. Former historians showed their sense of the necessity of making professions to this effect in their writings. For when their subject was political, they were careful to state that the writer had of course been engaged in politics, and had had experience in matters of the sort; or if the subject was military, that he had served a campaign and been actually engaged; and again, when the matter was one of everyday life, that he had brought up children and had been married; and so on in every department of life, which we may expect to find adequately treated by those writers alone who have had personal experience, and have accordingly made that branch of history their own. It is difficult perhaps for a man to have been actually and literally engaged in everything: but in the most important actions and most frequently occurring he must have been so.

(*i*) And that this is no impossibility, Homer is a convincing instance; for in him you may see this quality of personal knowledge frequently and conspicuously displayed. The upshot of all this is that the study of documents is only one of three elements in the preparation of an historian, and is only third in importance. And no clearer proof of this could be given than that furnished by the deliberative speeches, harangues of commanders, and orations of ambassadors as recorded by Timaeus. For the truth is, that the occasions are rare which admit of all possible arguments being set forth; as a rule, the circumstances of the case confine them to narrow limits. And of such speeches one sort are regarded with favour by men of our time, another by those of an earlier age; different styles again are popular with Aetolians, Peloponnesians, and Athenians. But to make digressions, in season and out of season, for the purpose of setting forth every possible speech that could be made, as Timaeus does by his trick of inventing words to suit every sort of occasion, is utterly misleading, pedantic, and worthy of a schoolboy essayist. And this practice has brought failure and discredit on many writers. Of course to select from time to time the proper and appropriate language is a necessary part of our art: but as there is no fixed rule to decide the quantity and quality of the words to be used on a particular occasion, great care and training is required if we are to instruct and not mislead our readers. The exact nature of the situation is difficult to communicate always; still it may be brought home to the mind by means of systematic demonstration, founded on personal and habitual experience. The best way of securing that this should be realised is for historians, first, to state clearly the position, the aims, and the circumstances of those deliberating; and then, recording the real speeches made, to explain to us the causes which contributed to the success or failure of the several speakers. Thus we should obtain a true conception of the situation, and by exercising our judgment upon it, and drawing analogies from it, should be able to form a thoroughly sound opinion upon the circumstances of the hour. But I suppose that tracing causes is difficult, while stringing words together in books is easy. Few again have the faculty of speaking briefly to the point, and getting the necessary training for doing so; while to produce a long and futile composition is within most people's capacity and is common enough.

25. (k) To confirm the judgment I have expressed of Timaeus, on his wilful misstatements as well as his ignorance, I shall now quote certain short passages from his acknowledged works as specimens. . . . Of all the men who have exercised sovereignty in Sicily, since the elder Gelo, tradition tells us that the most able

have been Hermocrates, Timoleon, and Pyrrhus of Epirus, who are the last persons in the world on whom to father pedantic and scholastic speeches. Now Timaeus tells us in his twenty-first book that on his arrival in Sicily Eurymedon urged the cities there to undertake the war against Syracuse; that subsequently the people of Gela becoming tired of the war, sent an embassy to Camarina to make a truce; that upon the latter gladly welcoming the proposal, each state sent ambassadors to their respective allies begging them to despatch men of credit to Gela to deliberate on a pacification, and to secure the common interests. Upon the arrival of these deputies in Gela and the opening of the conference, he represents Hermocrates as speaking to the following effect: "He praised the people of Gela and Camarina first, for having made the truce; secondly, because they were the cause of the assembling of this peace congress; and thirdly because they had taken precautions to prevent the mass of the citizens from taking part in the discussion, and had secured that it should be confined to the leading men in the states, who knew the difference between peace and war." Then after making two or three practical suggestions, Hermocrates is represented as expressing an opinion that "if they seriously consider the matter they will learn the profound difference between peace and war,"—although just before he had said that it was precisely this which moved his gratitude to the men of Gela, that "the discussion did not take place in the mass assembly, but in a congress of men who knew the difference between peace and war." This is an instance in which Timaeus not only fails to show the ability of an historian, but sinks below the level of a school theme. For, I presume, it will be universally admitted that what an audience requires is a demonstration of that about which they are in ignorance or uncertainty; but to exhaust one's ingenuity in finding arguments to prove what is known already is the most futile waste of time. But besides his cardinal mistake of directing the greater part of the speech to points which stood in need of no arguments at all, Timaeus also puts into the mouth of Hermocrates certain sentences of which one could scarcely believe that any commonplace youth would have been capable, much less the colleague of the

Lacedaemonians in the battle of Aegospotami, and the sole conqueror of the Athenian armies and generals in Sicily.

* * *

For whereas he is thought to have possessed great and wide knowledge, a faculty for historical inquiry, and extraordinary industry in the execution of his work, in certain cases he appears to have been the most ignorant and indolent person that ever called himself an historian. And the following considerations will prove it. Nature has bestowed on us two instruments of inquiry and research, hearing and sight. Of these sight is, according to Heracleitus, by far the truer; for eyes are surer witnesses than ears. And of these channels of learning Timaeus has chosen the pleasanter and the worse; for he entirely refrained from looking at things with his own eyes, and devoted himself to learning by hearsay. But even the ear may be instructed in two ways, reading and answers to personal inquiries: and in the latter of these he was very indolent, as I have already shown. The reason of his preference for the other it is easy to divine. Study of documents involves no danger or fatigue, if one only takes care to lodge in a city rich in such records, or to have a library in one's neighbourhood. You may then investigate any question while reclining on your couch, and compare the mistakes of former historians without any fatigue to yourself. But personal investigation demands great exertion and expense; though it is exceedingly advantageous, and in fact is the very corner-stone of history. This is evident from the writers of history themselves. Ephorus says, "if writers could only be present at the actual transactions, it would be far the best of all modes of learning." Theopompus says, "the best military historian is he who has been present at the greatest number of battles; the best speech maker is he who has been engaged in most political contests." . . .

28. Plato says that "human affairs will not go well until either philosophers become kings or kings become philosophers." So I should say that history will never be properly written, until either men of action undertake to write it (not as they do now, as a matter of secondary importance; but, with the conviction that it is their

most necessary and honourable employment, shall devote themselves through life exclusively to it), or historians become convinced that practical experience is of the first importance for historical composition. Until that time arrives there will always be abundance of blunders in the writings of historians. Timaeus, however, quite disregarded all this. He spent his life in one place, of which he was not even a citizen; and thus deliberately renounced all active career either in war or politics, and all personal exertion in travel and inspection of localities: and yet, somehow or another, he has managed to obtain the reputation of a master in the art of history. To prove that I have not misrepresented him, it is easy to bring the evidence of Timaeus himself. In the preface to his sixth book he says that "some people suppose that more genius, industry, and preparation are required for rhetorical than for historical composition." And that "this opinion had been formerly advanced against Ephorus." Then because this writer had been unable to refute those who held it, he undertakes himself to draw a comparison between history and rhetorical compositions: a most unnecessary proceeding altogether. In the first place he misrepresents Ephorus. For in truth, admirable as Ephorus is throughout his whole work, in style, treatment, and argumentative acuteness, he is never more brilliant than in his digressions and statements of his personal views: in fact, whenever he is adding anything in the shape of a commentary or a note. And it so happens that his most elegant and convincing digression is on this very subject of a comparison between historians and speech-writers. But Timaeus is anxious not to be thought to follow Ephorus. Therefore, in addition to misrepresenting him and condemning the rest, he enters upon a long, confused, and in every way inferior, discussion of what had been already sufficiently handled by others; and expected that no one living would detect him.

(*a*) However, he wished to exalt history; and, in order to do so, he says that "history differs from rhetorical composition as much as real buildings differ from those represented in scene-paintings." And again, that "to collect the necessary materials for writing history is by itself more laborious than the whole process of producing rhetorical compositions." He mentions, for instance, the expense and labour which he underwent in collecting records from Assyria, and in studying the customs of the Ligures, Celts, and Iberians. But he exaggerates these so much, that he could not have himself expected to be believed. One would be glad to ask the historian which of the two he thinks is the more expensive and laborious,— to remain quietly at home and collect records and study the customs of Ligures and Celts, or to obtain personal experience of all the tribes possible, and see them with his own eyes? To ask questions about manœuvres on the field of battle and the sieges of cities and fights at sea from those who were present, or to take personal part in the dangers and vicissitudes of these operations as they occur? For my part I do not think that real buildings differ so much from those in stage-scenery, nor history from rhetorical compositions, as a narrative drawn from actual and personal experience differs from one derived from hearsay and the report of others. But Timaeus had no such experience: and he therefore naturally supposed that the part of an historian's labour which is the least important and lightest, that namely of collecting records and making inquiries from those who had knowledge of the several events, was in reality the most important and most difficult. And, indeed, in this particular department of research, men who have had no personal experience must necessarily fall into grave errors. For how is a man, who has no knowledge of such things, to put the right questions as to manœuvering of troops, sieges of cities, and fights at sea? And how can he understand the details of what is told him? Indeed, the questioner is as important as the narrator for getting a clear story. For in the case of men who have had experience of real action, memory is a sufficient guide from point to point of a narrative: but a man who has had no such experience can neither put the right questions, nor understand what is happening before his eyes. Though he is on the spot, in fact, he is as good as absent. . . .

Polybius' Account of Intrigue and Corruption at the Court of Ptolemy in Alexandria
Book XV: 25–36

25. Sosibius, the unfaithful guardian of Ptolemy Epiphanes, was a creature of extraordinary cunning, who long retained his power, and was the instrument of many crimes at court: he contrived first the murder of Lysimachus, son of Arsinoe, daughter of Ptolemy and Berenice; secondly, that of Maga, son of Ptolemy and Berenice the daughter of Maga; thirdly, that of Berenice the mother of Ptolemy Philopator; fourthly, that of Cleomenes of Sparta; and fifthly, that of Arsinoe the daughter of Berenice. . . .

Three or four days after the death of Ptolemy Philopator [205 B.C.], having caused a platform to be erected in the largest court of the palace Agathocles and Sosibius summoned a meeting of the footguards and the household, as well as the officers of the infantry and cavalry. The assembly being formed, they mounted the platform, and first of all announced the deaths of the king and queen, and proclaimed the customary period of mourning for the people. After that they placed a diadem upon the head of the child, Ptolemy Epiphanes, proclaimed him king, and read a forged will, in which the late king nominated Agathocles and Sosibius guardians of his son. They ended by an exhortation to the officers to be loyal to the boy and maintain his sovereignty. They next brought in two silver urns, one of which they declared contained the ashes of the king, the other those of Arsinoe. And in fact one of them did really contain the king's ashes, the other was filled with spices. Having done this they proceeded to complete the funeral ceremonies. It was then that all the world at last learnt the truth about the death of Arsinoe. For now that her death was clearly established, the manner of it began to be a matter of speculation. Though rumours which turned out to be true had found their way among the people, they had up to this time been disputed; now there was no possibility of hiding the truth, and it became deeply impressed in the minds of all. Indeed there was great excitement among the populace: no one thought about the king; it was the fate of Arsinoe that moved them. Some recalled her orphanhood; others the tyranny and insult she had endured from her earliest days; and when her miserable death was added to these misfortunes, it excited such a passion of pity and sorrow that the city was filled with sighs, tears, and irrepressible lamentation. Yet it was clear to the thoughtful observer that these were not so much signs of affection for Arsinoe as of hatred towards Agathocles.

The first measure of this minister, after depositing the urns in the royal mortuary, and giving orders for the laying aside of mourning, was to gratify the army with two months' pay; for he was convinced that the way to deaden the resentment of the common soldiers was to appeal to their interests. He then caused them to take the oath customary at the proclamation of a new king; and next took measures to get all who were likely to be formidable out of the country. Philammon, who had been employed in the murder of Arsinoe, he sent out as governor of Cyrene, while he committed the young king to the charge of Oenanthe and Agathocleia. Next, Pelops the son of Pelops he despatched to the court of Antiochus in Asia, to urge him to maintain his friendly relations with the court of Alexandria, and not to violate the treaty he had made with the young king's father. Ptolemy, son of Sosibius, he sent to Philip to arrange for a treaty of intermarriage between the two countries, and to ask for assistance in case Antiochus should make a serious attempt to play them false in any matter of importance.

He also selected Ptolemy, son of Agesarchus, as ambassador to Rome: not with a view of his seriously prosecuting the embassy, but because he thought that, if he once entered Greece, he would find himself among friends and kinsfolk, and would stay there; which would suit his policy of getting rid of eminent men. Scopas the Aetolian also he sent to Greece to recruit foreign mercenaries, giving him a large sum in gold for bounties. He had two objects in view in this measure: one was to use the soldiers so recruited in the war with Antiochus; another was to get rid of the mercenary troops already existing, by sending them on garrison duty in the various forts and settlements about the country; while he used the new recruits to fill up the numbers of the household regiments with new men, as well as the pickets immediately round the palace, and in other parts of the city. For he believed that men who had been hired by himself, and were taking his pay, would have no feelings in common with the old soldiers, with whom they would be totally unacquainted; but that, having all their hopes of safety and profit in him, he would find them ready to co-operate with him and carry out his orders.

Now all this took place before the intrigue of Philip, though it was necessary for the sake of clearness to speak of that first, and to describe the transactions which took place, both at the audience and the dispatch of the ambassadors.

To return to Agathocles: when he had thus got rid of the most eminent men, and had to a great degree quieted the wrath of the common soldiers by his present of pay, he returned quickly to his old way of life. Drawing round him a body of friends, whom he selected from the most frivolous and shameless of his personal attendants or servants, he devoted the chief part of the day and night to drunkenness and all the excesses which accompany drunkenness, sparing neither matron, nor bride, nor virgin, and doing all this with the most offensive ostentation. The result was a widespread outburst of discontent; and when there appeared no prospect of reforming this state of things, or of obtaining protection against the violence, insolence and debauchery of the court, which on the contrary grew daily more outrageous, their old hatred blazed up once more in the hearts of the common people, and all began again to recall the misfortunes which the kingdom already owed to these very men. But the absence of any one fit to take the lead, and by whose means they could vent their wrath upon Agathocles and Agathocleia, kept them quiet. Their one remaining hope rested upon Tlepolemus, and on this they fixed their confidence.

As long as the late king was alive Tlepolemus remained in retirement; but upon his death he quickly propitiated the common soldiers, and became once more governor of Pelusium. At first he directed all his actions with a view to the interest of the king, believing that there would be some council of regency to take charge of the boy and administer the government. But when he saw that all those who were fit for this charge were got out of the way, and that Agathocles was boldly monopolising the supreme power, he quickly changed his purpose; because he suspected the danger that threatened him from the hatred which they mutually entertained. He therefore began to draw his troops together, and bestir himself to collect money, that he might not be an easy prey to any one of his enemies. At the same time he was not without hope that the guardianship of the young king, and the chief power in the state might devolve upon him; both because, in his own private opinion, he was much more fit for it in every respect than Agathocles, and because he was informed that his own troops and those in Alexandria were looking to him to put an end to the minister's outrageous conduct. When such ideas were entertained by Tlepolemus, it did not take long to make the quarrel grow, especially as the partisans of both helped to inflame it. Being eager to secure the adhesion of the generals of divisions and the captains of companies, he frequently invited them to banquets; and at these assemblies, instigated partly by the flattery of his guests and partly by his own impulse (for he was a young man and the conversation was over the wine), he used to throw out sarcastic remarks against the family of Agathocles. At first they were covert and enigmatic, then merely ambiguous, and finally undisguised, and containing the bitterest reflections. He proposed the health of the scribbler of pasquinades, the sackbut-girl and waiting-woman; and spoke of his shameful boyhood, when as cupbearer of the king he had submitted to the foulest treatment. His guests were always ready to laugh at his words and add their quota to the sum of vituperation. It was not long before this reached the ears of Agathocles: and the breach between the two thus becoming an open one, Agathocles immediately began bringing charges against Tlepolemus, declaring that he was a traitor to the king, and was inviting Antiochus to come and seize the government. And he brought many plausible proofs of this forward, some of which he got by distorting facts that actually occurred, while others were pure invention. His object in so doing was to excite the wrath of the common people against Tlepolemus. But the result was the reverse; for the populace had long fixed their hopes on Tlepolemus, and were only too delighted to see the quarrel growing hot between them. The actual popular outbreak which did occur began from the following circumstances. Nicon, a relation of Agathocles, was in the lifetime of the late king commander of the navy. . . .

26. (a) Another murder committed by Agathocles was that of

Deinon, son of Deinon. But this, as the proverb has it, was the fairest of his foul deeds. For the letter ordering the murder of Arsinoe had fallen into this man's hands, and he might have given information about the plot and saved the Queen; but at the time he chose rather to help Philammon, and so became the cause of all the misfortunes which followed; while, after the murder was committed, he was always recalling the circumstances, commiserating the unhappy woman, and expressing repentance at having let such an opportunity slip: and this he repeated in the hearing of many, so that Agathocles heard of it, and he met with his just punishment in losing his life. . . .

THE DEATH OF AGATHOCLES AND HIS FAMILY

26. (b) The first step of Agathocles was to summon a meeting of the Macedonian guards. He entered the assembly accompanied by the young king and his own sister Agathocleia. At first he feigned not to be able to say what he wished for tears; but after again and again wiping his eyes with his chlamys he at length mastered his emotion, and, taking the young king in his arms, spoke as follows: "Take this boy, whom his father on his death-bed placed in this lady's arms" (pointing to his sister) "and confided to your loyalty, men of Macedonia! That lady's affection has but little influence in securing the child's safety: it is on you that that safety now depends; his fortunes are in your hands. It has long been evident to those who had eyes to see, that Tlepolemus was aiming at something higher than his natural rank; but now he has named the day and hour on which he intends to assume the crown. Do not let your belief of this depend upon my words; refer to those who know the real truth and have but just come from the very scene of his treason." With these words he brought forward Critolaus, who deposed that he had seen with his own eyes the altars being decked, and the victims being got ready by the common soldiers for the ceremony of a coronation.

When the Macedonian guards had heard all this, far from being moved by his appeal, they showed their contempt by hooting and loud murmurs, and drove him away under such a fire of derision that he got out of the assembly without being conscious how he did it. And similar scenes occurred among other corps of the army at their meetings. Meanwhile great crowds kept pouring into Alexandria from the up-country stations, calling upon kinsmen or friends to help the movement, and not to submit to the unbridled tyranny of such unworthy men. But what inflamed the populace against the government more than anything else was the knowledge that, as Tlepolemus had the absolute command of all the imports into Alexandria, delay would be a cause of suffering to themselves.

27. Moreover, an action of Agathocles himself served to heighten the anger of the multitude and of Tlepolemus. For he took Danae, the latter's mother-in-law, from the temple of Demeter, dragged her through the middle of the city unveiled, and cast her into prison. His object in doing this was to manifest his hostility to Tlepolemus; but its effect was to loosen the tongues of the people. In their anger they no longer confined themselves to secret murmurs: but some of them in the night covered the walls in every part of the city with pasquinades; while others in the day time collected in groups and openly expressed their loathing for the government.

Seeing what was taking place, and beginning to fear the worst, Agathocles at one time meditated making his escape by secret flight; but as he had nothing ready for such a measure, thanks to his own imprudence, he had to give up that idea. At another time he set himself to drawing out lists of men likely to assist him in a bold *coup d'état*, by which he should put to death or arrest his enemies, and then possess himself of absolute power. While still meditating these plans he received information that Moeragenes, one of the body-guard, was betraying all the secrets of the palace to Tlepolemus, and was co-operating with him on account of his relationship with Adaeus, at that time the commander of Bubastus. Agathocles immediately ordered his secretary Nicostratus to arrest Moeragenes, and extract the truth from him by every possible kind of torture. Being promptly arrested by Nicostratus, and taken to a retired part of the palace, he was at first examined directly as to the facts alleged; but, refusing to confess anything, he was stripped. And now some of the torturers were preparing their instruments, and others with scourges in their hands were just taking off their outer garments, when just at that very moment a servant ran in, and, whispering something in the ear of Nicostratus, hurried out again. Nicostratus followed close behind him, without a word, frequently slapping his thigh with his hand.

28. The predicament of Moeragenes was now indescribably strange. There stood the executioners by his side on the point of raising their scourges, while others close to him were getting ready their instruments of torture: but when Nicostratus withdrew they all stood silently staring at each other's faces, expecting him every moment to return; but as time went on they one by one slipped away, until Moeragenes was left alone. Having made his way through the palace, after this unhoped-for escape, he rushed in his half-clothed state into a tent of the Macedonian guards which was situated close to the palace. They chanced to be at breakfast, and therefore a good many were collected together; and to them he narrated the story of his wonderful escape. At first they would not believe it, but ultimately were convinced by his appearing without his clothes. Taking advantage of this extraordinary occurrence, Moeragenes besought the Macedonian guards with tears not only to help him to secure his own safety, but the king's also, and above all their own. "For certain destruction stared them in the face," he said, "unless they seized the moment when the hatred of the populace was at its height, and every one was ready to wreak vengeance on Agathocles. That moment was *now*, and all that was wanted was some one to begin."

29. The passions of the Macedonians were roused by these words, and they finally agreed to do as Moeragenes advised. They at once went round to the tents, first those of their own corps, and then those of the other soldiers; which were all close together, facing the same quarter of the city. The wish was one which had for a long time been formed in the minds of the soldiery, wanting nothing but some one to call it forth, and with courage to begin. No sooner, therefore, had a commencement been made than it blazed out like a fire: and before four hours had elapsed every class, whether military or civil, had agreed to make the attempt.

At this crisis, too, chance contributed a great deal to the final catastrophe. For a letter addressed by Tlepolemus to the army as well as some of his spies, had fallen into the hands of Agathocles. The letter announced that he would be at Alexandria shortly, and the spies informed Agathocles that he was already there. This news so distracted Agathocles that he gave up taking any measures at all or even thinking about the dangers which surrounded him, but departed at his usual hour to his wine, and kept up the carouse to the end in his usual licentious fashion. But his mother Oenanthe went in great distress to the temple of Demeter and Persephone, which was open on account of a certain annual sacrifice; and there first of all she besought the aid of those goddesses with bendings of the knee and strange incantations, and then sat down close to the altar and remained motionless. Most of the women present, delighted to witness her dejection and distress, kept silence: but the ladies of the family of Polycrates, and certain others of the nobility, being as yet unaware of what was going on around them, approached Oenanthe and tried to comfort her. But she cried out in a loud voice: "Do not come near me, you monsters! I know you well! Your hearts are always against us; and you pray the goddess for all imaginable evil upon us. Still I trust and believe that, God willing, you shall one day taste the flesh of your own children." With these words she ordered her female attendants to drive them away, and strike them with their staves if they refused to go. The ladies availed themselves of this excuse for quitting the temple in a body, raising their hands and praying that she might herself have experience of those very miseries with which she had threatened her neighbours.

30. The men having by this time decided upon a revolution, now that in every house the anger of the women was added to the general resentment, the popular hatred blazed out with redoubled violence. As soon as night fell the whole city was filled with tumult, torches, and hurrying feet. Some were assembling with shouts in the stadium; some were calling upon others to join them; some were running backwards and forwards seeking to conceal themselves in houses and places least likely to be suspected. And now the open spaces round the palace, the stadium, and the street were filled with a motley crowd, as well as the area in front of the Dionysian Theatre. Being informed of this, Agathocles roused himself from a

drunken lethargy,—for he had just dismissed his drinking party,—and, accompanied by all his family, with the exception of Philo, went to the king. After a few words of lamentation over his misfortunes addressed to the child, he took him by the hand, and proceeded to the covered walk which runs between the Maeander garden and the Palaestra, and leads to the entrance of the theatre. Having securely fastened the two first doors through which he passed, he entered the third with two or three bodyguards, his own family, and the king. The doors, however, which were secured by double bars, were only of lattice work and could therefore be seen through.

By this time the mob had collected from every part of the city in such numbers, that, not only was every foot of ground occupied, but the doorsteps and roofs also were crammed with human beings; and such a mingled storm of shouts and cries arose, as might be expected from a crowd in which women and children were mixed with men: for in Alexandria, as in Carthage, the children perform as conspicuous a part in such commotions as the men.

31. Day now began to break and the uproar was still a confused babel of voices; but one cry made itself heard conspicuously above the rest, it was a call for THE KING. The first thing actually done was by the Macedonian guard: they left their quarters and seized the vestibule which served as the audience hall of the palace; then, after a brief pause, having ascertained whereabouts in the palace the king was, they went round to the covered walk, burst open the first doors, and, when they came to the next, demanded with loud shouts that the young king should be surrendered to them. Agathocles, recognising his danger, begged his bodyguards to go in his name to the Macedonians, to inform them that "he resigned the guardianship of the king, and all offices, honours, or emoluments which he possessed, and only asked that his life should be granted him with a bare maintenance; that by sinking to his original situation in life he would be rendered incapable, even if he wished it, of being henceforth oppressive to any one." All the bodyguards refused except Aristomenes, who afterwards obtained the chief power in the state.

This man was an Acarnanian, and, though far advanced in life when he obtained supreme power, he is thought to have made a most excellent and blameless guardian of the king and kingdom. And as he was distinguished in that capacity, so had he been remarkable before for his adulation of Agathocles in the time of his prosperity. He was the first, when entertaining Agathocles at his house, to distinguish him among his guests by the present of a gold diadem, an honour reserved by custom to the kings alone; he was the first too who ventured to wear his likeness on his ring; and when a daughter was born to him he named her Agathocleia.

But to return to my story. Aristomenes undertook the mission, received his message, and made his way through a certain wicket-gate to the Macedonians. He stated his business in few words: the first impulse of the Macedonians was to stab him to death on the spot; but some of them held up their hands to protect him, and successfully begged his life. He accordingly returned with orders to bring the king or to come no more himself. Having dismissed Aristomenes with these words, the Macedonians proceeded to burst open the second door also. When convinced by their proceedings, no less than by the answers they had returned, of the fierce purpose of the Macedonians, the first idea of Agathocles was to thrust his hand through the latticed door,—while Agathocleia did the same with her breasts which she said had suckled the king,—and by every kind of entreaty to beg that the Macedonians would grant him bare life.

32. But finding that his long and piteous appeals produced no effect, at last he sent out the young king with the bodyguards. As soon as they had got the king, the Macedonians placed him on a horse and conducted him to the stadium. His appearance being greeted with loud shouts and clapping of hands, they stopped the horse, and dismounting the child, ushered him to the royal stall and seated him there. But the feelings of the crowd were divided: they were delighted that the young king had been brought, but they were dissatisfied that the guilty persons had not been arrested and met with the punishment they deserved. Accordingly, they continued with loud cries to demand that the authors of all the mischief should be brought out and made an example. The day was wearing away, and yet the crowd had found no one on whom to

wreak their vengeance, when Sosibius, who, though a son of the elder Sosibius, was at that time a member of the bodyguard, and as such had a special eye to the safety of the king and the State,—seeing that the furious desire of the multitude was implacable, and that the child was frightened at the unaccustomed faces that surrounded him and the uproar of the crowd, asked the king whether he would "surrender to the populace those who had injured him or his mother." The boy having nodded assent, Sosibius bade some of the bodyguard announce the king's decision, while he raised the young child from his seat and took him to his own house which was close by to receive proper attention and refreshment. When the message from the king was declared, the whole place broke out into a storm of cheering and clapping of hands. But meanwhile Agathocles and Agathocleia had separated and gone each to their own lodgings. Without loss of time soldiers, some voluntarily and others under pressure from the crowd, started in search of them.

33. The beginning of actual bloodshed, however, was this. One of the servants and flatterers of Agathocles, whose name was Philo, came out to the stadium still flustered with wine. Seeing the fury of the multitude, he said to some bystanders that they would have cause to repent it again, as they had only the other day, if Agathocles were to come there. Of those who heard him some began to abuse him, while others pushed him about; and on his attempting to defend himself, some tore his cloak off his back, while others thrust their spears into him and wounded him mortally. He was dragged into the middle of the crowd breathing his last gasp; and, having thus tasted blood, the multitude began to look impatiently for the coming of the other victims. They had not to wait long. First appeared Agathocles dragged along bound hand and foot. No sooner had he entered than some soldiers rushed at him and struck him dead. And in doing so they were his friends rather than enemies, for they saved him from the horrible death which he deserved. Nicon was brought next, and after him Agathocleia stripped naked, with her two sisters; and following them the whole family. Last of all some men came bringing Oenanthe, whom they had torn from the temple of Demeter and Persephone, riding stripped naked upon a horse. They were all given up to the popu-

lace, who bit, and stabbed them, and knocked out their eyes, and, as soon as any one of them fell, tore him limb from limb, until they had utterly annihilated them all: for the savagery of the Egyptians when their passions are roused is indeed terrible. At the same time some young girls who had been brought up with Arsinoe, having learnt that Philammon, the chief agent in the murder of that Queen, had arrived three days before from Cyrene, rushed to his house; forced their way in; killed Philammon with stones and sticks; strangled his infant son; and, not content with this, dragged his wife naked into the street and put her to death.

Such was the end of Agathocles and Agathocleia and their kinsfolk.

34. I am quite aware of the miraculous occurrences and embellishments which the chroniclers of this event have added to their narrative with a view of producing a striking effect upon their hearers, making more of their comments on the story than of the story itself and the main incidents. Some ascribe it entirely to Fortune, and take the opportunity of expatiating on her fickleness and the difficulty of being on one's guard against her. Others dwell upon the unexpectedness of the event, and try to assign its causes and probabilities. It was not my purpose, however, to treat this episode in this way, because Agathocles was not a man of conspicuous courage or ability as a soldier; nor particularly successful or worth imitating as a statesman; nor, lastly, eminent for his acuteness as a courtier or cunning as an intriguer, by which latter accomplishments Sosibius and many others have managed to keep one king after another under their influence to the last day of their lives. The very opposite of all this may be said of this man. For though he obtained high promotion owing to Philopator's feebleness as a king; and though after his death he had the most favourable opportunity of consolidating his power, he yet soon fell into contempt, and lost his position and his life at once, thanks to his own want of courage and vigour.

35. To such a story then no such dissertation is required, as was in place, for instance, in the case of the Sicilian monarchs, Agathocles and Dionysius, and certain others who have administered governments with reputation. For the former of these, starting from

a plebeian and humble position—having been, as Timaeus sneeringly remarks, a potter—came from the wheel, clay, and smoke, quite a young man to Syracuse. And, to begin with, both these men in their respective generations became tyrants of Syracuse, a city that had obtained at that time the greatest reputation and the greatest wealth of any in the world; and afterwards were regarded as suzerains of all Sicily, and lords of certain districts in Italy. While, for his part, Agathocles not only made an attempt upon Africa, but eventually died in possession of the greatness he had acquired. It is on this account that the story is told of Publius Scipio, the first conqueror of the Carthaginians, that being asked whom he considered to have been the most skilful administrators and most distinguished for boldness combined with prudence, he replied, "the Sicilians Agathocles and Dionysius." Now, in the case of such men as these, it is certainly right to try to arrest the attention of our readers, and, I suppose, to speak of Fortune and the mutability of human affairs, and in fact to point a moral: but in the case of such men as we have been speaking of, it is quite out of place to do so.

36. For these reasons I have rejected all idea of making too much of the story of Agathocles. But another and the strongest reason was that all such wonderful and striking catastrophes are only worth listening to once; not only are subsequent exhibitions of them unprofitable to ear and eye, but elaborate harping upon soon becomes simply troublesome. For those who are engaged on representing anything either to eye or ear can have only two objects to aim at,—pleasure and profit; and in history, more than in anything else, excessive prolixity on events of tragic interest fails of both these objects. . . .

> *Polybius' further assertions on the historian's impartial pursuit of truth*
> Book XXXVIII: 6

6. IN REGARD to these men, it should not be a matter of surprise if we leave for a while the ordinary method and spirit of our narrative to give a clearer and more elaborate exposition of their

character. I am aware that some may be found, regarding it as their first duty to cast a veil over the errors of the Greeks, to accuse us of writing in a spirit of malevolence. But for myself, I conceive that with right-minded persons a man will never be regarded as a true friend who shrinks from and is afraid of plain speech, nor indeed as a good citizen who abandons the truth because of the offence he will give to certain persons at the time. But a writer of public history above all deserves no indulgence whatever, who regards anything of superior importance to truth. For in proportion as written history reaches larger numbers, and survives for longer time, than words spoken to suit an occasion, both the writer ought to be still more particular about truth, and his readers ought to admit his authority only so far as he adheres to this principle. At the actual hour of danger it is only right that Greeks should help Greeks in every possible way, by protecting them, veiling their errors or deprecating the wrath of the sovereign people,—and this I genuinely did for my part at the actual time: but it is also right, in regard to the record of events to be transmitted to posterity, to leave them unmixed with any falsehood: so that readers should not be merely gratified for the moment by a pleasant tale, but should receive in their souls a lesson which will prevent a repetition of similar errors in the future. Enough, however, on this subject. . . .

Pericles

PLUTARCH · PERICLES*

CAESAR** ONCE, seeing some wealthy strangers at Rome, carrying up and down with them in their arms and bosoms young puppy-dogs and monkeys, embracing and making much of them, took occasion not unnaturally to ask whether the women in their country were not used to bear children; by that prince-like reprimand gravely reflecting upon persons who spend and lavish upon brute beasts that affection and kindness which nature has implanted in us to be bestowed on those of our own kind. With like reason may we blame those who misuse that love of inquiry and observation which nature has implanted in our souls, by expending it on objects unworthy of the attention either of their eyes or their ears, while they disregard such as are excellent in themselves, and would do them good.

The mere outward sense, being passive in responding to the impression of the objects that come in its way and strike upon it, perhaps cannot help entertaining and taking notice of every thing that addresses it, be it what it will, useful or unuseful; but, in the exercise of his mental perception, every man, if he chooses, has a natural power to turn himself upon all occasions, and to change and shift with the greatest ease to what he shall himself judge desirable. So that it becomes a man's duty to pursue and make after the best and choicest of every thing, that he may not only employ his contemplation, but may also be improved by it. For as that color is most suitable to the eye whose freshness and pleasantness stimulates and strengthens the sight, so a man ought to apply his intellectual per-

---

* Reprinted, with revisions, from *Plutarch's Lives of Illustrious Men*, edited by Arthur H. Clough (Boston: Little, Brown, 1895).
** Probably Augustus.

ception to such objects as, with the sense of delight, are apt to call it forth, and allure it to its own proper good and advantage.

Such objects we find in the acts of virtue, which also produce in the minds of mere readers about them, an emulation and eagerness that may lead them on to imitation. In other things there does not immediately follow upon the admiration and liking of the thing done, any strong desire of doing the like. Nay, many times, on the very contrary, when we are pleased with the work, we slight and set little by the workman or artist himself, as, for instance, in perfumes and purple dyes, we are taken with the things themselves well enough, but do not think dyers and perfumers otherwise than low and sordid people. It was not said amiss by Antisthenes, when people told him that one Ismenias was an excellent piper, "It may be so," said he, "but he is but a wretched human being, otherwise he would not have been an excellent piper." And king Philip, to the same purpose, told his son Alexander, who once at a merry-meeting played a piece of music charmingly and skilfully, "Are you not ashamed, son, to play so well?" For it is enough for a king or prince to find leisure sometimes to hear others sing, and he does the muses quite honor enough when he pleases to be but present, while others engage in such exercises and trials of skill.

He who busies himself in mean occupations produces, in the very pains he takes about things of little or no use, an evidence against himself of his negligence and indisposition to what is really good. Nor did any generous and ingenuous young man, at the sight of the statue of Jupiter at Pisa, ever desire to be a Phidias, or, on seeing that of Juno at Argos, long to be a Polycletus, or feel induced by his pleasure in their poems to wish to be an Anacreon or Philetas or Archilochus. For it does not necessarily follow, that, if a piece of work please for its gracefulness, therefore he that wrought it deserves our admiration. Whence it is that neither do such things really profit or advantage the beholders, upon the sight of which no zeal arises for the imitation of them, nor any impulse or inclination, which may prompt any desire or endeavor of doing the like. But virtue, by the bare statement of its actions, can so affect men's minds as to create at once both admiration of the things done and desire to imitate the doers of them. The goods of fortune we would possess and would enjoy; those of virtue we long to practise and exercise; we are content to receive the former from others, the latter we wish others to experience from us. Moral good is a practical stimulus; it is no sooner seen, than it inspires an impulse to practise; and influences the mind and character not by a mere imitation which we look at, but, by the statement of the fact, creates a moral purpose which we form.

And so we have thought fit to spend our time and pains in writing of the lives of famous persons; and have composed this tenth book upon that subject, containing the life of Pericles, and that of Fabius Maximus, who carried on the war against Hannibal, men alike, as in their other virtues and good parts, so especially in their mild and upright temper and demeanor, and in that capacity to bear the cross-grained humors of their fellow-citizens and colleagues in office which made them both most useful and serviceable to the interests of their countries. Whether we take a right aim at our intended purpose, it is left to the reader to judge by what he shall here find.

PERICLES was of the tribe Acamantis, and the township Cholargus, of the noblest birth both on his father's and mother's side. Xanthippus, his father, who defeated the king of Persia's generals in the battle at Mycale, took to wife Agariste, the grandchild of Clisthenes, who drove out the sons of Pisistratus, and nobly put an end to their tyrannical usurpation, and moreover made a body of laws, and settled a model of government admirably tempered and suited for the harmony and safety of the people.

His mother, being near her time, fancied in a dream that she was brought to bed of a lion, and a few days after was delivered of Pericles, in other respects perfectly formed, only his head was somewhat longish and out of proportion. For which reason almost all the images and statues that were made of him have the head covered with a helmet, the workmen apparently being willing not to expose him. The poets of Athens called him *Schinocephalos*, or squill-head, from *schinos*, a squill, or sea-onion. One of the comic poets, Cratinus, in the Chirons, tells us that—

> Old Chronos once took queen Sedition to wife;
> Which two brought to life
> That tyrant far-famed,
> Whom the gods the supreme skull-compeller* have named.

And, in the Nemesis, addresses him—

> Come, Jove, thou *head* of gods.

And a second, Teleclides, says, that now, in embarrassment with political difficulties, he sits in the city,—

> Fainting underneath the load
> Of his own head; and now abroad,
> From his huge gallery of a pate,
> Sends forth trouble to the state.

And a third, Eupolis, in the comedy called the Demi, in a series of questions about each of the demagogues, whom he makes in the play to come up from hell, upon Pericles being named last, exclaims,—

> And here by way of summary, now we've done,
> Behold, in brief, the heads of all in one.

The master that taught him music, most authors are agreed, was Damon (whose name, they say, ought to be pronounced with the first syllable short). Though Aristotle tells us that he was thoroughly practised in all accomplishments of this kind by Pythoclides. Damon, it is not unlikely, being a sophist, out of policy, sheltered himself under the profession of music to conceal from people in general his skill in other things, and under this pretence attended Pericles, the young athlete of politics, so to say, as his training-master in these exercises. Damon's lyre, however, did not prove altogether a successful blind; he was banished [from] the country by ostracism for ten years, as a dangerous intermeddler and a favorer of arbitrary power, and, by this means, gave the stage occasion to play upon him. As, for instance, Plato, the comic poet, introduces a character, who questions him—

---

* Kephalegeretes, a play on Nephelegeretes, the cloud-compeller.—tr.

> Tell me, if you please,
> Since you're the Chiron who taught Pericles.

Pericles, also, was a hearer of Zeno, the Eleatic, who treated of natural philosophy in the same manner as Parmenides did, but had also perfected himself in an art of his own for refuting and silencing opponents in argument: as Timon of Phlius describes it,—

> Also the two-edged tongue of mighty Zeno, who,
> Say what one would, could argue it untrue.

But he that saw most of Pericles, and furnished him most especially with a weight and grandeur of sense, superior to all arts of popularity, and in general gave him his elevation and sublimity of purpose and of character, was Anaxagoras of Clazomenæ; whom the men of those times called by the name of Nous, that is, mind, or intelligence, whether in admiration of the great and extraordinary gift he displayed for the science of nature, or because that he was the first of the philosophers who did not refer the first ordering of the world to fortune or chance, nor to necessity or compulsion, but to a pure, unadulterated intelligence, which in all other existing mixed and compound things acts as a principle of discrimination, and of combination of like with like.

For this man, Pericles entertained an extraordinary esteem and admiration, and, filling himself with this lofty, and, as they call it, up-in-the-air sort of thought, derived hence not merely, as was natural, elevation of purpose and dignity of language, raised far above the base and dishonest buffooneries of mob-eloquence, but, besides this, a composure of countenance, and a serenity and calmness in all his movements, which no occurrence whilst he was speaking could disturb, a sustained and even tone of voice, and various other advantages of a similar kind, which produced the greatest effect on his hearers. Once, after being reviled and ill-spoken of all day long in his own hearing by some vile and abandoned fellow in the open market-place, where he was engaged in the despatch of some urgent affair, he continued his business in perfect silence, and in the evening returned home composedly, the man still dogging him at the heels, and pelting him all the way with abuse and foul language; and stepping into his house, it being by this time dark, he ordered one of his servants to take a light, and to go along with the man and see him safe home. Ion, it is true, the dramatic poet, says that Pericles's manner in company was somewhat over-assuming and pompous; and that into his high bearing there entered a good deal of slightingness and scorn of others; he reserves his commendation for Cimon's ease and pliancy and natural grace in society. Ion, however, who must needs make virtue, like a show of tragedies, include some comic scenes,* we shall not altogether rely upon; Zeno used to bid those who called Pericles's gravity the affectation of a charlatan, to go and affect the like themselves; inasmuch as this mere counterfeiting might in time insensibly instil into them a real love and knowledge of those noble qualities.

Nor were these the only advantages which Pericles derived from Anaxagoras's acquaintance; he seems also to have become, by his instructions, superior to that superstition with which an ignorant wonder at appearances, for example, in the heavens possesses the minds of people unacquainted with their causes, eager for the supernatural, and excitable through an inexperience which the knowledge of natural causes removes, replacing wild and timid superstition by the good hope and assurance of an intelligent piety.

There is a story, that once Pericles had brought to him from a country farm of his, a ram's head with one horn, and that Lampon, the diviner, upon seeing the horn grow strong and solid out of the midst of the forehead, gave it as his judgment, that, there being at that time two potent factions, parties, or interests in the city, the one of Thucydides** and the other of Pericles, the government would come about to that one of them in whose ground or estate this token or indication of fate had shown itself. But that Anaxagoras, cleaving the skull in sunder, showed to the bystanders that the brain had not filled up its natural place, but being oblong, like an

---

* Three tragedies represented in succession were followed by a burlesque, the so-called *satyric* drama, which has no connection, it must be remembered, with the moral satire of the Romans, but takes its name from the grotesque satyrs of the Greek woods.—tr.

** Not Thucydides the historian.

egg, had collected from all parts of the vessel which contained it, in a point to that place from whence the root of the horn took its rise. And that, for that time, Anaxagoras was much admired for his explanation by those that were present; and Lampon no less a little while after, when Thucydides was overpowered, and the whole affairs of the state and government came into the hands of Pericles.

And yet, in my opinion, it is no absurdity to say that they were both in the right, both natural philosopher and diviner, one justly detecting the cause of this event, by which it was produced, the other the end for which it was designed. For it was the business of the one to find out and give an account of what it was made, and in what manner and by what means it grew as it did; and of the other to foretell to what end and purpose it was so made, and what it might mean or portend. Those who say that to find out the cause of a prodigy is in effect to destroy its supposed signification as such, do not take notice that, at the same time, together with divine prodigies, they also do away with signs and signals of human art and concert, as, for instance, the clashings of quoits, sun beacons, and the shadows on sun-dials, every one of which things has its cause, and by that cause and contrivance is a sign of something else. But these are subjects, perhaps, that would better befit another place.

PERICLES, while yet but a young man, stood in considerable apprehension of the people, as he was thought in face and figure to be very like the tyrant Pisistratus, and those of great age remarked upon the sweetness of his voice, and his volubility and rapidity in speaking, and were struck with amazement at the resemblance. Reflecting, too, that he had a considerable estate, and was descended of a noble family, and had friends of great influence, he was fearful all this might bring him to be banished as a dangerous person; and for this reason meddled not at all with state affairs, but in military service showed himself of a brave and intrepid nature. But when Aristides was now dead, and Themistocles driven out, and Cimon was for the most part kept abroad by the expeditions he made outside of Greece, Pericles, seeing things in this posture, now advanced and took his side, not with the rich and few, but with the many and poor, contrary to his natural bent, which was far from democratical; but, most likely, fearing he might fall under suspicion of aiming at arbitrary power, and seeing Cimon on the side of the aristocracy, and much beloved by the better and more distinguished people, he joined the party of the people, with a view at once both to secure himself and procure means against Cimon.

He immediately entered, also, on quite a new course of life and management of his time. For he was never seen to walk in any street but that which led to the market-place and the council-hall, and he avoided invitations of friends to supper, and all friendly visiting and intercourse whatever; in all the time he had to do with the public, which was not a little, he was never known to have gone to any of his friends to a supper, except that once when his near kinsman Euryptolemus married, he remained present till the ceremony of the drink-offering,* and then immediately rose from table and went his way. For these friendly meetings are very quick to defeat any assumed superiority, and in intimate familiarity an exterior of gravity is hard to maintain. Real excellence, indeed, is most recognized when most openly looked into; and in really good men, nothing which meets the eyes of external observers so truly deserves their admiration, as their daily common life does that of their nearer friends. Pericles, however, to avoid any feeling of commonness, or any satiety on the part of the people, presented himself at intervals only, not speaking to every business, nor at all times coming into the assembly, but, as Critolaus says, reserving himself, like the Salamian galley,** for great occasions, while matters of lesser importance were despatched by friends or other speakers under his direction. And of this number we are told Ephialtes made one, who broke the power of the council of Areopagus, giving the people, according to Plato's expression, so copious and so strong a draught of liberty, that, growing wild and unruly, like an unmanageable horse, it, as the comic poets say,—

"—— got beyond all keeping in,
Champing at Eubœa, and among the islands leaping in."

* The *spondai*, or libations, which concluded the meal.—tr.
** The Salaminia and the Paralus were the two sacred state-galleys of Athens, used only on special missions.—tr.

The style of speaking most consonant to his form of life and the dignity of his views he found, so to say, in the tones of that instrument with which Anaxagoras had furnished him; of his teaching he continually availed himself, and deepened the colors of rhetoric with the dye of natural science. For having, in addition to his great natural genius, attained, by the study of nature, to use the words of the divine Plato, this height of intelligence, and this universal consummating power, and drawing hence whatever might be of advantage to him in the art of speaking, he showed himself far superior to all others. Upon which account, they say, he had his nickname given him, though some are of opinion he was named the Olympian from the public buildings with which he adorned the city; and others again, from his great power in public affairs, whether of war or peace. Nor is it unlikely that the confluence of many attributes may have conferred it on him. However, the comedies represented at the time, which, both in good earnest and in merriment, let fly many hard words at him, plainly show that he got that appellation especially from his speaking; they speak of his "thundering and lightning" when he harangued the people, and of his wielding a dreadful thunderbolt in his tongue.

A saying also of Thucydides, the son of Melesias, stands on record, spoken by him by way of pleasantry upon Pericles's dexterity. Thucydides was one of the noble and distinguished citizens, and had been his greatest opponent; and, when Archidamus, the king of the Lacedæmonians, asked him whether he or Pericles were the better wrestler, he made this answer: "When I," said he, "have thrown him and given him a fair fall, by persisting that he had no fall, he gets the better of me, and makes the bystanders, in spite of their own eyes, believe him." The truth, however, is, that Pericles himself was very careful what and how he was to speak, insomuch that, whenever he went up to the hustings, he prayed the gods that no one word might unawares slip from him unsuitable to the matter and the occasion.

He has left nothing in writing behind him, except some decrees; and there are but very few of his sayings recorded; one, for example, is, that he said Ægina must, like a gathering in a man's eye, be removed from Piræus; and another, that he said he saw already war moving on its way towards them out of Peloponnesus. Again, when once . . . Sophocles, who was his fellow-commissioner in the generalship, was going on board with him, and praised the beauty of a youth they met with in the way to the ship, "Sophocles," said he, "a general ought not only to have clean hands, but also clean eyes." And Stesimbrotus tells us, that, in his encomium on those who fell in battle at Samos, he said they were become immortal, as the gods were. "For," said he, "we do not see them themselves, but only by the honors we pay them, and by the benefits they do us, attribute to them immortality; and the like attributes belong also to those that die in the service of their country."

SINCE Thucydides describes the rule of Pericles as an aristocratical government, that went by the name of a democracy, but was, indeed, the supremacy of a single great man, while many others say, on the contrary, that by him the common people were first encouraged and led on to such evils as appropriations of subject territory; allowances for attending theatres, payments for performing public duties, and by these bad habits were, under the influence of his public measures, changed from a sober, thrifty people, that maintained themselves by their own labors, to lovers of expense, intemperance, and license, let us examine the cause of this change by the actual matters of fact.

At the first, as has been said, when he set himself against Cimon's great authority, he did caress the people. Finding himself come short of his competitor in wealth and money, by which advantages the other was enabled to take care of the poor, inviting every day some one or other of the citizens that was in want to supper, and bestowing clothes on the aged people, and breaking down the hedges and enclosures of his grounds, that all that would might freely gather what fruit they pleased, Pericles, thus outdone in popular arts, by the advice of one Damonides of Œa, as Aristotle states, turned to the distribution of the public moneys; and in a short time having bought the people over, what with moneys allowed for shows and for service on juries, and what with other forms of pay and largess, he made use of them against the council of Areopagus, of which he himself was no member, as having never been appointed by lot either chief archon, or lawgiver, or king, or captain.* For from of old these offices were conferred on persons by lot, and they who had acquitted themselves duly in the discharge of them were advanced to the court of Areopagus. And so Pericles, having secured his power and interest with the populace, directed the exertions of his party against this council with such success, that most of those causes and matters which had been used to be tried there, were, by the agency of Ephialtes, removed from its cognizance, Cimon, also, was banished by ostracism as a favorer of the Lacedæmonians and a hater of the people, though in wealth and noble birth he was among the first, and had won several most glorious victories over the barbarians, and had filled the city with money and spoils of war; as is recorded in the history of his life. So vast an authority had Pericles obtained among the people.

The ostracism was limited by law to ten years; but the Lacedæmonians, in the mean time, entering with a great army into the territory of Tanagra, and the Athenians going out against them, Cimon, coming from his banishment before his time was out, put himself in arms and array with those of his fellow-citizens that were of his own tribe, and desired by his deeds to wipe off the suspicion of his favoring the Lacedæmonians, by venturing his own person along with his countrymen. But Pericles's friends, gathering in a body, forced him to retire as a banished man. For which cause also Pericles seems to have exerted himself more in that than in any battle, and to have been conspicuous above all for his exposure of himself to danger. All Cimon's friends, also, to a man, fell together side by side, whom Pericles had accused with him of taking part with the Lacedæmonians. Defeated in this battle on their own frontiers, and expecting a new and perilous attack with return of spring, the Athenians now felt regret and sorrow for the loss of Cimon, and repentance for their expulsion of him. Pericles, being sensible of their feelings, did not hesitate or delay to gratify it, and himself made the motion for recalling him home. He, upon his return, concluded a peace betwixt the two cities; for the Lacedæ-

* Eponymus, Thesmothetes, Basileus, Polemarchus; titles of the different archons, the chief civic dignitaries, who, after the period of the Persian wars, were appointed, not by election, but simply by lot, from the whole body of citizens. Hence, at this time, the importance of the board of the ten *strategi*, or generals, who were elected, and were always persons of real or supposed capacity.—tr.

monians entertained as kindly feelings towards him as they did the reverse towards Pericles and the other popular leaders.

Yet some there are who say that Pericles did not propose the order for Cimon's return till some private articles of agreement had been made between them, and this by means of Elpinice, Cimon's sister; that Cimon, namely, should go out to sea with a fleet of two hundred ships, and be commander-in-chief abroad, with a design to reduce the king of Persia's territories, and that Pericles should have the power at home.

This Elpinice, it was thought, had before this time procured some favor for her brother Cimon at Pericles's hands, and induced him to be more remiss and gentle in urging the charge when Cimon was tried for his life; for Pericles was one of the committee appointed by the commons to plead against him. And when Elpinice came and besought him in her brother's behalf, he answered, with a smile, "O Elpinice, you are too old a woman to undertake such business as this." But, when he appeared to impeach him, he stood up but once to speak, merely to acquit himself of his commission, and went out of court, having done Cimon the least prejudice of any of his accusers.

How, then, can one believe Idomeneus, who charges Pericles as if he had by treachery procured the murder of Ephialtes, the popular statesman, one who was his friend, and of his own party in all his political course, out of jealousy, forsooth, and envy of his great reputation? This historian, it seems, having raked up these stories, I know not whence, has befouled with them a man who, perchance, was not altogether free from fault or blame, but yet had a noble spirit, and a soul that was bent on honor; and where such qualities are, there can no such cruel and brutal passion find harbor or gain admittance. As to Ephialtes, the truth of the story, as Aristotle has told it, is this: that having made himself formidable to the oligarchical party, by being an uncompromising asserter of the people's rights in calling to account and prosecuting those who any way wronged them, his enemies, lying in wait for him, by the means of Aristodicus the Tanagræan, privately despatched him.

Cimon, while he was admiral, ended his days in the Isle of Cyprus. And the aristocratical party, seeing that Pericles was already before this grown to be the greatest and foremost man of all the city, but nevertheless wishing there should be somebody set up against him, to blunt and turn the edge of his power, that it might not altogether prove a monarchy, put forward Thucydides of Alopece, a discreet person, and a near kinsman of Cimon's, to conduct the opposition against him; who, indeed, though less skilled in warlike affairs than Cimon was, yet was better versed in speaking and political business, and keeping close guard in the city, and engaging with Pericles on the hustings, in a short time brought the government to an equality of parties. For he would not suffer those who were called the honest and good (persons of worth and distinction) to be scattered up and down and mix themselves and be lost among the populace, as formerly, diminishing and obscuring their superiority amongst the masses; but taking them apart by themselves and uniting them in one body, by their combined weight he was able, as it were upon the balance, to make a counterpoise to the other party.

For, indeed, there was from the beginning a sort of concealed split, or seam, as it might be in a piece of iron, marking the different popular and aristocratical tendencies; but the open rivalry and contention of these two opponents made the gash deep, and severed the city into the two parties of the people and the few. And so Pericles, at that time more than at any other, let loose the reins to the people, and made his policy subservient to their pleasure, contriving continually to have some great public show or solemnity, some banquet, or some procession or other in the town to please them, coaxing his countrymen like children, with such delights and pleasures as were not, however, unedifying. Besides that every year he sent out threescore galleys, on board of which there went numbers of the citizens, who were in pay eight months, learning at the same time and practising the art of seamanship.

He sent, moreover, a thousand of them into the Chersonese as planters, to share the land among them by lot, and five hundred more into the isle of Naxos, and half that number to Andros, a thousand into Thrace to dwell among the Bisaltæ, and others into Italy, when the city Sybaris, which now was called Thurii, was to be repeopled. And this he did to ease and discharge the city of an idle, and, by reason of their idleness, a busy, meddling crowd of people; and at the same time to meet the necessities and restore the fortunes of the poor townsmen, and to intimidate, also, and check their allies from attempting any change, by posting such garrisons, as it were, in the midst of them.

That which gave most pleasure and ornament to the city of Athens, and the greatest admiration and even astonishment to all strangers, and that which now is Greece's only evidence that the power she boasts of and her ancient wealth are no romance or idle story, was his construction of the public and sacred buildings. Yet this was that of all his actions in the government which his enemies most looked askance upon and cavilled at in the popular assemblies, crying out . . . that the commonwealth of Athens had lost its reputation and was ill-spoken of abroad for removing the common treasure of the Greeks from the isle of Delos into their own custody; and how that their fairest excuse for so doing, namely, that they took it away for fear the barbarians should seize it, and on purpose to secure it in a safe place, this Pericles had made unavailable, and how that "Greece cannot but resent it as an insufferable affront, and consider herself to be tyrannized over openly, when she sees the treasure, which was contributed by her upon a necessity for the war, wantonly lavished out by us upon our city, to gild her all over, and to adorn and set her forth, as it were some vain woman, hung round with precious stones and figures and temples, which cost a world of money."

PERICLES, on the other hand, informed the people, that they were in no way obliged to give any account of those moneys to their allies, so long as they maintained their defence, and kept off the barbarians from attacking them; while in the mean time they did not so much as supply one horse or man or ship, but only found money for the service; "which money," said he, "is not theirs that give it, but theirs that receive it, if so be they perform the conditions upon which they receive it." And that it was good reason, that, now the city was sufficiently provided and stored with all things necessary for the war, they should convert the overplus of its wealth to such undertakings, as would hereafter, when completed, give them eternal honor, and, for the present, while in process, freely supply all the inhabitants with plenty. With their variety of workmanship and of occasions for service, which summon all arts and trades and require all hands to be employed about them, they do actually put the whole city, in a manner, into state-pay; while at the same time she is both beautified and maintained by herself. For as those who are of age and strength for war are provided for and maintained in the armaments abroad by their pay out of the public stock, so, it being his desire and design that the undisciplined mechanic multitude that stayed at home should not go without their share of public salaries, and yet should not have them given them for sitting still and doing nothing, to that end he thought fit to bring in among them, with the approbation of the people, these vast projects of buildings and designs of works, that would be of some continuance before they were finished, and would give employment to numerous arts, so that the part of the people that stayed at home might, no less than those that were at sea or in garrisons or on expeditions, have a fair and just occasion of receiving the benefit and having their share of the public moneys.

The materials were stone, brass, ivory, gold, ebony cypress-wood; and the arts or trades that wrought and fashioned them were smiths and carpenters, moulders, founders and braziers, stone-cutters, dyers, goldsmiths, ivory-workers, painters, embroiderers, turners; those again that conveyed them to the town for use, merchants and mariners and ship-masters by sea, and by land, cartwrights, cattle-breeders, waggoners, rope-makers, flax-workers, shoe-makers and leather-dressers, road-makers, miners. And every trade in the same nature, as a captain in an army has his particular company of soldiers under him, had its own hired company of journeymen and laborers belonging to it banded together as in array, to be as it were the instrument and body for the performance of the service. Thus, to say all in a word, the occasions and services of these public works distributed plenty through every age and condition.

As then grew the works up, no less stately in size than exquisite in form, the workmen striving to outvie the material and the design with the beauty of their workmanship, yet the most wonderful thing of all was the rapidity of their execution. Undertakings, any one of which singly might have required, they thought, for their completion, several successions and ages of men, were every one of them accomplished in the height and prime of one man's political service. Although they say, too, that Zeuxis once, having heard Agatharchus the painter boast of despatching his work with speed and ease, replied, "I take a long time." For ease and speed in doing a thing do not give the work lasting solidity or exactness of beauty; the expenditure of time allowed to a man's pains beforehand for the production of a thing is repaid by way of interest with a vital force for its preservation when once produced. For which reason Pericles's works are especially admired, as having been made quickly, to last long. For every particular piece of his work was immediately, even at that time, for its beauty and elegance, antique; and yet in its vigour and freshness looks to this day as if it were just executed. There is a sort of bloom of newness upon those works of his, preserving them from the touch of time, as if they had some perennial spirit and undying vitality mingled in the composition of them.

Phidias had the oversight of all the works, and was surveyor-general, though upon the various portions other great masters and workmen were employed. For Callicrates and Ictinus built the Parthenon; the chapel at Eleusis, where the mysteries were celebrated, was begun by Corœbus, who erected the pillars that stand upon the floor or pavement, and joined them to the architraves; and after his death Metagenes of Xypete added the frieze and the upper line of columns; Xenocles of Cholargus roofed or arched the lantern on the top of the temple of Castor and Pollux; and the long wall, which Socrates says he himself heard Pericles propose to the people, was undertaken by Callicrates. This work Cratinus ridicules, as long in finishing,—

> 'T is long since Pericles, if words would do it,
> Talk'd up the wall; yet adds not one mite to it.

The Odeum, or music-room, which in its interior was full of seats and ranges of pillars, and outside had its roof made to slope and descend from one single point at the top, was constructed, we are told, in imitation of the king of Persia's Pavilion; this likewise by Pericles's order; which Cratinus again, in his comedy called The Thracian Women, made an occasion of raillery,—

So, we see here,
Jupiter Long-pate Pericles appear,
Since ostracism time, he's laid aside his head,
And wears the new Odeum in its stead.

Pericles, also, eager for distinction, then first obtained the decree for a contest in musical skill to be held yearly at the Panathenæa, and he himself, being chosen judge, arranged the order and method in which the competitors should sing and play on the flute and on the harp. And both at that time, and at other times also, they sat in this music-room to see and hear all such trials of skill.

The propylæa, or entrances to the Acropolis, were finished in five years' time, Mnesicles being the principal architect. A strange accident happened in the course of building, which showed that the goddess was not averse to the work, but was aiding and coöperating to bring it to perfection. One of the artificers, the quickest and the handiest workman among them all, with a slip of his foot fell down from a great height, and lay in a miserable condition, the physicians having no hopes of his recovery. When Pericles was in distress about this, Athena appeared to him at night in a dream, and ordered a course of treatment, which he applied, and in a short time and with great ease cured the man. And upon this occasion it was that he set up a brass statue of Athena, surnamed Health, in the citadel near the altar, which they say was there before. But it was Phidias who wrought the goddess's image in gold, and he has his name inscribed on the pedestal as the workman of it; and indeed the whole work in a manner was under his charge, and he had, as we have said already, the oversight over all the artists and workmen, through Pericles's friendship for him; and this, indeed, made him much envied, and his patron shamefully slandered with stories, as if Phidias were in the habit of receiving, for Pericles's use, freeborn women that came to see the works. The comic writers of the town, when they had got hold of this story, made much of it, and bespattered him with all the ribaldry they could invent, charging him falsely with the wife of Menippus, one who was his friend and served as lieutenant under him in the wars; and with the birds kept by Pyrilampes, an acquaintance of Pericles, who, they pretended, used to give presents of peacocks to Pericles's female friends. And how can one wonder at any number of strange assertions from men whose whole lives were devoted to mockery, and who were ready at any time to sacrifice the reputation of their superiors to vulgar envy and spite, as to some evil genius, when even Stesimbrotus the Thasian has dared to lay to the charge of Pericles a monstrous and fabulous piece of criminality with his son's wife? So very difficult a matter is it to trace and find out the truth of any thing by history, when, on the one hand, those who afterwards write it find long periods of time intercepting their view, and, on the other hand, the contemporary records of any actions and lives, partly through envy and ill-will, partly through favor and flattery, pervert and distort truth.

WHEN the orators, who sided with Thucydides and his party, were at one time crying out, as their custom was, against Pericles, as one who squandered away the public money, and made havoc of the state revenues, he rose in the open assembly and put the question to the people, whether they thought that he had laid out much; and they saying, "Too much, a great deal," "Then," said he, "since it is so, let the cost not go to your account, but to mine; and let the inscription upon the buildings stand in my name." When they heard him say thus, whether it were out of a surprise to see the greatness of his spirit, or out of emulation of the glory of the works, they cried aloud, bidding him to spend on, and lay out what he thought fit from the public purse, and to spare no cost, till all were finished.

At length, coming to a final contest with Thucydides, which of the two should ostracize the other out of the country, and having gone through this peril, he threw his antagonist out, and broke up the confederacy that had been organized against him. So that now all schism and division being at an end, and the city brought to evenness and unity, he got all Athens and all affairs that pertained to the Athenians into his own hands, their tributes, their armies, and their galleys, the islands, the sea, and their wide-extended power, partly over other Greeks and partly over barbarians, and all that empire, which they possessed, founded and fortified upon subject nations and royal friendships and alliances.

After this he was no longer the same man he had been before, nor as tame and gentle and familiar as formerly with the populace, so as readily to yield to their pleasures and to comply with the desires of the multitude, as a steersman shifts with the winds. Quitting that loose, remiss, and, in some cases, licentious court of the popular will, he turned those soft and flowery modulations to the austerity of aristocratical and regal rule; and employing this uprightly and undeviatingly for the country's best interests, he was able generally to lead the people along, with their own wills and consents, by persuading and showing them what was to be done; and sometimes, too, urging and pressing them forward extremely against their will, he made them, whether they would or no, yield submission to what was for their advantage. In which, to say the truth, he did but like a skilful physician, who, in a complicated and chronic disease, as he sees occasion, at one time allows his patient the moderate use of such things as please him, at another time gives him keen pains and drugs to work the cure. For there arising and growing up, as was natural, all manner of distempered feelings among a people which had so vast a command and dominion, he alone, as a great master, knowing how to handle and deal fitly with each one of them, and, in an especial manner, making that use of hopes and fears, as his two chief rudders, with the one to check the career of their confidence at any time, with the other to raise them up and cheer them when under any discouragement, plainly showed by this, that rhetoric, or the art of speaking, is, in Plato's language, the government of the souls of men, and that her chief business is to address the affections and passions, which are as it were the strings and keys to the soul, and require a skilful and careful touch to be played on as they should be. The source of this predominance was not merely his power of language, but, as Thucydides assures us, the reputation of his life, and the confidence felt in his character; his manifest freedom from every kind of corruption, and superiority to all considerations of money. Notwithstanding he had made the city Athens, which was great of itself, as great and rich as can be imagined, and though he were himself in power and interest more than equal to many kings and absolute rulers, some of whom also bequeathed by will their power to their children, he, for his part, did not make the patrimony his father left him greater than it was by one drachma.

Thucydides, indeed, gives a plain statement of the greatness of his power; and the comic poets, in their spiteful manner, more than hint at it, styling his companions and friends the new Pisistratidæ, and calling on him to abjure any intention of usurpation, as one whose eminence was too great to be any longer proportionable to and compatible with a democracy or popular government. And Teleclides says the Athenians had surrendered up to him—

> The tribute of the cities, and with them, the cities too, to do with them as he pleases, and undo;
> To build up, if he likes, stone walls around a town; and again, if so he likes, to pull them down;
> Their treaties and alliances, power, empire, peace, and war, their wealth and their success forevermore.

Nor was all this the luck of some happy occasion; nor was it the mere bloom and grace of a policy that flourished for a season. For forty years he maintained the first place among statesmen such as Ephialtes and Leocrates and Myronides and Cimon and Tolmides and Thucydides. For no less than fifteen years after the banishment of Thucydides he remained in continuous command in the office of General to which he was annually reelected. Throughout this period he preserved his integrity unspotted, though otherwise he was not altogether idle or careless in looking after his pecuniary advantage. His paternal estate, which of right belonged to him, he so ordered that it might neither through negligence be wasted or lessened, nor yet, being so full of business as he was, cost him any great trouble or time with taking care of it; and put it into such a way of management as he thought to be the most easy for himself, and the most exact. All his yearly products and profits he sold together in a lump, and supplied his household needs afterward by buying every thing that he or his family wanted out of the market. Upon which account, his children, when they grew to age, were not well pleased with his management, and the women that lived with him were treated with little cost, and complained of this way of housekeeping, where every thing was ordered and set down from day to day, and reduced to the greatest exactness; since there was not there, as is usual in a great family and a plentiful estate, any thing to spare, or over and above; but all that went out or came in, all disbursements and all receipts, proceeded as it were by number and measure. His manager in all this was a single servant, Evangelus by name, a man either naturally gifted or instructed by Pericles so as to excel every one in this art of domestic economy.

All this, in truth, was very little in harmony with Anaxagoras's wisdom; if, indeed, it be true that he, by a kind of divine impulse and greatness of spirit, voluntarily quitted his house, and left his land to lie fallow and to be grazed by sheep like a common. But the life of a contemplative philosopher and that of an active statesman are, I presume, not the same thing; for the one merely employs, upon great and good objects of thought, an intelligence that requires no aid of instruments nor supply of any external materials; whereas the other, who tempers and applies his virtue to human uses, may have occasion for affluence, not as a matter of mere necessity, but as a noble thing; which was Pericles's case, who relieved numerous poor citizens.

However, there is a story, that Anaxagoras himself, while Pericles was taken up with public affairs, lay neglected, and that, now being grown old, he wrapped himself up with a resolution to die for want of food; which being by chance brought to Pericles's ear, he was horror-struck, and instantly ran thither, and used all the arguments and entreaties he could to him, lamenting not so much Anaxagoras's condition as his own, should he lose such a counsellor as he had found him to be; and that, upon this, Anaxagoras unfolded his robe, and showing himself, made answer: "Pericles," said he, "even those who have occasion for a lamp supply it with oil."

The Lacedæmonians beginning to show themselves troubled at the growth of the Athenian power, Pericles, on the other hand, to elevate the people's spirit yet more, and to raise them to the thought of great actions, proposed a decree, to summon all the Greeks in every part, whether of Europe or Asia, every city, little as well as great, to send their deputies to Athens to a general assembly, or convention, there to consult and advise concerning the Greek temples which the barbarians had burnt down, and the sacrifices which were due from them upon vows they had made to their gods for the safety of Greece when they fought against the barbarians; and also concerning the navigation of the sea, that they might henceforward all of them pass to and fro and trade securely, and be at peace among themselves.

Upon this errand, there were twenty men, of such as were above fifty years of age, sent by commission; five to summon the Ionians and Dorians in Asia, and the islanders as far as Lesbos and Rhodes; five to visit all the places in the Hellespont and Thrace, up to Byzantium; and another five besides these to go to Bœotia and Phocis and Peloponnesus, and from hence to pass through the Locrians over to the neighboring continent, as far as Acarnania and Ambracia; and the rest to take their course through Eubœa to the Œtæans and the Malian Gulf, and to the Achæans of Phthiotis and the Thessalians; all of them to treat with the people as they passed, and to persuade them to come and take their part in the debates for settling the peace and jointly regulating the affairs of Greece.

Nothing was effected, nor did the cities meet by their deputies, as was desired; the Lacedæmonians, as it is said, crossing the design underhand, and the attempt being disappointed and baffled first in Peloponnesus. I thought fit, however, to introduce the mention of it, to show the spirit of the man and the greatness of his thoughts.

In his military conduct, he gained a great reputation for wariness; he would not by his good-will engage in any fight which had much uncertainty or hazard; he did not envy the glory of generals whose rash adventures fortune favored with brilliant success, however they were admired by others; nor did he think them worthy his imitation, but always used to say to his citizens that, so far as lay in his power, they should continue immortal, and live forever. Seeing Tolmides, the son of Tolmæus, upon the confidence of his former successes, and flushed with the honor his military actions had procured him, making preparation to attack the Bœotians in their own country, when there was no likely opportunity, and that he had prevailed with the bravest and most enterprising of the youth to enlist themselves as volunteers in the service, who besides his other force made up a thousand, he endeavored to withhold him and to advise him from it in the public assembly, telling him in a memorable saying of his, which still goes about, that, if he would not take Pericles's advice, yet he would not do amiss to wait and be ruled by time, the wisest counsellor of all. This saying, at that time, was but slightly commended; but within a few days after, when news was brought that Tolmides himself had been defeated and slain in battle near Coronea, and that many brave citizens had fallen with him, it gained him great repute as well as good-will among the people, for wisdom and for love of his countrymen.

But of all his expeditions, that to the Chersonese gave most satisfaction and pleasure, having proved the safety of the Greeks who inhabited there. For not only by carrying along with him a thousand fresh citizens of Athens he gave new strength and vigor to the cities, but also by belting the neck of land, which joins the peninsula to the continent, with bulwarks and forts from sea to sea, he put a stop to the inroads of the Thracians, who lay all about the Chersonese, and closed the door against a continual and grievous war, with which that country had been long harassed, lying exposed to the encroachments and influx of barbarous neighbors, and groaning under the evils of a predatory population both upon and within its borders.

Nor was he less admired and talked of abroad for his sailing round the Peloponnesus, having set out from Pegæ, or The Fountains, the port of Megara, with a hundred galleys. For he not only laid waste the sea-coast, as Tolmides had done before, but also, advancing far up into main land with the soldiers he had on board, by the terror of his appearance drove many within their walls; and at Nemea, with main force, routed and raised a trophy over the Sicyonians, who stood their ground and joined battle with him. And having taken on board a supply of soldiers into the galleys, out of Achaia, then in league with Athens, he crossed with the fleet to the opposite continent, and, sailing along by the mouth of the river Achelous, overran Acarnania, and shut up the Œniadæ within their city walls, and having ravaged and wasted their country, weighed anchor for home with the double advantage of having shown himself formidable to his enemies, and at the same time safe and energetic to his fellow-citizens; for there was not so much as any chance-miscarriage that happened, the whole voyage through, to those who were under his charge.

Entering also the Euxine Sea with a large and finely equipped fleet, he obtained for the Greek cities any new arrangements they wanted, and entered into friendly relations with them; and to the barbarous nations, and kings and chiefs round about them, displayed the greatness of the power of the Athenians, their perfect ability and confidence to sail wherever they had a mind, and to bring the whole sea under their control. He left the Sinopians thirteen ships of war, with soldiers under the command of Lamachus, to assist them against Timesileus the tyrant; and when he and his accomplices had been thrown out, obtained a decree that six hundred of the Athenians that were willing should sail to Sinope and plant themselves there with the Sinopians, sharing among them the houses and land which the tyrant and his party had previously held.

But in other things he did not comply with the giddy impulses of the citizens, nor quit his own resolutions to follow their fancies, when, carried away with the thought of their strength and great success, they were eager to interfere again in Egypt, and to disturb the king of Persia's maritime dominions. Nay, there were a good many who were, even then, possessed with that unblest and inauspicious passion for Sicily, which afterward the orators of Alcibiades's party blew up into a flame. There were some also who dreamt of Tuscany and of Carthage, and not without plausible reason in their present large dominion and the prosperous course of their affairs.

But Pericles curbed this passion for foreign conquest, and unsparingly pruned and cut down their ever busy fancies for a multitude of undertakings; and directed their power for the most part to securing and consolidating what they had already got, supposing it would be quite enough for them to do, if they could keep the Lacedæmonians in check; to whom he entertained all along a sense of opposition; which, as upon many other occasions, so he particularly showed by what he did in the time of the holy war. The Lacedæmonians, having gone with an army to Delphi, restored

Apollo's temple, which the Phocians had got into their possession, to the Delphians; immediately after their departure, Pericles, with another army, came and restored the Phocians. And the Lacedæmonians having engraven the record of their privilege of consulting the oracle before others, which the Delphians gave them, upon the forehead of the brazen wolf which stands there, he, also, having received from the Phocians the like privilege for the Athenians, had it cut upon the same wolf of brass on his right side.

That he did well and wisely in thus restraining the exertions of the Athenians within the compass of Greece, the events themselves that happened afterward bore sufficient witness. For, in the first place, the Eubœans revolted, against whom he passed over with forces; and then, immediately after, news came that the Megarians were turned their enemies, and a hostile army was upon the borders of Attica, under the conduct of Plistoanax, king of the Lacedæmonians. Wherefore Pericles came with his army back again in all haste out of Eubœa, to meet the war which threatened at home; and did not venture to engage a numerous and brave army eager for battle; but perceiving that Plistoanax was a very young man, and governed himself mostly by the counsel and advice of Cleandrides, whom the ephors had sent with him, by reason of his youth, to be a kind of guardian and assistant to him, he privately made trial of this man's integrity, and, in a short time, having corrupted him with money, prevailed with him to withdraw the Peloponnesians out of Attica. When the army had retired and dispersed into their several states, the Lacedæmonians in anger fined their king in so large a sum of money, that, unable to pay it, he quitted Lacedæmon; while Cleandrides fled, and had sentence of death passed upon him in his absence. This was the father of Gylippus, who overpowered the Athenians in Sicily. And it seems that this covetousness was an hereditary disease transmitted from father to son; for Gylippus also afterwards was caught in foul practices, and expelled from Sparta for it. But this we have told at large in the account of Lysander.

WHEN Pericles, in giving his accounts of this expedition, stated a disbursement of ten talents, as laid out upon fit occasion, the people, without any question, nor troubling themselves to investigate the mystery, freely allowed of it. And some historians, among them Theophrastus the philosopher, have given it as a truth that Pericles every year used to send privately the sum of ten talents to Sparta, with which he complimented those in office, to keep off the war; not to purchase peace . . . , but time, that he might prepare at leisure, and be the better able to carry on war hereafter.

Immediately after this, turning his forces against the revolters, and passing over into the island of Eubœa with fifty . . . ships and five thousand men in arms, he reduced their cities, and drove out the citizens of the Chalcidians, called Hippobotæ, horsefeeders, the chief persons for wealth and reputation among them; and removing all the Histiæans out of the country, brought in a plantation of Athenians in their place, making them his one example of severity, because they had captured an Attic ship and killed all on board.

After this, having made a truce between the Athenians and Lacedæmonians for thirty years, he ordered, by public decree, the expedition against the Isle of Samos, on the ground, that, when they were bid to leave off their war with the Milesians, they had not complied. And as these measures against the Samians are thought to have been taken to please Aspasia, this may be a fit point for inquiry about the woman, what art or charming faculty she had that enabled her to captivate, as she did, the greatest statesmen, and to give the philosophers occasion to speak so much about her, and that, too, not to her disparagement. That she was a Milesian by birth, the daughter of Axiochus, is a thing acknowledged. And they say it was in emulation of Thargelia, a courtesan of the old Ionian times, that she made her addresses to men of great power. Thargelia was a great beauty, extremely charming, and at the same time sagacious; she had numerous suitors among the Greeks, and brought all who had to do with her over to the Persian interest, and by their means, being men of the greatest power and station, sowed the seeds of the Median faction up and down in several cities.* Aspasia, some say, was courted and caressed by Pericles upon account of her knowledge and skill in politics. Socrates himself would sometimes go to visit her, and some of his acquaintance with him;

---

* She was married, says Athenæus, to fourteen husbands; a woman of great beauty and intellect.—tr.

and those who frequented her company would carry their wives with them to listen to her. Her occupation was any thing but creditable, her house being a home for young courtesans. Æschines tells us also, that Lysicles, a sheep-dealer, a man of low birth and character, by keeping Aspasia company after Pericles's death, came to be a chief man in Athens. And in Plato's Menexenus, though we do not take the introduction as quite serious, still this much seems to be historical, that she had the repute of being resorted to by many of the Athenians for instruction in the art of speaking. Pericles's inclination for her seems, however, to have rather proceeded from the passion of love. He had a wife that was near of kin to him, who had been married first to Hipponicus, by whom she had Callias, surnamed the Rich; and also she brought Pericles, while she lived with him, two sons, Xanthippus and Paralus. Afterwards, when they did not well agree nor like to live together, he parted with her, with her own consent, to another man, and himself took Aspasia, and loved her with wonderful affection; every day, both as he went out and as he came in from the market-place, he saluted and kissed her.

In the comedies she goes by the nicknames of the new Omphale and Deianira, and again is styled Juno. Cratinus, in downright terms, calls her a harlot.

> To find him a Juno the goddess of lust
> Bore that harlot past shame,
> Aspasia by name.

It should seem, also, that he had a son by her; Eupolis, in his Demi, introduced Pericles asking after his safety, and Myronides replying,

> "My son?" "He lives; a man he had been long,
> But that the harlot-mother did him wrong."

Aspasia, they say, became so celebrated and renowned, that Cyrus also, who made war against Artaxerxes for the Persian monarchy, gave her whom he loved the best of all his concubines the name of Aspasia, who before that was called Milto. She was a Phocæan by birth, the daughter of one Hermotimus, and, when Cyrus fell in battle, was carried to the king, and had great influence at court.

These things coming into my memory as I am writing this story, it would be unnatural for me to omit them.

Pericles, however, was particularly charged with having proposed to the assembly the war against the Samians, from favor to the Milesians, upon the entreaty of Aspasia. For the two states were at war for the possession of Priene; and the Samians, getting the better, refused to lay down their arms and to have the controversy between them decided by arbitration before the Athenians. Pericles, therefore, fitting out a fleet, went and broke up the oligarchical government at Samos, and, taking fifty of the principal men of the town as hostages, and as many of their children, sent them to the isle of Lemnos, there to be kept, though he had offers, as some relate, of a talent a piece for himself from each one of the hostages, and of many other presents from those who were anxious not to have a democracy. Moreover, Pissuthnes the Persian, one of the king's lieutenants, bearing some good-will to the Samians, sent him ten thousand pieces of gold to excuse the city. Pericles, however, would receive none of all this; but after he had taken that course with the Samians which he thought fit, and set up a democracy among them, sailed back to Athens.

But they, however, immediately revolted, Pissuthnes having privily got away their hostages for them, and provided them with means for the war. Whereupon Pericles came out with a fleet a second time against them, and found them not idle nor slinking away, but manfully resolved to try for the dominion of the sea. The issue was, that, after a sharp sea-fight about the island called Tragia, Pericles obtained a decisive victory, having with forty-four ships routed seventy of the enemy's, twenty of which were carrying soldiers.

Together with his victory and pursuit, having made himself master of the port, he laid siege to the Samians, and blocked them up, who yet, one way or other, still ventured to make sallies, and fight under the city walls. But after . . . another greater fleet from Athens had arrived, and . . . the Samians were now shut up with a close leaguer on every side, Pericles, taking with him sixty galleys, sailed out into the main sea, with the intention, as most authors give the account, to meet a squadron of Phœnician ships that were coming for the Samians' relief, and to fight them at as great distance as could be from the island; but, as Stesimbrotus says, with a design of putting over to Cyprus; which does not seem to be probable. But whichever of the two was his intent, it seems to have been a miscalculation. For on his departure, Melissus, the son of Ithagenes, a philosopher, being at that time general in Samos, despising either the small number of the ships that were left or the inexperience of the commanders, prevailed with the citizens to attack the Athenians. And the Samians having won the battle, and taken several of the men prisoners, and disabled several of the ships, were masters of the sea, and brought into port all necessaries they wanted for the war, which they had not before. Aristotle says, too, that Pericles himself had been once before this worsted by this Melissus in a sea-fight.

The Samians, that they might requite an affront which had before been put upon them, branded the Athenians, whom they took prisoners, in their foreheads, with the figure of an owl. For so the Athenians had marked them before with a Samæna, which is a sort of ship, low and flat in the prow, so as to look snub-nosed, but wide and large and well-spread in the hold, by which it both carries a large cargo and sails well. And it was so called, because the first of that kind was seen at Samos, having been built by order of Polycrates the tyrant. These brands upon the Samians' foreheads, they say, are the allusion in the passage of Aristophanes, where he says,—

> For, oh, the Samians are a lettered people.

PERICLES, as soon as news was brought him of the disaster that had befallen his army, made all the haste he could to come in to their relief, and having defeated Melissus, who bore up against him, and put the enemy to flight, he immediately proceeded to hem them in with a wall, resolving to master them and take the town, rather with some cost and time, than with the wounds and hazards of his citizens. But as it was a hard matter to keep back the Athenians, who were vexed at the delay, and were eagerly bent to fight, he divided the whole multitude into eight parts, and arranged by lot that that part which had the white bean should have leave to feast and take their ease, while the other seven were fighting. And this is the reason, they say, that people, when at any time they have been merry, and enjoyed themselves, call it white day, in allusion to this white bean.

Ephorus the historian tells us besides, that Pericles made us of engines of battery in this siege, being much taken with the curiousness of the invention, with the aid and presence of Artemon himself, the engineer, who, being lame, used to be carried about in a litter, where the works required his attendance, and for that reason was called Periphoretus. But Heraclides Ponticus disproves this out of Anacreon's poems, where mention is made of this Artemon Periphoretus several ages before the Samian war, or any of these occurrences. And he says that Artemon, being a man who loved his ease, and had a great apprehension of danger, for the most part kept close within doors, having two of his servants to hold a brazen shield over his head, that nothing might fall upon him from above; and if he were at any time forced upon necessity to go abroad, that he was carried about in a little hanging bed, close to the very ground, and that for this reason he was called Periphoretus.

In the ninth month, the Samians surrendering themselves and delivering up the town, Pericles pulled down their walls, and seized their shipping, and set a fine of a large sum of money upon them, part of which they paid down at once, and they agreed to bring in the rest by a certain time, and gave hostages for security. Duris the Samian makes a tragical drama out of these events, charging the Athenians and Pericles with a great deal of cruelty, which neither Thucydides, nor Ephorus, nor Aristotle have given any account of, and probably with little regard to truth; how, for example, he brought the captains and soldiers of the galleys into the market-place at Miletus, and there having bound them fast to boards for ten days, then, when they were already all but half dead, gave order to have them killed by beating out their brains with clubs, and their dead bodies to be flung out into the open streets and fields, unburied. Duris, however, who even where he has no private feeling concerned, is not wont to keep his narrative within the limits of truth, is the more likely upon this occasion to have exaggerated the calamities which befell his country, to create odium against the Athenians. Pericles, however, after the reduction of

Samos, returning back to Athens, took care that those who died in the war should be honorably buried, and made a funeral harangue, as the custom is, in their commendation at their graves, for which he gained great admiration. As he came down from the stage on which he spoke, the rest of the women came and complimented him, taking him by the hand, and crowning him with garlands and ribbons, like a victorious athlete in the games; but Elpinice, coming near to him, said, "These are brave deeds, Pericles, that you have done, and such as deserve our chaplets; who have lost us many a worthy citizen, not in a war with Phœnicians or Medes, like my brother Cimon, but for the overthrow of an allied and kindred city." As Elpinice spoke these words, he, smiling quietly, as it is said, returned her answer with this verse,—

Old women should not seek to be perfumed.

Ion says of him, that, upon this exploit of his, conquering the Samians, he indulged very high and proud thoughts of himself: whereas Agamemnon was ten years a taking a barbarous city, he had in nine months' time vanquished and taken the greatest and most powerful of the Ionians. And indeed it was not without reason that he assumed this glory to himself, for, in real truth, there was much uncertainty and great hazard in this war, if so be, as Thucydides tells us, the Samian state were within a very little of wresting the whole power and dominion of the sea out of the Athenians' hands.

After this was over, the Peloponnesian war beginning to break out in full tide, he advised the people to send help to the Corcyræans, who were attacked by the Corinthians, and to secure to themselves an island possessed of great naval resources, since the Peloponnesians were already all but in actual hostilities against them. The people readily consenting to the motion, and voting an aid and succor for them, he despatched Lacedæmonius, Cimon's son, having only ten ships with him, as it were out of a design to affront him; for there was a great kindness and friendship betwixt Cimon's family and the Lacedæmonians; so, in order that Lacedæmonius might lie the more open to a charge, or suspicion at least, of favoring the Lacedaemonians and playing false, if he performed no considerable exploit in this service, he allowed him a small number of ships, and sent him out against his will; and indeed he made it somewhat his business to hinder Cimon's sons from rising in the state, professing that by their very names they were not to be looked upon as native and true Athenians, but foreigners and strangers, one being called Lacedæmonius, another Thessalus, and the third Eleus; and they were all three of them, it was thought, born of an Arcadian woman. Being, however, ill spoken of on account of these ten galleys, as having afforded but a small supply to the people that were in need, and yet given a great advantage to those who might complain of the act of intervention, Pericles sent out a larger force afterward to Corcyra, which arrived after the fight was over. And when now the Corinthians, angry and indignant with the Athenians, accused them publicly at Lacedæmon, the Megarians joined with them, complaining that they were, contrary to common right and the articles of peace sworn to among the Greeks, kept out and driven away from every market and from all ports under the control of the Athenians. The Æginetans, also, professing to be ill-used and treated with violence, made supplications in private to the Lacedæmonians for redress, though not daring openly to call the Athenians in question. In the mean time, also, the city Potidæa, under the dominion of the Athenians, but a colony formerly of the Corinthians, had revolted, and was beset with a formal siege, and was a further occasion of precipitating the war.

Yet notwithstanding all this, there being embassies sent to Athens, and Archidamus, the king of the Lacedæmonians, endeavoring to bring the greater part of the complaints and matters in dispute to a fair determination, and to pacify and allay the heats of the allies, it is very likely that the war would not upon any other grounds of quarrel have fallen upon the Athenians, could they have been prevailed with to repeal the ordinance against the Megarians, and to be reconciled to them. Upon which account, since Pericles was the man who mainly opposed it, and stirred up the people's passions to persist in their contention with the Megarians, he was regarded as the sole cause of the war.

They say, moreover, that ambassadors went, by order, from Lacedæmon to Athens about this very business, and that when Pericles was urging a certain law which made it illegal to take down or withdraw the tablet of the decree, one of the ambassadors, Polyalces by name, said, "Well, do not take it down then, but *turn* it; there is no law, I suppose, which forbids that;"* which, though prettily said, did not move Pericles from his resolution. There may have been, in all likelihood, something of a secret grudge and private animosity which he had against the Megarians. Yet, upon a public and open charge against them, that they had appropriated part of the sacred land on the frontier, he proposed a decree that a herald should be sent to them, and the same also to the Lacedæmonians, with an accusation of the Megarians; an order which certainly shows equitable and friendly proceeding enough. And after . . . the herald who was sent, by name Anthemocritus, died, and it was believed that the Megarians had contrived his death, then Charinus proposed a decree against them, that there should be an irreconcilable and implacable enmity thenceforward between the two commonwealths; and that if any one of the Megarians should but set his foot in Attica, he should be put to death; and that the commanders, when they take the usual oath, should, over and above that, swear that they will twice every year make an inroad into the Megarian country; and that Anthemocritus should be buried near the Thriasian Gates, which are now called the Dipylon, or Double Gate.

On the other hand, the Megarians, utterly denying and disowning the murder of Anthemocritus, throw the whole matter upon Aspasia and Pericles, availing themselves of the famous verses in the Acharnians,

> To Megara some of our madcaps ran,
> And stole Simætha thence, their courtesan.
> Which exploit the Megarians to outdo,
> Came to Aspasia's house, and took off two.

---

* The word for *taking down*, in the literal sense, is also the technical term for revoking, or repealing; hence the Spartans play upon the two senses. "If you may not take it down, turn it, with its face to the wall."—tr.

THE true occasion of the quarrel is not so easy to find out. But of inducing the refusal to annul the decree, all alike charge Pericles. Some say he met the request with a positive refusal, out of high spirit and a view of the state's best interests, accounting that the demand made in those embassies was designed for a trial of their compliance, and that a concession would be taken for a confession of weakness, as if they dared not do otherwise; while others . . . say that it was rather out of arrogance and a wilful spirit of contention, to show his own strength, that he took occasion to slight the Lacedæmonians. The worst motive of all, which is confirmed by most witnesses, is to the following effect. Phidias the Sculptor had, as has before been said, undertaken to make the statue of Minerva [Athena]. Now he, being admitted to friendship with Pericles, and a great favorite of his, had many enemies upon this account, who envied and maligned him; who also, to make trial in a case of his, what kind of judges the commons would prove, should there be occasion to bring Pericles himself before them, having tampered with Menon, one who had been a workman with Phidias, stationed him in the market-place, with a petition desiring public security upon his discovery and impeachment of Phidias. The people admitting the man to tell his story, and the prosecution proceeding in the assembly, there was nothing of theft or cheat proved against him; for Phidias, from the very first beginning, by the advice of Pericles, had so wrought and wrapt the gold that was used in the work about the statue, that they might take it all off and make out the just weight of it, which Pericles at that time bade the accusers do. But the reputation of his works was what brought envy upon Phidias, especially that where he represents the fight of the Amazons upon the goddesses' shield, he had introduced a likeness of himself as a bald old man holding up a great stone with both hands, and had put in a very fine representation of Pericles fighting with an Amazon. And the position of the hand, which holds out the spear in front of the face, was ingeniously contrived to conceal in some degree the likeness, which, meantime, showed itself on either side.

Phidias then was carried away to prison, and there died of a disease: but, as some say, of poison, administered by the enemies of

Pericles, to raise a slander, or a suspicion, at least, as though he had procured it. The informer Menon, upon Glycon's proposal, the people made free from payment of taxes and customs, and ordered the generals to take care that nobody should do him any hurt. About the same time, Aspasia was indicted of impiety, upon the complaint of Hermippus the comedian, who also laid further to her charge that she received into her house freeborn women for the uses of Pericles. And Diopithes proposed a decree, that public accusation should be laid against persons who neglected religion, or taught new doctrines about things above,* directing suspicion, by means of Anaxagoras, against Pericles himself. The people receiving and admitting these accusations and complaints, at length, by this means, they came to enact a decree, at the motion of Dracontides, that Pericles should bring in the accounts of the moneys he had expended, and lodge them with the Prytanes; and that the judges, carrying their suffrage from the altar in the Acropolis, should examine and determine the business in the city. This last clause Hagnon took out of the decree, and moved that the causes should be tried before fifteen hundred jurors, whether they should be styled prosecutions for robbery, or bribery, or any kind of malversation. Aspasia, Pericles begged off, shedding, as Æschines says, many tears at the trial, and personally entreating the jurors. But fearing how it might go with Anaxagoras, he sent him out of the city. And finding that in Phidias's case he had miscarried with the people, being afraid of impeachment, he kindled the war, which hitherto had lingered and smothered, and blew it up into a flame; hoping, by that means, to disperse and scatter these complaints and charges, and to allay their jealousy; the city usually throwing herself upon him alone, and trusting to his sole conduct, upon the urgency of great affairs and public dangers, by reason of his authority and the sway he bore.

These are given out to have been the reasons which induced Pericles not to suffer the people of Athens to yield to the proposals of the Lacedæmonians; but their truth is uncertain.

The Lacedæmonians, for their part, feeling sure that if they

---

* "Supera ac cœlestia," as Cicero translates the words *meteōra* and *metarsia*, whence we have formed our *meteorology*.

could once remove him, they might be at what terms they pleased with the Athenians, sent them word that they should expel the "Pollution" with which Pericles on the mother's side was tainted, as Thucydides tells us. But the issue proved quite contrary to what those who sent the message expected; instead of bringing Pericles under suspicion and reproach, they raised him into yet greater credit and esteem with the citizens, as a man whom their enemies most hated and feared. In the same way, also, before Archidamus, who was at the head of the Peloponnesians, made his invasion into Attica, he told the Athenians beforehand, that if Archidamus, while he laid waste the rest of the country, should forbear and spare his estate, either on the ground of friendship or right of hospitality that was betwixt them, or on purpose to give his enemies an occasion of traducing him, that then he did freely bestow upon the state all that his land and the buildings upon it for the public use. The Lacedæmonians, therefore, and their allies, with a great army, invaded the Athenian territories, under the conduct of king Archidamus, and laying waste the country, marched on as far as Acharnæ, and there pitched their camp, presuming that the Athenians would never endure that, but would come out and fight them for their country's and their honor's sake. But Pericles looked upon it as dangerous to engage in battle, to the risk of the city itself, against sixty thousand . . . Peloponnesians and Bœotians; for so many they were in number that made the inroad at first; and he endeavored to appease those who were desirous to fight, and were grieved and discontented to see how things went, and gave them good words, saying, that "trees, when they are lopped and cut, grow up again in a short time but men, being once lost, cannot easily be recovered." He did not convene the people into an assembly, for fear lest they should force him to act against his judgment; but, like a skilful steersman or pilot of a ship, who, when a sudden squall comes on, out at sea, makes all his arrangements, sees that all is tight and fast, and then follows the dictates of his skill, and minds the business of the ship, taking no notice of the tears and entreaties of the sea-sick and fearful passengers, so he, having shut up the city gates, and placed guards at all posts for security, followed his own reason and judgment, little regarding those that cried out against him and were angry at his mangement, although there were a great many of his friends that urged him with requests, and many of his enemies threatened and accused him for doing as he did, and many made songs and lampoons upon him, which were sung about the town to his disgrace, reproaching him with the cowardly exercise of his office of general, and the tame abandonment of every thing to the enemy's hands.

Cleon, also, already was among his assailants, making use of the feeling against him as a step to the leadership of the people, as appears in the anapæstic verses of Hermippus—

> Satyr-king, instead of swords,
> Will you always handle words?
> Very brave indeed we find them,
> But a Teles* lurks behind them.
>
> Yet to gnash your teeth you're seen,
> When the little dagger keen,
> Whetted every day anew,
> Of sharp Cleon touches you.

PERICLES, however, was not at all moved by any attacks, but took all patiently, and submitted in silence to the disgrace they threw upon him and the ill-will they bore him; and, sending out a fleet of a hundred galleys to Peloponnesus, he did not go along with it in person, but stayed behind, that he might watch at home and keep the city under his own control, till the Peloponesians broke up their camp and were gone. Yet to soothe the common people, jaded and distressed with the war, he relieved them with distributions of public moneys, and ordained new divisions of subject land. For having turned out all the people of Ægina, he parted the island among the Athenians, according to lot. Some comfort, also, and ease in their miseries, they might receive from what their enemies endured. For the fleet, sailing round the Peloponnese, ravaged a great deal of the country, and pillaged and plundered the towns and smaller cities; and by land he himself entered with an army the Megarian country, and made havoc of it all. Whence it is clear that

---

* Apparently some notorious coward.—tr.

the Peloponnesians, though they did the Athenians much mischief by land, yet suffering as much themselves from them by sea, would not have protracted the war to such a length, but would quickly have given it over, as Pericles at first foretold they would, had not some divine power crossed human purposes.

In the first place, the pestilential disease, or plague, seized upon the city, and ate up all the flower and prime of their youth and strength. Upon occasion of which, the people, distempered and afflicted in their souls, as well as in their bodies, were utterly enraged like madmen against Pericles, and, like patients grown delirious, sought to lay violent hands on their physician, or, as it were, their father. They had been possessed, by his enemies, with the belief that the occasion of the plague was the crowding of the country people together into the town, forced as they were now, in the heat of the summer-weather, to dwell many of them together even as they could, in small tenements and stifling hovels, and to be tied to a lazy course of life within doors, whereas before they lived in a pure, open, and free air. The cause and author of all this, said they, is he who on account of the war has poured a multitude of people from the country in upon us within the walls, and uses all these many men that he has here upon no employ or service, but keeps them pent up like cattle, to be overrun with infection from one another, affording them neither shift of quarters nor any refreshment.

With the design to remedy these evils, and do the enemy some inconvenience, Pericles got a hundred and fifty galleys ready, and having embarked many tried soldiers, both foot and horse, was about to sail out, giving great hope to his citizens, and no less alarm to his enemies, upon the sight of so great a force. And now the vessels having their complement of men, and Pericles being gone aboard his own galley, it happened that the sun was eclipsed, and it grew dark on a sudden, to the affright of all, for this was looked upon as extremely ominous. Pericles, therefore, perceiving the steersman seized with fear and at a loss what to do, took his cloak and held it up before the man's face, and, screening him with it so that he could not see, asked him whether he imagined there was any great hurt, or the sign of any great hurt in this, and he answering No, "Why," said he, "and what does that differ from this, only that what has caused that darkness there, is something greater than a cloak?" This is a story which philosophers tell their scholars. Pericles, however, after putting out to sea, seems not to have done any other exploit befitting such preparations, and when he had laid siege to the holy city Epidaurus, which gave him some hope of surrender, miscarried in his design by reason of the sickness. For it not only seized upon the Athenians, but upon all others, too, that held any sort of communication with the army. Finding after this the Athenians ill affected and highly displeased with him, he tried and endeavored what he could to appease and re-encourage them. But he could not pacify or allay their anger, nor persuade or prevail with them any way, till they freely passed their votes upon him, resumed their power, took away his command from him, and fined him in a sum of money; which, by their account that say least, was fifteen talents, while they who reckon most, name fifty. The name prefixed to the accusation was Cleon, as Idomeneus tells us; Simmias, according to Theophrastus; and Heraclides Ponticus gives it as Lacratidas.

After this, public troubles were soon to leave him unmolested; the people, so to say, discharged their passion in their stroke, and lost their stings in the wound. But his domestic concerns were in an unhappy condition, many of his friends and acquaintance having died in the plague time, and those of his family having long since been in disorder and in a kind of mutiny against him. For the eldest of his lawfully begotten sons, Xanthippus by name, being naturally prodigal, and marrying a young and expensive wife, the daughter of Tisander, son of Epilycus, was highly offended at his father's economy in making him but a scanty allowance, by little and little at a time. He sent, therefore, to a friend one day and borrowed some money of him in his father Pericles's name, pretending it was by his order. The man coming afterward to demand the debt, Pericles was so far from yielding to pay it, that he entered an action against him. Upon which the young man, Xanthippus, thought himself so ill-used and disobliged that he openly reviled his father; telling first, by way of ridicule, stories about his conversations at home, and the discourses he had with the sophists and scholars that came to his house. As, for instance, how one who was a practiser of the five games of skill, having with a dart or javelin unawares against his will struck and killed Epitimus the Pharsalian, his father spent a whole day with Protagoras in a serious dispute, whether the javelin, or the man that threw it, or the masters of the games who appointed these sports, were, according to the strictest and best reason, to be accounted the cause of this mischance. Besides this, Stesimbrotus tells us that it was Xanthippus who spread abroad among the people the infamous story concerning his own wife; and in general that this difference of the young man's with his father, and the breach between them, continued never to be healed or made up till his death. For Xanthippus died in the plague time of the sickness. At which time Pericles also lost his sister, and the greatest part of his relations and friends, and those who had been most useful and serviceable to him in managing the affairs of state. However, he did not shrink or give in upon these occasions, nor betray or lower his high spirit and the greatness of his mind under all his misfortunes; he was not even so much as seen to weep or to mourn, or even attend the burial of any of his friends or relations, till at last he lost his only remaining legitimate son. Subdued by this blow, and yet striving still, as far as he could, to maintain his principle, and to preserve and keep up the greatness of his soul, when he came, however, to perform the ceremony of putting a garland of flowers upon the head of the corpse, he was vanquished by his passion at the sight, so that he burst into exclamations, and shed copious tears, having never done any such thing in all his life before.

The city having made trial of other generals for the conduct of war, and orators for business of state, when they found there was no one who was of weight enough for such a charge, or of authority sufficient to be trusted with so great a command, regretted the loss of him, and invited him again to address and advise them, and to reassume the office of general. He, however, lay at home in dejection and mourning; but was persuaded by Alcibiades and others of his friends to come abroad and show himself to the people; who having, upon his appearance, made their acknowledgments, and apologised for their untowardly treatment of him, he undertook the public affairs once more; and, being chosen general, requested that the statute concerning base-born children, which he himself had formerly caused to be made, might be suspended; that so the name and race of his family might not, for absolute want of a lawful heir to succeed, be wholly lost and extinguished. The case of the statute was thus: Pericles, when long ago at the height of his power in the state, having then, as has been said, children lawfully begotten, proposed a law that those only should be reputed true citizens of Athens who were born of such parents as were both Athenians. After this, the king of Egypt having sent to the people, by way of present, forty thousand bushels of wheat, which were to be shared out among the citizens, a great many actions and suits about legitimacy occurred, by virtue of that edict; cases which, till that time, had not been known nor taken notice of; and several persons suffered by false accusations. There were little less than five thousand who were convicted and sold for slaves; those who, enduring the test, remained in the government and passed muster for true Athenians were found upon the poll to be fourteen thousand and forty persons in number.

It looked strange, that a law, which had been carried so far against so many people, should be cancelled again by the same man that made it; yet the present calamity and distress which Pericles labored under in his family broke through all objections, and prevailed with the Athenians to pity him, as one whose losses and misfortunes had sufficiently punished his former arrogance and haughtiness. His sufferings deserved, they thought, their pity, and even indignation, and his request was such as became a man to ask and men to grant; they gave him permission to enroll his son in the register of his fraternity, giving him his own name. This son afterward, after having defeated the Peloponnesians at Arginusæ, was, with his fellow-generals, put to death by the people.

About the time when his son was enrolled, it should seem, the plague seized Pericles, not with sharp and violent fits, as it did others that had it, but with a dull and lingering distemper, attended with various changes and alterations, leisurely, by little and little, wasting the strength of his body, and undermining the noble faculties of his soul. So that Theophrastus, in his Morals, when discussing whether men's characters change with their circumstances, and their moral habits, disturbed by the ailings of their bodies, start aside from the rules of virtue, has left it upon record, that Pericles, when he was sick, showed one of his friends that came to visit him, an amulet or charm that the women had hung about his neck; as much as to say, that he was very sick indeed when he would admit of such a foolery as that was.

When he was now near his end, the best of the citizens and those of his friends who were left alive, sitting about him, were speaking of the greatness of his merit, and his power, and reckoning up his famous actions and the number of his victories; for there were no less than nine trophies, which, as their chief commander and conqueror of their enemies, he had set up, for the honor of the city. They talked thus together among themselves, as though he were unable to understand or mind what they said, but had now lost his consciousness. He had listened, however, all the while, and attended to all, and speaking out among them, said, that he wondered they should commend and take notice of things which were as much owing to fortune as to any thing else, and had happened to many other commanders, and, at the same time, should not speak or make mention of that which was the most excellent and greatest thing of all. "For," said he, "no Athenian, through my means, ever wore mourning."

He was indeed a character deserving our high admiration, not only for his equitable and mild temper, which all along in the many affairs of his life, and the great animosities which he incurred, he constantly maintained; but also for the high spirit and feeling which made him regard it the noblest of all his honors that, in the exercise of such immense power, he never had gratified his envy or his passion, nor ever had treated any enemy as irreconcilably opposed to him. And to me it appears that this one thing gives that otherwise childish and arrogant title a fitting and becoming significance; so dispassionate temper, a life so pure and unblemished, in the height of power and place, might well be called Olympian, in accordance with our conceptions of the divine beings, to whom, as the natural authors of all good and of nothing evil, we ascribe the rule and government of the world. Not as the poets represent, who, while confounding us with their ignorant fancies, are themselves confuted by their own poems and fictions, and call the place, indeed, where they say the gods make their abode, a secure and quiet seat, free from all hazards and commotions, untroubled with winds or with clouds, and equally through all time illumined with a soft serenity and a pure light, as though such were a home most agreeable for a blessed and immortal nature; and yet, in the mean while, affirm that the gods themselves are full of trouble and enmity and anger and other passions, which no way become or belong to even men that have any understanding. But this will, perhaps, seem a subject fitter for some other consideration, and that ought to be treated of in some other place.

The course of public affairs after his death produced a quick and speedy sense of the loss of Pericles. Those who, while he lived, resented his great authority, as that which eclipsed themselves, presently after his quitting the stage, making trial of other orators and demagogues, readily acknowledged that there never had been in nature such a disposition as his was, more moderate and reasonable in the height of that state he took upon him, or more grave and impressive in the mildness which he used. And that invidious arbitrary power, to which formerly they gave the name of monarchy and tyranny, did then appear to have been the chief bulwark of public safety; so great a corruption and such a flood of mischief and vice followed, which he, by keeping weak and low, had witheld from notice, and had prevented from attaining incurable height through a licentious impunity.

SELECT BIBLIOGRAPHY

R. H. Barrow, *Plutarch and His Times* (Bloomington: Indiana University Press, 1967).
Truesdell S. Brown, ed., *Ancient Greece* (London: Collier-Macmillan, Free Press of Glencoe, "Sources in Western Civilization" No. 2). Documentary history of Greece.
J. B. Bury, *The Ancient Greek Historians* (New York: Dover Press, 1958).
John H. Finley, *Thucydides* (Cambridge, Mass.: Harvard University Press, 1942).
Moses I. Finley, ed., *The Greek Historians* (New York: Viking Press, 1954).
———, *The Ancient Greeks* (New York: Viking Press, 1963).
A. W. Gomme, *Essays in Greek History and Literature* (Oxford: Basil Blackwell, 1937).
———, *More Essays in Greek History and Literature* (Oxford: Basil Blackwell, 1962).
Eric A. Havelock, *Preface to Plato* (Cambridge, Mass.: Harvard University Press, 1963).
H. D. F. Kitto, *The Greeks*, rev. ed. (Baltimore: Penguin Press, 1957).
J. L. Myres, *Herodotus the Father of History* (Oxford: Clarendon Press, 1953).
Lionel Pearson, *The Early Ionian Historians* (Oxford: Clarendon Press, 1939).